SOURCE
The Prentice Hall
ENGINEERING SOURCE

MATLAB Programming

David C. Kuncicky

Pearson Education, Inc.
Upper Saddle River, NJ 07458

Library of Congress Cataloging-in-Publication Data

Kuncicky, David C.
    Matlab programming / David C. Kuncicky
       p. cm.—(ESource—the Prentice Hall engineering source)
    Includes index.
    ISBN 0-13-035127-X
    1. MATLAB. 2. Numerical analysis—Data processing. I. Title. II. Series.

    QA297.K768 2003
    519.4'0285—dc21

                      2003042860

Vice President and Editorial Director, ECS: *Marcia J. Horton*
Executive Editor: *Eric Svendsen*
Associate Editor: *Dee Bernhard*
Vice President and Director of Production and Manufacturing, ESM: *David W. Riccardi*
Executive Managing Editor: *Vince O'Brien*
Managing Editor: *David A. George*
Production Editor: *Barbara A. Till*
Director of Creative Services: *Paul Belfanti*
Creative Director: *Carole Anson*
Art Director: *Jayne Conte*
Art Editor: *Greg Dulles*
Manufacturing Manager: *Trudy Pisciotti*
Manufacturing Buyer: *Lisa McDowell*
Marketing Manager: *Holly Stark*

© 2004 by Pearson Education, Inc.
Pearson Prentice Hall
Pearson Education, Inc.
Upper Saddle River, NJ 074588

All rights reserved. No part of this book may be reproduced, in any form or by any means, without permission in writing from the publisher.

The author and publisher of this book have used their best efforts in preparing this book. These efforts include the development, research, and testing of the theories and programs to determine their effectiveness. The author and publisher make no warranty of any kind, expressed or implied, with regard to these programs or the documentation contained in this book. The author and publisher shall not be liable in any event for incidental or consequential damages in connection with, or arising out of, the furnishing, performance, or use of these programs.

Macintosh is a registered trademark of Apple Computer, Inc. Maple and Maple VIII are registered trademarks of Waterloo Maple, Inc. MATLAB is a registered trademark of The MathWorks, Inc. PostScript is a registered trademark of Adobe Systems, Inc. Unix is a registered trademark of the Open Group. Windows is a registered trademark of Microsoft, Inc.

Printed in the United States of America.

10 9 8 7 6 5 4 3 2

ISBN 0-13-035127-X

Pearson Education Ltd., *London*
Pearson Education Australia Pty. Ltd., *Sydney*
Pearson Education Singapore, Pte. Ltd.
Pearson Education North Asia Ltd., *Hong Kong*
Pearson Education Canada, Inc., *Toronto*
Pearson Educación de Mexico, S.A. de C.V.
Pearson Education—Japan, *Tokyo*
Pearson Education Malaysia, Pte. Ltd.
Pearson Education, *Upper Saddle River, New Jersey*

About ESource

ESource—The Prentice Hall Engineering Source—
www.prenhall.com/esource

ESource—The Prentice Hall Engineering Source gives professors the power to harness the full potential of their text and their first-year engineering course. More than just a collection of books, ESource is a unique publishing system revolving around the ESource website—www.prenhall.com/esource. ESource enables you to put your stamp on your book just as you do your course. It lets you:

Control   You choose exactly what chapters are in your book and in what order they appear. Of course, you can choose the entire book if you'd like and stay with the authors' original order.

Optimize   Get the most from your book and your course. ESource lets you produce the optimal text for your students needs.

Customize   You can add your own material anywhere in your text's presentation, and your final product will arrive at your bookstore as a professionally formatted text. Of course, all titles in this series are available as stand-alone texts, or as bundles of two or more books sold at a discount. Contact your PH sales rep for discount information.

ESource ACCESS

Professors who choose to bundle two or more texts from the ESource series for their class, or use an ESource custom book will be providing their students with an on-line library of intro engineering content—ESource Access. We've designed ESource ACCESS to provide students a flexible, searchable, on-line resource. Free access codes come in bundles and custom books are valid for one year after initial log-on. Contact your PH sales rep for more information.

ESource Content

All the content in ESource was written by educators specifically for freshman/first-year students. Authors tried to strike a balanced level of presentation, an approach that was neither formulaic nor trivial, and one that did not focus too heavily on advanced topics that most introductory students do not encounter until later classes. Because many professors do not have extensive time to cover these topics in the classroom, authors prepared each text with the idea that many students would use it for self-instruction and independent study. Students should be able to use this content to learn the software tool or subject on their own.

While authors had the freedom to write texts in a style appropriate to their particular subject, all followed certain guidelines created to promote a consistency that makes students comfortable. Namely, every chapter opens with a clear set of **Objectives**, includes **Practice Boxes** throughout the chapter, and ends with a number of **Problems**, and a list of **Key Terms**. **Applications Boxes** are spread throughout the book with the intent of giving students a real-world perspective of engineering. **Success Boxes** provide the student with advice about college study skills, and help students avoid the common pitfalls of first-year students. In addition, this series contains an entire book titled *Engineering Success* by Peter Schiavone of the University of Alberta intended to expose students quickly to what it takes to be an engineering student.

Creating Your Book

Using ESource is simple. You preview the content either on-line or through examination copies of the books you can request on-line, from your PH sales rep, or by calling 1-800-526-0485. Create an on-line outline of the content you want, in the order you want, using ESource's simple interface. Insert your own material into the text flow. If you are not ready to order, ESource will save your work. You can come back at any time and change, re-arrange, or add more material to your creation. Once you're finished you'll automatically receive an ISBN. Give it to your bookstore and your book will arrive on their shelves four to six weeks after they order. Your custom desk copies with their instructor supplements will arrive at your address at the same time.

To learn more about this new system for creating the perfect textbook, go to www.prenhall.com/esource. You can either go through the on-line walkthrough of how to create a book, or experiment yourself.

Supplements

Adopters of ESource receive an instructor's CD that contains professor and student code from the books in the series, as well as other instruction aides provided by authors. The website also holds approximately **350 PowerPoint transparencies** created by Jack Leifer of University of Kentucky–Paducah. Professors can either follow these transparencies as pre-prepared lectures or use them as the basis for their own custom presentations.

Titles in the ESource Series

About the Authors

No project could ever come to pass without a group of authors who have the vision and the courage to turn a stack of blank paper into a book. The authors in this series, who worked diligently to produce their books, provide the building blocks of the series.

Martin D. Bradshaw was born in Pittsburg, KS in 1936, grew up in Kansas and the surrounding states of Arkansas and Missouri, graduating from Newton High School, Newton, KS in 1954. He received the B.S.E.E. and M.S.E.E. degrees from the University of Wichita in 1958 and 1961, respectively. A Ford Foundation fellowship at Carnegie Institute of Technology followed from 1961 to 1963 and he received the Ph.D. degree in electrical engineering in 1964. He spent his entire academic career with the Department of Electrical and Computer Engineering at the University of New Mexico (1961-1963 and 1991-1996). He served as the Assistant Dean for Special Programs with the UNM College of Engineering from 1974 to 1976 and as the Associate Chairman for the EECE Department from 1993 to 1996. During the period 1987-1991 he was a consultant with his own company, EE Problem Solvers. During 1978 he spent a sabbatical year with the State Electricity Commission of Victoria, Melbourne, Australia. From 1979 to 1981 he served an IPA assignment as a Project Officer at the U.S. Air Force Weapons Laboratory, Kirkland AFB, Albuquerque, NM. He has won numerous local, regional, and national teaching awards, including the George Westinghouse Award from the ASEE in 1973. He was awarded the IEEE Centennial Medal in 2000.

Acknowledgments: Dr. Bradshaw would like to acknowledge his late mother, who gave him a great love of reading and learning, and his father, who taught him to persist until the job is finished. The encouragement of his wife, Jo, and his six children is a never-ending inspiration.

Stephen J. Chapman received a B.S. degree in Electrical Engineering from Louisiana State University (1975), the M.S.E. degree in Electrical Engineering from the University of Central Florida (1979), and pursued further graduate studies at Rice University. Mr. Chapman is currently Manager of Technical Systems for British Aerospace Australia, in Melbourne, Australia. In this position, he provides technical direction and design authority for the work of younger engineers within the company. He also continues to teach at local universities on a part-time basis.

Mr. Chapman is a Senior Member of the Institute of Electrical and Electronics Engineers (and several of its component societies). He is also a member of the Association for Computing Machinery and the Institution of Engineers (Australia).

Steven C. Chapra presently holds the Louis Berger Chair for Computing and Engineering in the Civil and Environmental Engineering Department at Tufts University. Dr. Chapra received engineering degrees from Manhattan College and the University of Michigan. Before joining the faculty at Tufts, he taught at Texas A&M University, the University of Colorado, and Imperial College, London. His research interests focus on surface water-quality modeling and advanced computer applications in environmental engineering. He has published over 50 refereed journal articles, 20 software packages and 6 books. He has received a number of awards including the 1987 ASEE Merriam/Wiley Distinguished Author Award, the 1993 Rudolph Hering Medal, and teaching awards from Texas A&M, the University of Colorado, and the Association of Environmental Engineering and Science Professors.

Acknowledgments: To the Berger Family for their many contributions to engineering education. I would also like to thank David Clough for his friendship and insights, John Walkenbach for his wonderful books, and my colleague Lee Minardi and my students Kenny William, Robert Viesca and Jennifer Edelmann for their suggestions.

Mark Dix began working with AutoCAD in 1985 as a programmer for CAD Support Associates, Inc. He helped design a system for creating estimates and bills of material directly from AutoCAD drawing databases for use in the automated conveyor industry. This system became the basis for systems still widely in use today. In 1986 he began collaborating with Paul Riley to create AutoCAD training materials, combining Riley's background in industrial design and training with Dix's background in writing, curriculum development, and programming. Mr. Dix received the M.S. degree in education from the University of Massachusetts. He is currently the Director of Dearborn Academy High School in Arlington, Massachusetts.

Delores M. Etter is a Professor of Electrical and Computer Engineering at the University of Colorado. Dr. Etter was a faculty member at the University of New Mexico and also a Visiting Professor at Stanford University. Dr. Etter was responsible for the Freshman Engineering Program at the University of New Mexico and is active in the Integrated Teaching Laboratory at the University of Colorado. She was elected a Fellow of the Institute of Electrical and Electronics Engineers for her contributions to education and for her technical leadership in digital signal processing.

Charles B. Fleddermann is a professor in the Department of Electrical and Computer Engineering at the University of New Mexico in Albuquerque, New Mexico. All of his degrees are in electrical engineering: his Bachelor's degree from the University of Notre Dame, and the Master's and Ph.D. from the University of Illinois at Urbana-Champaign. Prof. Fleddermann developed an engineering ethics course for his department in response to the ABET requirement to incorporate ethics topics into the undergraduate engineering curriculum. *Engineering Ethics* was written as a vehicle for presenting ethical theory,

analysis, and problem solving to engineering undergraduates in a concise and readily accessible way.

Acknowledgments: I would like to thank Profs. Charles Harris and Michael Rabins of Texas A & M University whose NSF sponsored workshops on engineering ethics got me started thinking in this field. Special thanks to my wife Liz, who proofread the manuscript for this book, provided many useful suggestions, and who helped me learn how to teach "soft" topics to engineers.

Kirk D. Hagen is a professor at Weber State University in Ogden, Utah. He has taught introductory-level engineering courses and upper-division thermal science courses at WSU since 1993. He received his B.S. degree in physics from Weber State College and his M.S. degree in mechanical engineering from Utah State University, after which he worked as a thermal designer/analyst in the aerospace and electronics industries. After several years of engineering practice, he resumed his formal education, earning his Ph.D. in mechanical engineering at the University of Utah. Hagen is the author of an undergraduate heat transfer text.

Mark N. Horenstein is a Professor in the Department of Electrical and Computer Engineering at Boston University. He has degrees in Electrical Engineering from M.I.T. and U.C. Berkeley and has been involved in teaching engineering design for the greater part of his academic career. He devised and developed the senior design project class taken by all electrical and computer engineering students at Boston University. In this class, the students work for a virtual engineering company developing products and systems for real-world engineering and social-service clients.

Acknowledgments: I would like to thank Prof. James Bethune, the architect of the Peak Performance event at Boston University, for his permission to highlight the competition in my text. Several of the ideas relating to brainstorming and teamwork were derived from a workshop on engineering design offered by Prof. Charles Lovas of Southern Methodist University. The principles of estimation were derived in part from a freshman engineering problem posed by Prof. Thomas Kincaid of Boston University.

Steven Howell is the Chairman and a Professor of Mechanical Engineering at Lawrence Technological University. Prior to joining LTU in 2001, Dr. Howell led a knowledge-based engineering project for Visteon Automotive Systems and taught computer-aided design classes for Ford Motor Company engineers. Dr. Howell also has a total of 15 years experience as an engineering faculty member at Northern Arizona University, the University of the Pacific, and the University of Zimbabwe. While at Northern Arizona University, he helped develop and implement an award-winning interdisciplinary series of design courses simulating a corporate engineering-design environment.

Douglas W. Hull is a graduate student in the Department of Mechanical Engineering at Carnegie Mellon University in Pittsburgh, Pennsylvania. He is the author of *Mastering Mechanics I Using Matlab 5*, and contributed to *Mechanics of Materials* by Bedford and Liechti. His research in the Sensor Based Planning lab involves motion planning for hyper-redundant manipulators, also known as serpentine robots.

Scott D. James is a staff lecturer at Kettering University (formerly GMI Engineering & Management Institute) in Flint, Michigan. He is currently pursuing a Ph.D. in Systems Engineering with an emphasis on software engineering and computer-integrated manufacturing. He chose teaching as a profession after several years in the computer industry. "I thought that it was really important to know what it was like outside of academia. I wanted to provide students with classes that were up to date and provide the information that is really used and needed."

Acknowledgments: Scott would like to acknowledge his family for the time to work on the text and his students and peers at Kettering who offered helpful critiques of the materials that eventually became the book.

Joe King received the B.S. and M.S. degrees from the University of California at Davis. He is a Professor of Computer Engineering at the University of the Pacific, Stockton, CA, where he teaches courses in digital design, computer design, artificial intelligence, and computer networking. Since joining the UOP faculty, Professor King has spent yearlong sabbaticals teaching in Zimbabwe, Singapore, and Finland. A licensed engineer in the state of California, King's industrial experience includes major design projects with Lawrence Livermore National Laboratory, as well as independent consulting projects. Prof. King has had a number of books published with titles including *Matlab*, MathCAD, Exploring Engineering, and Engineering and Society.

David C. Kuncicky is a native Floridian. He earned his Baccalaureate in psychology, Master's in computer science, and Ph.D. in computer science from Florida State University. He has served as a faculty member in the Department of Electrical Engineering at the FAMU–FSU College of Engineering and the Department of Computer Science at Florida State University. He has taught computer science and computer engineering courses for over 15 years. He has published research in the areas of intelligent hybrid systems and neural networks. He is currently the Director of Engineering at Bioreason, Inc. in Sante Fe, New Mexico.

Acknowledgments: Thanks to Steffie and Helen for putting up with my late nights and long weekends at the computer. Finally, thanks to Susan Bassett for having faith in my abilities, and for providing continued tutelage and support.

Ron Larsen is a Professor of Chemical Engineering at Montana State University, and received his Ph.D. from the Pennsylvania State University. He was initially attracted to engineering by the challenges the profession offers, but also appreciates that engineering is a serving profession. Some of the greatest challenges he has faced while teaching have involved non-traditional teaching methods, including evening courses for practicing engineers and teaching through an interpreter at the Mongolian National University. These experiences have provided tremendous opportunities to learn new ways to communicate technical material. Dr. Larsen views modern software as one of the new tools that will radically alter the way engineers work, and his book *Introduction to Math-CAD* was written to help young engineers prepare to meet the challenges of an ever-changing workplace.

Acknowledgments: To my students at Montana State University who have endured the rough drafts and typos, and who still allow me to experiment with their classes—my sincere thanks.

Sanford Leestma is a Professor of Mathematics and Computer Science at Calvin College, and received his Ph.D. from New Mexico State University. He has been the long-time co-author of successful textbooks on Fortran, Pascal, and data structures in Pascal. His current research interest are in the areas of algorithms and numerical computation.

Jack Leifer is an Assistant Professor in the Department of Mechanical Engineering at the University of Kentucky Extended Campus Program in Paducah, and was previously with the Department of Mathematical Sciences and Engineering at the University of South Carolina–Aiken. He received his Ph.D. in Mechanical Engineering from the University of Texas at Austin in December 1995. His current research interests include the analysis of ultra-light and inflatable (Gossamer) space structures.

Acknowledgments: I'd like to thank my colleagues at USC–Aiken, especially Professors Mike May and Laurene Fausett, for their encouragement and feedback; and my parents, Felice and Morton Leifer, for being there and providing support (as always) as I completed this book.

Richard M. Lueptow is the Charles Deering McCormick Professor of Teaching Excellence and Associate Professor of Mechanical Engineering at Northwestern University. He is a native of Wisconsin and received his doctorate from the Massachusetts Institute of Technology in 1986. He teaches design, fluid mechanics, an spectral analysis techniques. Rich has an active research program on rotating filtration, Taylor Couette flow, granular flow, fire suppression, and acoustics. He has five patents and over 40 refereed journal and proceedings papers along with many other articles, abstracts, and presentations.

Acknowledgments: Thanks to my talented and hardworking co-authors as well as the many colleagues and students who took the tutorial for a "test drive." Special thanks to Mike Minbiole for his major contributions to Graphics Concepts with SolidWorks. Thanks also to Northwestern University for the time to work on a book. Most of all, thanks to my loving wife, Maiya, and my children, Hannah and Kyle, for supporting me in this endeavor. (Photo courtesy of Evanston Photographic Studios, Inc.)

Larry Nyhoff is a Professor of Mathematics and Computer Science at Calvin College. After doing bachelor's work at Calvin, and Master's work at Michigan, he received a Ph.D. from Michigan State and also did graduate work in computer science at Western Michigan. Dr. Nyhoff has taught at Calvin for the past 34 years—mathematics at first and computer science for the past several years.

Acknowledgments: We thank our families—Shar, Jeff, Dawn, Rebecca, Megan, Sara, Greg, Julie, Joshua, Derek, Tom, Joan; Marge, Michelle, Sandy, Lory, Michael—for being patient and understanding. We thank God for allowing us to write this text.

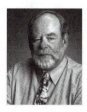

Paul Riley is an author, instructor, and designer specializing in graphics and design for multimedia. He is a founding partner of CAD Support Associates, a contract service and professional training organization for computer-aided design. His 15 years of business experience and 20 years of teaching experience are supported by degrees in education and computer science. Paul has taught AutoCAD at the University of Massachusetts at Lowell and is presently teaching AutoCAD at Mt. Ida College in Newton, Massachusetts. He has developed a program, Computer-aided Design for Professionals that is highly regarded by corporate clients and has been an ongoing success since 1982.

Robert Rizza is an Assistant Professor of Mechanical Engineering at North Dakota State University, where he teaches courses in mechanics and computer-aided design. A native of Chicago, he received the Ph.D. degree from the Illinois Institute of Technology. He is also the author of *Getting Started with Pro/ENGINEER*. Dr. Rizza has worked on a diverse range of engineering projects including projects from the railroad, bioengineering, and aerospace industries. His current research interests include the fracture of composite materials, repair of cracked aircraft components, and loosening of prostheses.

Peter Schiavone is a professor and student advisor in the Department of Mechanical Engineering at the University of Alberta, Canada. He received his Ph.D. from the University of Strathclyde, U.K. in 1988. He has authored several books in the area of student academic success as well as numerous papers in international scientific research journals. Dr. Schiavone has worked in private industry in several different areas of engineering including aerospace and systems engineering. He founded the first Mathematics Resource Center at the University of Alberta, a unit designed specifically to teach new students the necessary *survival skills* in mathematics and the physical sciences required for success in first-year engineering. This led to the Students' Union Gold Key Award for outstanding contributions to the university. Dr. Schiavone lectures regularly to freshman engineering students and to new engineering professors on engineering success, in particular about maximizing students' academic performance.

Acknowledgements: Thanks to Richard Felder for being such an inspiration; to my wife Linda for sharing my dreams and believing in me; and to Francesca and Antonio for putting up with Dad when working on the text.

David I. Schneider holds an A.B. degree from Oberlin College and a Ph.D. degree in Mathematics from MIT. He has taught for 34 years, primarily at the University of Maryland. Dr. Schneider has authored 28 books, with one-half of them computer programming books. He has developed three customized software packages that are supplied as supplements to over 55 mathematics textbooks. His involvement with computers dates back to 1962, when he programmed a special purpose computer at MIT's Lincoln Laboratory to correct errors in a communications system.

David I. Schwartz is an Assistant Professor in the Computer Science Department at Cornell University and earned his B.S., M.S., and Ph.D. degrees in Civil Engineering from State University of New York at Buffalo. Throughout his graduate studies, Schwartz combined principles of computer science to applications of civil engineering. He became interested in helping students learn how to apply software tools for solving a variety of engineering problems. He teaches his students to learn incrementally and practice frequently to gain the maturity to tackle other subjects. In his spare time, Schwartz plays drums in a variety of bands.

Acknowledgments: I dedicate my books to my family, friends, and students who all helped in so many ways.

Many thanks go to the schools of Civil Engineering and Engineering & Applied Science at State University of New York at Buffalo where I originally developed and tested my UNIX and Maple books. I greatly appreciate the opportunity to explore my goals and all the help from everyone at the Computer Science Department at Cornell.

 **John T. Sears** received the Ph.D. degree from Princeton University. Currently, he is a Professor and the head of the Department of Chemical Engineering at Montana State University. After leaving Princeton he worked in research at Brookhaven National Laboratory and Esso Research and Engineering, until he took a position at West Virginia University. He came to MSU in 1982, where he has served as the Director of the College of Engineering Minority Program and Interim Director for BioFilm Engineering. Prof. Sears has written a book on air pollution and economic development, and over 45 articles in engineering and engineering education.

 **Michael T. Snyder** is President of Internet startup company Appointments123.com. He is a native of Chicago, and he received his Bachelor of Science degree in Mechanical Engineering from the University of Notre Dame. Mike also graduated with honors from Northwestern University's Kellogg Graduate School of Management in 1999 with his Masters of Management degree. Before Appointments123.com, Mike was a mechanical engineer in new product development for Motorola Cellular and Acco Office Products. He has received four patents for his mechanical design work. "Pro/ ENGINEER was an invaluable design tool for me, and I am glad to help students learn the basics of Pro/ ENGINEER."

Acknowledgments: Thanks to Rich Lueptow and Jim Steger for inviting me to be a part of this great project. Of course, thanks to my wife Gretchen for her support in my various projects.

 **Jim Steger** is currently Chief Technical Officer and cofounder of an Internet applications company. He graduated with a Bachelor of Science degree in Mechanical Engineering from Northwestern University. His prior work included mechanical engineering assignments at Motorola and Acco Brands. At Motorola, Jim worked on part design for two-way radios and was one of the lead mechanical engineers on a cellular phone product line. At Acco Brands, Jim was the sole engineer on numerous office product designs. His Worx stapler has won design awards in the United States and in Europe. Jim has been a Pro/ENGINEER user for over six years.

Acknowledgments: Many thanks to my co-authors, especially Rich Lueptow for his leadership on this project. I would also like to thank my family for their continuous support.

 **Royce Wilkinson** received his undergraduate degree in chemistry from Rose-Hulman Institute of Technology in 1991 and the Ph.D. degree in chemistry from Montana State University in 1998 with research in natural product isolation from fungi. He currently resides in Bozeman, MT and is involved in HIV drug research. His research interests center on biological molecules and their interactions in the search for pharmaceutical advances.

Reviewers

We would like to thank everyone who has reviewed texts in this series.

Christopher Rowe *Vanderbilt University*
Steve Yurgartis *Clarkson University*
Heidi A. Diefes-Dux *Purdue University*
Howard Silver *Fairleigh Dickenson University*
Jean C. Malzahn Kampe *Virginia Polytechnic Institute and State University*
Malcolm Heimer *Florida International University*
Stanley Reeves *Auburn University*
John Demel *Ohio State University*
Shahnam Navee *Georgia Southern University*
Heshem Shaalem *Georgia Southern University*
Terry L. Kohutek *Texas A & M University*
Liz Rozell *Bakersfield College*
Mary C. Lynch *University of Florida*
Ted Pawlicki *University of Rochester*
James N. Jensen *SUNY at Buffalo*
Tom Horton *University of Virginia*
Eileen Young *Bristol Community College*
James D. Nelson *Louisiana Tech University*
Jerry Dunn *Texas Tech University*
Howard M. Fulmer *Villanova University*
Naeem Abdurrahman *University of Texas, Austin*
Stephen Allan *Utah State University*
Anil Bajaj *Purdue University*
Grant Baker *University of Alaska–Anchorage*
William Beckwith *Clemson University*
Haym Benaroya *Rutgers University*
John Biddle *California State Polytechnic University*
Tom Bledsaw *ITT Technical Institute*
Fred Boadu *Duke University*
Tom Bryson *University of Missouri, Rolla*
Ramzi Bualuan *University of Notre Dame*
Dan Budny *Purdue University*
Betty Burr *University of Houston*
Dale Calkins *University of Washington*
Harish Cherukuri *University of North Carolina –Charlotte*
Arthur Clausing *University of Illinois*
Barry Crittendon *Virginia Polytechnic and State University*

James Devine *University of South Florida*
Ron Eaglin *University of Central Florida*
Dale Elifrits *University of Missouri, Rolla*
Patrick Fitzhorn *Colorado State University*
Susan Freeman *Northeastern University*
Frank Gerlitz *Washtenaw College*
Frank Gerlitz *Washtenaw Community College*
John Glover *University of Houston*
John Graham *University of North Carolina–Charlotte*
Ashish Gupta *SUNY at Buffalo*
Otto Gygax *Oregon State University*
Malcom Heimer *Florida International University*
Donald Herling *Oregon State University*
Thomas Hill *SUNY at Buffalo*
A.S. Hodel *Auburn University*
James N. Jensen *SUNY at Buffalo*
Vern Johnson *University of Arizona*
Autar Kaw *University of South Florida*
Kathleen Kitto *Western Washington University*
Kenneth Klika *University of Akron*
Terry L. Kohutek *Texas A&M University*
Melvin J. Maron *University of Louisville*
Robert Montgomery *Purdue University*
Mark Nagurka *Marquette University*
Romarathnam Narasimhan *University of Miami*
Soronadi Nnaji *Florida A&M University*
Sheila O'Connor *Wichita State University*
Michael Peshkin *Northwestern University*
Dr. John Ray *University of Memphis*
Larry Richards *University of Virginia*
Marc H. Richman *Brown University*
Randy Shih *Oregon Institute of Technology*
Avi Singhal *Arizona State University*
Tim Sykes *Houston Community College*
Neil R. Thompson *University of Waterloo*
Dr. Raman Menon Unnikrishnan *Rochester Institute of Technology*
Michael S. Wells *Tennessee Tech University*
Joseph Wujek *University of California, Berkeley*
Edward Young *University of South Carolina*
Garry Young *Oklahoma State University*
Mandochehr Zoghi *University of Dayton*

Contents

http://emissary.prenhall.com/esource/

http://emissary.prenhall.com/esource/

1

Introduction

1.1 ORIENTATION TO THE TEXT

1.1.1 Purpose

This book is intended to serve as your text for an introductory course in computer programming that uses the MATLAB scripting language. The text explains how to write computer programs and how to write them well. It provides scores of easy-to-follow examples and practice problems, as well as an introduction to programming methodology.

You will likely use MATLAB as a tool in several more of your engineering courses. The MATLAB system is also widely used by professional engineers and scientists. Thus, what you learn here will be useful throughout your academic and professional career as an engineer or scientist.

As an engineering student, you may study other programming languages in addition to MATLAB. Your second language will be a natural extension of the material in this text. Many of the topics and skills learned in the text will be directly applicable to other languages such as C++, Java, or FORTRAN. MATLAB even provides a means for interfacing with other programming languages from within your MATLAB code.

MATLAB includes many built-in functions that are not typically available in the core of other programming languages. This is especially true for matrix operations, which are MATLAB's specialty, allowing you, the engineering student, to focus sooner on the solution of engineering problems, rather than to focus on low-level computer-science problems. Professional engineers use this feature of MATLAB to rapidly prototype engineering solutions.

The text emphasizes the procedural programming paradigm and briefly introduces object-oriented programming. It also introduces software development tools that help you

OBJECTIVES

After reading this chapter, you should be able to

- State the purpose and prerequisites for the text.
- Understand the typographical conventions used in the text.
- Explain the steps of the engineering method.
- Identify the major components of the MATLAB® system.
- Describe the differences between MATLAB's student edition and professional edition.
- Identify the main hardware components of a computer.
- Distinguish between computer hardware and software.

organize and maintain your code (source-code management), find and fix program bugs (**MATLAB** Debugger), and speed up your programs (**MATLAB** Profiler).

Throughout the book, you will find examples of code segments, practice problems, and programming hints. These are in separate boxes. The answers to the practice problems are at the end of each chapter.

1.1.2 How to Use This Book

You can do several things to make your study of **MATLAB** programming easier. First, make sure that you understand each essential concept before moving on. The text lists key concepts in the "Key Terms" section at the end of each chapter. Try to understand each concept before moving on. Topics build upon one another—if you do not understand a concept, it will return to haunt you later.

Second, practice, practice, practice! You cannot learn to program by reading a book any more than you can learn to cross-country ski by reading a book. Try every example and practice problem in the text—even if you think that you understand it. Experiment with each problem. Try changing portions of your code to see what happens—you will not break the computer, and you may learn something interesting.

Lastly, use the programming tips. They have been collected from professional programmers. They are not merely academic. If carefully followed, they will save you much time and frustration.

1.1.3 Prerequisites

The text presents a number of examples to show the application of **MATLAB** functions and programs to engineering and scientific problems. Some of these include subject matter that you will find later in your engineering course work. We assume that you have studied high school algebra and trigonometry. We will present any domain-specific information that is required to understand an example or an end-of-chapter problem within each example or problem.

1.1.4 Text Organization

The full text includes 10 chapters and five appendices. Your instructor may not have included all of the chapters in your version of the text. Chapter 2 presents the use of **MATLAB** as an interactive tool. In Chapter 2, you will be introduced to the **MATLAB** interface, the interpreter, the help features, the setting of preferences, and the printing facility. Chapter 3 introduces some of the elements that are common to most programming languages. These include the use of reserved words, the naming of variables, and mechanisms for data storage. Chapter 4 introduces you to the control logic of a program. Control logic allows you to make the program do what you want by using repetition structures and by branching within the program. The control logic is the meat of a program. Chapter 5 is an introduction to matrix manipulation and some of the extensive groups of built-in **MATLAB** matrix functions. This is an important chapter, since **MATLAB** excels with array and matrix manipulation (**MATLAB** stands for *matrix laboratory*). Chapter 6 discusses basic plotting commands. Chapter 7 describes the use of procedural abstraction to organize software and encapsulate algorithms. This involves writing functions and subfunctions. Chapter 8 introduces the special case of recursive functions. Chapter 9 introduces the object-oriented programming paradigm. In Chapter 9, we will show you how to encapsulate an abstraction into a class and how to create and use an instance of that class. Chapter 10 illustrates a collection of topics that roughly fall under the category of software development. Topics include detection and handling of programming errors and the use of support tools such as debuggers and software profilers. Chapter 10 briefly covers the MATLAB support for source-code control, the MATLAB compiler, and MATLAB interfaces to other programming languages.

1.1.5   Author Contact

If you find text errors, have questions, or want to make suggestions, you can send me e-mail at

kuncicky@pobox.com

The following Web page contains code for some of the text's examples and an errata sheet for the text:

http://www.pobox.com/~kuncicky/MATLAB2002

1.2   TYPOGRAPHIC CONVENTIONS USED IN THE TEXT

Throughout the text, the following typographic conventions are used:

1.2.1   Selections

We will frequently ask you to move the mouse cursor over a particular item and then click and release the left mouse button. The text repeats this sequence of actions so many times that it is abbreviated as:
Choose **Item**.
If you are not to release the mouse button or if you are not to use the mouse button, the instructions will be stated explicitly.
Any button, icon, or menu item that you are to select with the mouse will be displayed in boldface type. For example, if you are asked to choose the menu item at the top of the screen that is labeled "File," it will be written as
Choose **File** from the Menu bar.
Any key that you should press is also indicated in boldface type. For example, if you are asked to press the control key, it will be written as
Press the **Ctrl** key.
The book frequently refers to selections that require more than a single step. For example, to see your user preferences, you would perform the following steps:

1.   Choose **File** from the Menu bar (at the top of the screen).
2.   Choose **Preferences** from the drop-down menu that appears after performing Step 1.

The text abbreviates multiple selections such as this by separating steps with a right arrow. The abbreviation for the two steps listed above is:
Choose **File** → **Preferences** from the Menu bar.
If you are to press multiple keys simultaneously, that will be denoted by separating the named keys with a plus sign. For example, to undo a typing change, you can simultaneously press the **Ctrl** key and the **Z** key, which will be abbreviated as follows:
To undo typing, press **Ctrl** + **Z**.
(Note that you do not type the plus sign.)

1.2.2   Functions and Variables

The text italicizes MATLAB function names and variables. For example:
The MATLAB statement $A = factorial(5)$ will compute the product of the integers from one to five and store the result in the variable A.
In this example, A is a variable name, and *factorial* is a function name.

1.2.3 MATLAB Sessions

The text uses the `Courier` font to display examples of MATLAB interactive sessions. The following session demonstrates how to create a 2×3 matrix named *A* in the MATLAB Command window at the $>>$ prompt: The MATLAB Command window displays the result immediately below the typed command.

```
>> A = [1, 3, 5; 2, 4, 6]
A =
     1      3      5
     2      4      6
```

1.2.4 Key Terms

The first time an important or key term is used, it is italicized. There is a summary of key terms at the end of each chapter.

1.2.5 Syntax Definitions

The text uses the `Courier` font to display syntax definitions of MATLAB functions and statements. The key words and other symbols that you are to type literally are printed in regular face font. Variables are printed in italics. The following is part of the syntax definition for the MATLAB function *ones*:

```
Y = ones(d1,d2,d3,...)
```

The symbol "=", the name "*ones*", and the parentheses are to be typed literally. The variable *Y* is a placeholder. You could substitute any legitimate variable name for *Y*. You could substitute any legitimate argument list for *d*1, *d*2, *d*3. The ellipsis "..." indicates that MATLAB will accept a variable number of arguments. All of the following are legitimate instances of the syntax definition just described:

```
>> MyMatrix = ones(2,3)
>> F34_Extra = ones(4,4,4,4)
>> Z = ones(1)
>> A_Ones = ones(A,A,A)     % if A is defined
```

1.2.6 Code Segments

The text uses the `Courier` font to print segments of source code such as function definitions. At times, we will add line numbers along the left margin for easy reference. You should not type the line numbers into the MATLAB Editor as part of the source code. The MATLAB Editor automatically supplies the line number. Figure 1.1 is an example of a function definition with line numbers.

```
1 function Out = Fib(N)
2 % Fib(N) - Returns the Nth Fibonacci number.
3 switch N
4    case {1, 2}
5       Out = 1;
6    otherwise
7       Out  = feval(@Fib, N-1) + feval(@Fib, N-2);
8 end
```

Figure 1.1. Example function definition.

1.3   PROBLEM SOLVING AND THE ENGINEERING METHOD

Engineers are problem solvers. The ability to solve technical problems successfully is both an art and a science. The successful solution of engineering problems requires a broad background in a variety of technical areas, such as mathematics, physics, and computational science. The successful resolution of engineering problems also requires a set of broad general skills. Good reading comprehension, common sense, good judgement, logical thinking, and careful verification of results are examples of important general abilities.

Engineering solutions often involve balancing several competing factors. An example is the trade-off between cost and reliability. It costs money to remove impurities from an integrated circuit during manufacture. The impurities are directly related to the reliability of the chip. As the manufacturing and testing processes improve to produce a progressively more reliable chip, the costs continue to increase. At some point, it becomes too expensive to make the chip any more reliable. A common design decision is to balance cost and reliability. This can be expressed in a way that defines the level of reliability required:

A chip is reliable if there is a 90% probability that the chip will not fail in five years.

Similar trade-offs are made in software design. For example, the solution to a problem may require a *space-time trade-off*. Writing results to a hard disk on your computer is slower than writing the results to the computer's physical memory (called random access memory or RAM). If many partial results are stored on disk, then the solution may require less volatile memory (RAM). Less space is taken in (expensive) memory, but the solution will compute more slowly, because saving the partial results to disk is slower than simply storing them in memory.

In order to understand the scope and overall programming process, it is helpful to describe the large steps involved. The process described next, called the *engineering method*, is presented as a series of steps. However, this linear presentation is somewhat misleading. First, the steps are not always discrete. A single step may blend into another, or several steps may proceed in parallel. Second, the process is iterative. An engineer may take two steps forward and one step back or may revisit and refine a previous step. Nevertheless, the following steps in the engineering method serve as a model of the tasks and the general order in which they are accomplished:

1.   Problem Definition
2.   Information Gathering
3.   Selection of the Appropriate Theory or Methodology
4.   Generation of Simplifying Assumptions
5.   Solution and Refinement
6.   Testing and Verification

1.3.1   Problem Definition

The precise definition of a problem can be one of the most difficult phases of solving a problem. Often a client (or instructor) will present a problem with ambiguous specifications. At times, the client does not completely understand the problem. It is worth the effort to obtain missing requirements and reduce ambiguities as early as possible in the design process. A clear and precise written statement of a problem at this stage will save you much wasted expenditure of energy later.

Next, precise and detailed requirements documents are developed. A software requirement is a statement of how the software should perform in a given situation. The development of a requirements document serves both as a process for acquiring a mutually agreeable and precise problem definition and as a contract of that agreement.

1.3.2   Information Gathering

To design a proper solution for a specified problem, an engineer must first gather relevant information. At a minimum, this involves a thorough review of the relevant domain areas, which includes a review of previous solutions to similar problems. There is no need to "reinvent the wheel." An engineer may also perform experiments to gather the information needed to devise a problem solution.

1.3.3   Selection of the Appropriate Theory or Methodology

An engineer may formulate a problem solution using a variety of scientific principles. The engineer's educational background and training contribute strongly to the ability to succeed in this step. An expert consultant in the application domain is extremely useful during this stage. One of the values of a domain expert is that the expert retains a history of previously known solutions to similar problems.

1.3.4   Generation of Simplifying Assumptions

A theory is an abstraction of how the world works. To solve real-world problems, we need to simplify the solution by making assumptions about some of the theory's components. As an example, suppose that your boss assigns you the job of designing a kiln. Part of the design process involves calculating the heat loss from the kiln. Heat loss can occur through convection, conduction, and radiation. If you make the assumption that the convective loss is negligible, the calculation only has to account for heat loss due to conduction and radiation.

1.3.5   Solution and Refinement

The *top-down design* method is a time-honored way to structure large problems. Top-down design involves creating a general, overall solution and then partitioning that solution into subsystems. Afterward, the engineer finds solutions for the subsystems and describes the interfaces among the subsystems. A large application may involve several levels of subdivision. We call the partitioning of a software design into subsystems with well-defined interfaces *modularization*.

As an engineer, one of the methods that you will use to solve problems is to write software programs. An essential element of software design is the reduction of a problem solution to an algorithm. An *algorithm* is like a recipe for the solution. At first, the engineer describes the general algorithm for the solution of the problem.

There are several software-design tools that can assist you with this task. Examples of tools that help in the design of algorithmic solutions are flowcharts and pseudocode. A *flowchart* is a pictorial representation that shows the logical steps and decisions used to complete an algorithm. *Pseudocode* is a textual description of an algorithmic solution that resembles programming code, but avoids the strict use of syntax.

If you correctly use the design tools in preceding phases, you will have a clear blueprint for writing the code. That is, once you write a pseudocode solution, you can easily translate it to MATLAB code or to another programming language. The coding phase usually takes less time than the other steps in the problem-solving process.

Questions may arise during the solution phase, even in a well-defined project. You may need to review the solution with the client and then refine the application's documentation. In your case, this may consist of clarifying details of your assignment with your instructor.

A common scenario is for an engineer to test and refine potential solutions to a problem by building a *prototype*. A *prototype* is a model or mock-up solution. In the case of a software solution, the engineer will first test the prototype solution by using a small data set, which may consist of a subset of the overall data, data from a scaled-down version of the real problem, or data from an artificial problem that mimics the real-world problem.

When the engineer is satisfied that the prototype works, the solution may be translated to a more scalable and efficient implementation. The MATLAB interpreter is useful for building software prototypes, because solutions can be quickly developed and easily modified. Once a prototype solution has been tested and verified, it may be translated to another language to increase the speed of the program.

A prototype can serve to help the client visualize the potential application. A prototype of the application's interface can serve to help the client describe the desired interaction more accurately. A prototype of any underlying algorithm can serve to help validate the accuracy of the algorithmic solution.

Sometimes, a number of iterations are required to get the correct solution. Engineers frequently solve problems iteratively. Successive refinement of a solution is a time-honored process.

1.3.6   Testing and Verification

Testing and verification of an engineering solution is a critical step. It is important that the person performing the testing be involved in the analysis and design phases of the software development process. This is easy if the same person is responsible for all phases of the project. In real-world applications, a team will likely conduct a project, and the team member responsible for testing is usually called the *quality assurance engineer* or *QA engineer*. The QA engineer should verify that the requirements are clear and testable. While other members of the team are busy creating the solution, the QA engineer may write test cases that cover each requirement in the requirements document. The QA engineer then uses the test cases to verify that each requirement has been successfully met.

The software QA engineer uses a process that is similar to QA for manufacturing, but the types of errors are somewhat different. For example, in manufacturing, a typical error is that a machine part is out of tolerance. Software errors may come from a variety of sources. For instance, the incorrect placement of a comma or semicolon may cause an error. We call this a *syntax error*, because the programmer has incorrectly used the syntax of the programming language. Computers are very strict about syntax errors. We will discuss MATLAB's syntax more fully beginning in Chapter 3.

Other types of errors are structural, rather than syntactic. The syntax is correct, but the logic or algorithm is incorrect. For example, if you are writing a program to compute the area of a cylinder, but you incorrectly use the formula for the surface area of a cylinder to develop your code, you have committed an algorithmic error.

Other errors are computational or engineering errors. Examples are misplaced decimal points or incorrect unit conversions that produce unreasonable answers. Chapter 10 covers these types of errors and shows you ways to detect them.

The process of testing is complex. Sometimes, you can test solutions by choosing the endpoints of input parameter ranges. In this way, the limits of the solution are tested. In many cases, it is impossible to test all of the possible input sets. Consider a control unit with eight input controls, each of which has 10 calibration settings. There are 10^8 or 100 million possible input combinations for the control unit. It would be unreasonable to test every combination, so the QA engineer often chooses a representative sample and presents the results statistically.

As an engineer, you should realize that every project of any size *will* have errors. In the real world, the testing phase and correction of errors may continue for years. Consider the manufacture of airplanes or automobiles. Often, defective parts are detected years after the vehicle has been built and sold. The recall and replacement of defective parts is costly. Software solutions are no different. Software maintenance is extremely costly to organizations that develop software. In fact, software maintenance typically costs an organization more than the original software development.

1.4 THE MATLAB SYSTEM

1.4.1 Introduction

The MATLAB system began as a collection of matrix manipulation routines. Over the years, MATLAB has grown to include a large number of components. MATLAB is used for a variety of purposes: interactive problem solving, support for research and algorithm prototyping, and, more recently, the development of software applications. It is important that MATLAB can be used as both an interactive tool and as an environment to write and store computer programs. These advantages allow an engineer to both quickly prototype small solutions and build large, deliverable solutions.

MATLAB is used professionally in a number of domains, including engineering, finance, physics, mathematics, and chemistry. This introductory text will cover a very small part of MATLAB's capabilities. In particular, we will cover a small number of the built-in functions. The text will cover none of the domain-specific toolboxes. The following sections present a top-level view of the main components of MATLAB:

1.4.2 The Interactive Environment

The MATLAB interactive environment is a set of graphical interfaces that promotes the rapid solution of mathematical and engineering problems in a single session. The interfaces allow you to locate files, execute MATLAB functions, view a history of previously executed commands, view data structures, and create plots.

1.4.3 The Programming Environment

The MATLAB programming environment consists primarily of an interpreted scripting language and a set of programming support tools. The scripting language is the primary focus of this text, and we will describe it throughout the book.

The MATLAB development environment includes an Editor, Debugger, and Code Profiler. Support is also provided for accessing a source-code management system from MATLAB.

1.4.4 Built-In Functions

The heart of the MATLAB engine is a large number of high-level, optimized functions that enable the rapid prototyping of scientific and engineering solutions. The basic MATLAB engine includes functions for input–output operations, matrix manipulation, plotting, interpolation, data analysis, linear and nonlinear methods, sound processing, and numerical solutions.

You will realize the power of these built-in functions as you progress through your engineering courses and as you are required to solve complex or computationally intensive problems by hand. For example, calculating the determinant of a matrix or inverting a matrix can be very tedious to do manually. However, MATLAB makes these types of matrix operations trivial to perform.

1.4.5 Toolboxes

In addition to the primary MATLAB engine, a large number of add-on toolboxes and other components are available. These special purpose applications provide sets of functions for specific purposes such as control systems, data acquisition, symbolic mathematics, fuzzy logic, signal processing, neural networks, and statistics. As you progress through your engineering courses and professional career, you will probably see some of these toolboxes in use. The MATLAB website lists the available toolboxes, and you can access it at

```
http://www.mathworks.com/products
```

1.4.6   Supported Platforms

Release 12 of MATLAB supports the following operating systems: the Microsoft Windows™ operating systems, including Windows 95™, Windows 98™, Windows NT™, Windows ME™, and Windows 2000. Beginning with Release 13, MATLAB no longer supports Windows 95, but fully supports Windows XP™. In addition, MATLAB fully supports the Mac OS X™, Linux, and a variety of UNIX systems, including Sun Solaris™, Silicon Graphics IRIX™, and Compaq Alpha Tru64™.

The majority of deployed installations are in the Microsoft Windows environment and the screen shots in this textbook were taken by using Microsoft Windows and MATLAB Release 12. Except for initial start-up and file name limitations, most of the examples in this text will work on any platform. The examples have been tested with Release 12 and Release 13. If you are running MATLAB in a non-Microsoft environment, please refer to your MATLAB release notes to check for any peculiarities specific to your operating system.

1.4.7   MATLAB Student Version

MATLAB provides an inexpensive educational or student version of Release 12 for the Microsoft Windows and the Linux operating systems. The student version of MATLAB includes the following components of the professional version:

- The basic MATLAB engine and development environment
- The MATLAB notebook
- Simulink®
- Some of the Symbolic Math Toolbox functions

Matrix sizes are unlimited in the student version. The amount of memory on your computer is the limiting factor for maximum matrix size. This is the same for the professional version of MATLAB. The Simulink toolbox for the student version is limited to 300 modeling blocks. The student version's CD contains the full electronic documentation.

Other toolboxes must be purchased separately. Not all toolboxes are available for the student version. For more information, please see the MATLAB website.

The student version of MATLAB has a different prompt. Instead of >>, the prompt is EDU>>.

PRACTICE 1.1!

Log on to the MathWorks website at

```
http://www.mathworks.com
```

Familiarize yourself with the site, including the help features. Use the search feature to locate information about the student version of MATLAB. See if you can find the Technical Support Guide to the MATLAB student version.

1.5   INTRODUCTION TO COMPUTING

This section introduces important basic topics about computing. If the information is familiar to you, treat it as a review.

1.5.1   Computers and Programmers

A *computer* is literally any device that performs computations and makes logical decisions. Most computers today are electronic and many components are made out of silicon. However, working computers have been made out of a variety of materials. A notable example is a computer made out of Tinker Toys™ and fishing line by Danny Mills in the 1980's. The Tinker Toy computer demonstrated that almost any type of parts can be assembled to perform mathematical or logical computations. Scientists are currently exploring new media for computation, including the use of biological and optical components.

The mechanical and electronic devices that compose a computer, such as the monitor, keyboard, and floppy drive are called computer *hardware*. The programs that run on the hardware are called computer *software*. Examples of computer software are the Microsoft Windows operating system, the AOL® Instant Messenger™, MATLAB, and your favorite video game. Sometimes the dividing line between hardware and software is blurred. For example, short pieces of software that are used very frequently may be encoded directly into hardware to make the code execute faster. In this textbook, we will be concerned with writing computer software.

A person who uses computer applications is called a *computer user*. A person who writes computer programs is called a *computer programmer*. As an engineering student, you will use computer applications frequently. You will also have the opportunity to write computer programs to assist you in solving engineering problems.

1.5.2   Computer Organization

The typical computers of today share many common features. The core organization of a computer consists of the following components:

- a central processing unit
- volatile memory
- input and output devices
- peripheral devices

Central Processing Unit

The *central processing unit* or *CPU* is considered the brains of the computer. Typical components of a CPU are the arithmetic processing units, the control unit, very fast temporary storage units called *registers*, and slightly slower but somewhat larger capacity temporary storage units called *caches*. The *arithmetic processing units* are specialized units that perform arithmetic operations on either floating-point numbers or integers. The *control unit* reads the instructions that are fed to the computer and supervises the processing of the instructions.

Volatile Memory

Data are stored in a computer in a hierarchical fashion. Faster access to the data, in general, implies more costly storage mechanisms. The caches and registers on the CPU are the fastest and most expensive places to store data. The next level of hierarchical storage is called *volatile memory*, or *random access memory (RAM)*. The term *volatile* means that any data stored in this type of memory is lost when the computer is turned off. The term *random access* means that any location in memory can be accessed in about the same amount of time. An audio compact disc is random access in the sense that you can move quickly to the beginning of any song by pushing a button. An audio cassette is not random access since you must wind slowly forward or backwards to locate a song. If you are at the beginning of the tape, it takes you much longer to get to song eight than to song two. On a CD player, you can access song eight as rapidly as song two.

I/O Devices

The *input* and *output* or *I/O devices* may be the parts of a computer that are most familiar to you. These peripherals are the gates into and out of the CPU and memory. Typical *input devices* are a keyboard, a mouse, and a network connection. Typical *output devices* are a monitor, a printer, and a network card. A special class of I/O devices is called *secondary storage*. These are nonvolatile memory devices such as hard disks, floppy drives, compact disks, and data tape. Data that are stored on nonvolatile media do not disappear when you turn your computer off.

1.5.3   Program Execution

Computer software is typically stored in nonvolatile memory (secondary storage). When software is executed, part or the entire computer program is loaded into volatile memory. The control unit then reads and executes the program one instruction at a time.

A special piece of software that manages the resources of a computer is called the *operating system*. The kernel of the operating system is loaded when the computer is turned on, and it continues to run until the computer is turned off. The operating system acts as the master software. One of the primary tasks of the operating system is to schedule other programs to run. In modern operating systems, many programs are allowed to share the CPU at approximately the same time. The operating system schedules these jobs so that each one gets a fair chance to use the CPU.

The operating system also manages the data flow among the peripheral devices, the CPU, and memory. The peripheral devices typically communicate by sending data down an electronic highway called a *bus*. The operating system plays the role of traffic cop for the peripheral devices.

One of the differences between MATLAB and many other programming languages is that MATLAB is an interpreted language rather than a compiled language. If you are interested in this topic, Appendix B explains the difference between a compiled and an interpreted programming language.

KEY TERMS

algorithm	flowchart	RAM
arithmetic processing unit	hardware	random access memory
bus	I/O devices	registers
cache	input devices	secondary storage
central processing unit	matrix laboratory	software
computer	modularization	space-time trade-off
computer programmer	operating system	syntax errors
computer user	output devices	top-down design
control unit	prototype	volatile memory
CPU	pseudocode	
engineering method	QA engineer	

Problems

Section 1.1.

1. The term MATLAB stands for _____ _____.
2. MATLAB's mathematical specialty is _____ _____.
3. The prerequisites for this text are high school _____ and _____.

Section 1.2.

4. The text denotes pressing down two keys simultaneously by separating them with the _____ sign.
5. If you are to select two items one after the other, in text these items are separated with a _____ _____.
6. The ellipsis (...) indicates that a _____ _____ of arguments will be accepted by a function.

Section 1.3.

7. A common trade-off in software design is made between _____ and _____.
8. Before writing a complete software solution, a programmer may write a mock-up or _____.
9. Creating a general overall solution first and then partitioning that solution into subsystems is called _____ _____ _____.
10. A recipe for a solution to a problem is called an _____.
11. A comma placed incorrectly in a program's code is called a _____ error.

Section 1.4.

12. MATLAB's set of graphical interfaces is called its _____ environment.
13. MATLAB's interpreted scripting language and set of programming support tools is called its _____ environment.
14. The matrix sizes in the student version of MATLAB are smaller than the matrix sizes allowed in the professional version, true or false.
15. The software-development tool that assists you in finding program errors is called a _____.
16. Log on to the MathWorks website. Locate the list of available toolboxes. List three MATLAB toolboxes.

    _____
    _____
    _____

Section 1.5.

17. The fastest temporary storage units on a computer are called _____.
18. Floppy drives and zip disks are special types of I/O devices called _____ storage devices.
19. Which of the following are examples of software?

    ___ CPU
    ___ operating system
    ___ MATLAB
    ___ zip drives
    ___ control unit

2

The MATLAB Interactive Environment

2.1 THE MATLAB DESKTOP

2.1.1 Starting and Exiting MATLAB

In Microsoft Windows, you can start MATLAB in several ways. One way is to choose MATLAB from the Start menu. Click on the **Start** button (usually on the bottom left corner of your screen) and then choose

Programs → **MATLAB Release 12** → **MATLAB R12**

Depending on the installation, the MATLAB menu item may be in a different location on your computer. Figure 2.1 shows a typical location for the MATLAB menu item.

A second method for starting MATLAB is to type a command. From the Start menu, choose **Run**. When the Run dialog box appears, type

```
matlab
```

If typing the MATLAB command does not work, it may mean that your paths are not set up correctly. Please see your system administrator or local computer guru for help in locating the MATLAB executables and setting your paths correctly.

If you are using a UNIX system, you can start MATLAB by typing the following at the system prompt:

```
matlab
```

The first screen that appears is called the splash screen. If you are using the student version, the splash screen will announce that this is a student version. (See Figure 2.2.)

OBJECTIVES

After reading this chapter, you should be able to

- Start and exit MATLAB.
- Create, edit, and save MATLAB sessions to M-files.
- Save MATLAB data to MAT-files.
- Print MATLAB sessions.
- Find help on MATLAB topics.
- Modify and save your MATLAB preferences.

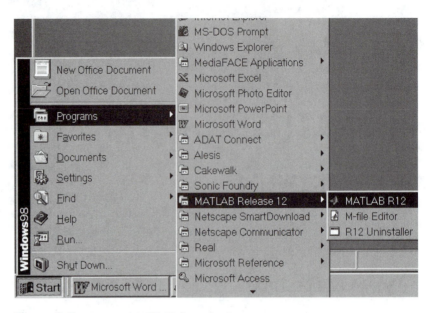

Figure 2.1. Starting MATLAB from the Start menu.

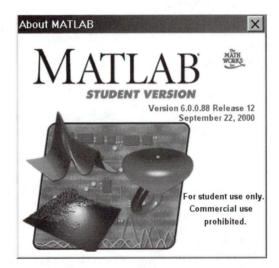

Figure 2.2. The MATLAB splash screen.

Figure 2.3 shows the default window setup, which happens to be the student version. Note that the prompt in the Command window reads

    EDU>>

to indicate that this is the student version. If you are not running the student version, the default prompt is

    >>

The list of items across the top of the MATLAB screen is called the *Menu bar*. From the Menu bar, choose **View → Desktop Layout**. You should see a list of layout options as depicted in Figure 2.4. Experiment with several of these options to see how

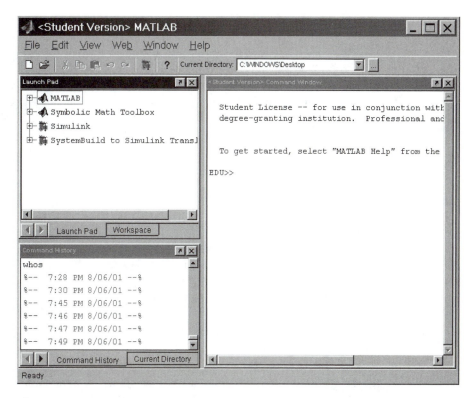

Figure 2.3.   The default MATLAB screen.

Figure 2.4.   The Desktop Layout menu.

Figure 2.5.   The Window control buttons.

they change the display. When you are finished experimenting, choose the **Default** layout.

If your MATLAB screen is not filling the whole screen, click on the icon in the top right that looks like the open square (the center icon in Figure 2.5). This is called the *Maximize button*.

To exit the MATLAB system, choose **File → Exit MATLAB** from the Menu bar. An alternate way to exit is to click on the button that looks like an **X** in the upper right portion of the MATLAB screen (the right icon in Figure 2.5). This is called the *Close button*. A third method is to type *quit* or *exit* at the MATLAB prompt.

The third control button (the one on the left in Figure 2.5) minimizes the MAT-LAB screen. It is called the *Minimize button*. A minimized application stays open, but it shrinks to an icon on the Task bar, which is typically located at the bottom of your screen. This is handy since your current workspace retains all of its values. Try minimizing the MATLAB screen, and then expand it by clicking on the MATLAB icon in the Task bar (the bar at the bottom of your screen). Once the application expands to full size, look at the screen components. The names of the MATLAB screen components, viewing roughly from top to bottom are as follows:

- Title bar
- Menu bar
- Desktop toolbar
- Launch Pad window
- Command window
- Command History window

There are tabs for accessing two other windows:

- Workspace window
- Current Directory window

Each of these components will be discussed in the next section.

2.1.2 The MATLAB Screen Components

The Title Bar

Figure 2.6 depicts the *Title bar*. The Title bar contains the program's logo and the Window Control buttons. Shown in Figure 2.6, it is the top item in the MATLAB screen.

The Menu Bar

Figure 2.7 depicts the Menu bar. In the example, the File menu item is selected. We will discuss each of the menu items in detail in subsequent sections. For now, take a few minutes and browse each menu item. Note that some items have a shortcut key to the right of the menu item name. For example, in Figure 2.7, the File, Open item has the notation Ctrl + O. This means that you can begin the process of opening a file by holding down the key labeled *Ctrl* and simultaneously pressing *O*. This action performs the same function as selecting *Open* from the File menu. Using our shortcut notation, we say that:

Choose **File → Open**

performs the same function as

Type **Ctrl + O**

Figure 2.6. The Title bar.

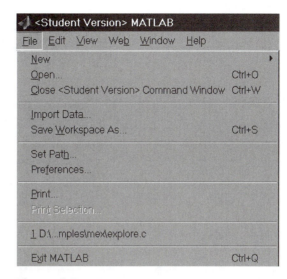

Figure 2.7. The Menu bar.

The Desktop Toolbar

The window depicted in Figure 2.8 is called the *Desktop toolbar*. On this toolbar, you will see icons for many of the same items that appear on the Menu bar. Slowly move your mouse over each item on the toolbar. You should see a small yellow box that describes the icon. We call this a *tool tip*. Figure 2.8 depicts the tool tip for Open File. Not all items that appear on the Menu bar are shown as icons on the Desktop toolbar. In addition, not all items that have icons on the toolbar appear in the menu.

The Launch Pad

The *Launch Pad window* is yet another method of accessing MATLAB resources. First, expand the Launch Pad window by separating it from the desktop. We call this action *undocking* the window. To undock the window, click on the ▣ icon at the top of the Launch Pad window. The launch pad will undock from the MATLAB window and the resulting window should be similar to Figure 2.9. You can expand or shrink menu icons in the Launch Pad window by clicking, respectively, on a plus or minus sign located to the left of the item. Figure 2.9 shows the MATLAB icon expanded.

If your system has any of the MATLAB toolboxes installed, they will appear in the Launch Pad. Figure 2.9 shows that the author's system has Simulink and the Symbolic Math toolboxes installed. Double-clicking on an expanded item will launch that module. Try the following:

1. Click on the plus sign to the left of the MATLAB icon to expand the selection.
2. Double-click on the item labeled *Demos*. The MATLAB Demo window should appear.

Figure 2.8. The Desktop toolbar with tool tip.

When you press the **Enter** key, the following should appear:

```
Width =
    2.3000
>>
```

Note that in the text, we often display MATLAB's results along with a command that you are to type. This is intended to help you verify that you are typing the correct command.

The effect of the command that you just executed is as follows:

1. A storage location is created.
2. The location is given the name *Width*.
3. The value 2.3 is stored in that location.
4. The results of the action are echoed back to you.
5. The prompt reappears, waiting for you to enter another command.

A named storage location is called a *variable*. In this example, the variable name is *Width*. If you do not give a variable a name, MATLAB will assign the results to the default variable *ans*. Type the following to see this effect:

```
>> 45 - 10
ans =
    35
```

You can change the contents of a variable simply by assigning it a new value. For example, type

```
>> Width = 3.7
Width =
    3.7000
```

Since the variable *Width* already exists, it is not recreated. The new value of 3.7 is now assigned to *Width* and the old value of 2.3 is overwritten. The results are echoed back when you press the **Enter** key.

If you do not want the results to be echoed in the Command window, you can suppress the output by typing a semicolon after the command. Try typing the previous command again, but this time, add a semicolon at the end. Your entry should look like this:

```
>> Width = 3.7;
```

Here, the Command window will display the results.

Note that MATLAB is case sensitive. The following names all refer to different variables: *width, Width, WIDTH*.

Now, type

```
>> Height = 4.1;
```

You have created a second variable named *Height* and assigned it a value of 4.1. We will use the variables *Width* and *Height* to compute the area of a rectangle. You have not yet been shown MATLAB's symbols for arithmetic operations, but, the symbol for multiplication is the asterisk (*).

Type the following:

```
>> Area = Height * Width
Area =
    15.1700
```

You have now computed the area of a rectangle with the given height and width and stored the result in a new variable named *Area*. Figure 2.10 displays the commands and results from this session.

You can undock the Command window by choosing **View → Undock Command Window** from the main MATLAB menu bar. You can redock the Command window by choosing **View → Dock Command Window** from the Command window menu bar. The other MATLAB windows share the same docking and undocking facility.

The Command window supports command line editing. *Command line editing* is the ability to edit each line interactively and to reexecute the line. MATLAB stores previously typed commands. You can press the up-arrow and down-arrow keys to locate the previously typed commands. You can use the left- and right-arrow keys to position the cursor and edit the command. When you have finished editing a command, press the **Enter** key to reexecute the command.

The Command History Window

The *Command History window* keeps a running history of the commands that have been typed and executed in the Command window. If you followed the previous examples, your Command History window should look like Figure 2.11. Note that the Command History window does not show the results of your commands.

You can clear selections from this window by choosing **Edit → Clear Command History** from the Menu bar. An alternate method is to first place the mouse cursor in the Command history window. We call this *focusing the mouse*. Then click the right mouse button and choose one of the delete items from the pop-up menu as depicted in Figure 2.12.

Look at the other menu items on the pop-up menu depicted in the figure. These allow you to copy previous commands (**Copy**), execute previous commands (**Evaluate Selection**), or save previous commands into a file (**Create M-File**).

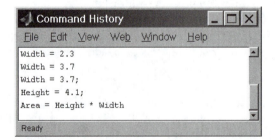

Figure 2.11.   The Command History window.

Figure 2.12.   The Command History pop-up menu.

The Workspace Window

Select the Workspace window by choosing the **Workspace** tab under the Launch Pad window. If you followed the examples, your Workspace window should be similar to Figure 2.13.

The *Workspace window* shows the variables that you have created during the current MATLAB session. The Workspace window displays some other information about the size and type of each variable. This information will make more sense later in the text after you have studied data types. For now, use the Workspace window to keep track of the variables in your workspace as you execute the examples in the text.

The variables in your workspace remain in existence only as long as the current session lasts, unless you explicitly delete them. If you minimize the MATLAB windows, the workspace does not change. However, if you exit MATLAB or if your computer crashes, the values will be lost.

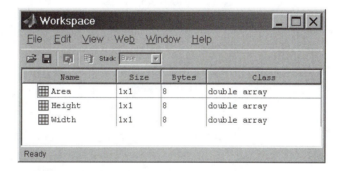

Figure 2.13.   The Workspace window.

The Current Directory Window

Select the *Current Directory window* by choosing the tab titled **Current Directory** under the Command History window. Figure 2.14 depicts the Current Directory window. This window contains a number of options that facilitate locating, opening, editing, and saving files. We will discuss many of the options in the next section.

2.2   CREATING, EDITING, AND SAVING SESSIONS

MATLAB makes it easy for you to interactively prototype solutions to a problem and then save the commands in a file. You can then retrieve, edit, or execute that file. Let us

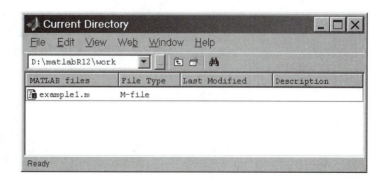

Figure 2.14.   The Current Directory window.

walk through creating, editing, and saving a file that contains a list of MATLAB commands. We will do so by using the MATLAB Editor/Debugger. As its name implies, you can use it to edit text files, as well as to debug code. We will use the Editor/Debugger extensively in later chapters, but, for now, we will use it to create and save a few lines of MATLAB code. Perform the following steps:

1. Choose **File → New → M-file** from the Menu bar. The Editor/Debugger will appear. (See Figure 2.15.)

2. Type the following three lines into the Editor:

    ```
    % My first M-file. Computes the area of a circle.
    Radius = 3.2;
    Area = pi * Radius^2
    ```

    The percent sign (%) denotes a comment. The MATLAB interpreter ignores everything on the same line that follows a percent sign.

    The commented line is colored green by default. The coloring of different elements is called *syntax highlighting*.

    The expression "pi" calls the internal MATLAB function named *pi* and returns an approximation of the mathematical constant π. The caret (^) symbol denotes raising the contents of the variable *Radius* to the power of the expression that follows it (2 in the example). Your Editor window should look like Figure 2.15.

3. Save the code to a file by choosing **File → Save As** from the Menu bar. The Save File As dialog box should appear as depicted in Figure 2.16.

4. Locate the directory in which you want to store your file. Click on the small arrow to the right of the box titled "Save in:". If you are using a networked computer, your instructor may have to tell you which drive and directory to use for storage.

5. In the box titled "File name:", type a name for your file. For example, you could name your file: example1.m. Make sure that your file has an *.m* extension; that is, the file name must end in a period, followed by the letter *m*. If you do not give an extension, MATLAB will add the extension by default. MATLAB calls a file that contains program code an *M-file*.

6. Close the Editor by selecting **File → Close** from the Menu bar. Note that the contents of the Current Directory window have changed to include your new M-file.

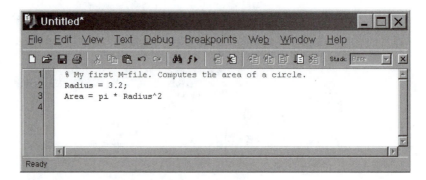

Figure 2.15.   The Editor/Debugger.

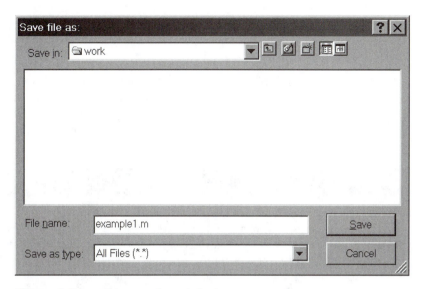

Figure 2.16.   The Save File As dialog box.

Now that you have saved your code to an M-file, you can open the file, edit it, or run the code. These are the steps to follow in order to run (also called execute) the program:

1.   Select the file in the Current Directory window by clicking on it once with the left mouse button.

2.   Once you have highlighted the file name, click the right mouse button. The Current Directory pop-up menu will appear as depicted in Figure 2.17.

3.   To execute the newly edited code, choose **Run** from the Current Directory pop-up menu. The new results will appear in the Command window.

There are four alternate ways to execute an open M-file:

1.   Press the **F5** key.

2.   Choose **Debug** → **Run** from the Editor's Menu bar.

Figure 2.17.   The Current Directory pop-up menu.

3. Type the name of the file at the MATLAB prompt.
4. Select the Run icon ⬚ from the Editor's toolbar.

The MATLAB Notebook is a feature that supports the creation of MATLAB macros inside of a Microsoft Word document. The MATLAB engine can evaluate the macros. The Notebook is useful for embedding MATLAB code into reports and technical papers. A Word document that contains embedded MATLAB commands is called an *M-book*. Appendix D describes the creation and use of M-books.

PROGRAMMING TIP 2.1!

Commenting code is an important part of documenting your work. You may understand your code the day that you write it, but it is surprising how much you can forget in six months time. Most professional programming is done by teams. Good commenting is essential when you are sharing code with others.

How much should you comment? Your instructor will probably have a strong opinion about this topic, and you should follow your instructor's guidelines.

More advice about commenting will be given as we progress, but, for now, make sure that, at a minimum, you comment every M-file by writing a short description of its contents in the first several lines of the file.

2.3 IMPORTING AND EXPORTING DATA

2.3.1 Saving and Retrieving MATLAB Data

In the previous section, you saved a few MATLAB commands to an M-file. You can also save MATLAB data to a file. A data file has the default extension *.mat*. MATLAB calls a data file a *MAT-file*.

To save all of your current variables (called your workspace), choose **File → Save Workspace As** from the Menu bar.

Follow these steps in order to save a subset of the workspace:

1. Select the variables to be saved by clicking on each variable in the Workspace window.
2. Select more than one variable by holding down the **Ctrl** key while left clicking the mouse. Alternatively, select a range of variables by holding down the **Shift** key while left clicking and dragging the mouse over the selection.
3. After you have selected the variables to save, hold down the right mouse key and choose **Save Selection As** from the drop-down menu.

To retrieve variables from a MAT-file,

1. Choose **File → Open** from the Menu bar.
2. You can limit your search for MAT files by choosing **Files of Type → MAT-files** from the dialog box, when the File Open dialog box appears.
3. Select the MAT file and then choose **Open**.

PRACTICE 2.1!

Practice creating, saving, and retrieving data by following these steps:

1. Clear the workspace by choosing **Edit → Clear Workspace** from the Menu bar (or by typing *clear* at the command prompt).
2. Create three variables by typing the following commands into the Command window:
   ```
   >> Resistance = 2500;
   >> Current = 14.7;
   >> Voltage = 110;
   ```
3. You should now see the variables *Resistance*, *Current*, and *Voltage* displayed in the Workspace window.
4. Select *Resistance* and *Voltage* with the mouse (use the **Ctrl** or **Shift** and arrow keys) and highlight both variables.
5. Click the right mouse button and choose **Save Selection As** from the drop-down menu.
6. From the Save As dialog box, choose a file name for your file and click **OK**. Make sure that the file has a *MAT* extension.
7. Clear the workspace by choosing **Edit → Clear Workspace** from the Menu bar.
8. Retrieve the data by choosing **File → Open** from the Menu bar. Note that *Resistance* and *Voltage* have reappeared in the Workspace window. However, the variable *Current* no longer exists because it was not saved in the MAT file.

An alternate method for saving and loading data is to use the save and load commands from the command prompt. To save the current workspace to a file name *my_vars*, type

```
>> save my_vars
```

To load the variables from the file *my_vars* to the workspace, type

```
>> load my_vars
```

Appendix E provides more information about importing external data.

2.4   PRINTING

2.4.1   Printing from the Command Window

To print text data from the Command window,

1. Select the data with the mouse until it is highlighted.
2. Choose **File → Print** from the Menu bar.

If you want to print everything in the Command window,

1. Choose **Edit → Select All** from the Menu bar.
2. Choose **File → Print** from the Menu bar.

2.4.2 Printing from the MATLAB Editor

To print an M-file,

1. First, open the file.
2. Choose **File → Print** from the Menu bar of the Editor.

To print a selection from an M-file,

1. Load the file into the MATLAB Editor.
2. Create a selection by using the mouse.
3. Choose **File → Print Selection** from the Menu bar of the Editor.

2.4.3 Printing Plots and Graphics

MATLAB has the facility for printing plots and graphics. We will discuss printing plots and graphics more fully in Chapter 6. For a simple demonstration, type the following statement into the Command window:

```
>> plot(sin(pi : 0.1 : 4*pi))
```

The basic MATLAB command for plotting is named *plot*. The effect of this command is to plot the sine function from π to $4*\pi$ in increments of 0.1. When you press the **Enter** key, the Plot Editor will appear as depicted in Figure 2.18. To print the plot, choose **File → Print** from the Menu bar of the Plot Editor.

MATLAB also has an online tutorial that demonstrates how to setup and print graphics. To view the tutorial,

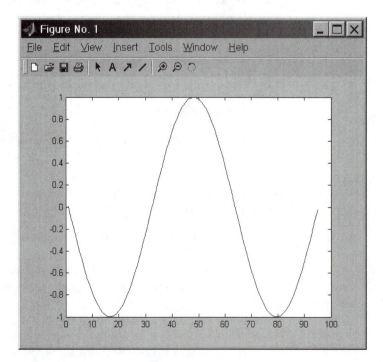

Figure 2.18. The Plot Editor.

1. Choose **MATLAB → Demos** from the Launch Pad. The MATLAB Demo window will appear as shown in Figure 2.19.

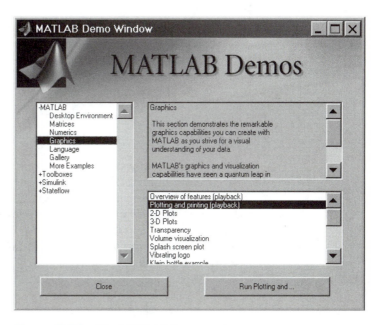

Figure 2.19.   The MATLAB Demo window.

2. Choose **Graphics → Plotting and printing (playback)** and then click the **Run** button to view the demo.

2.5   GETTING HELP

The MATLAB system provides a variety of ways to get help. It has a text-based and a graphical interface within the application. In addition, help is available on the World Wide Web.

2.5.1   Text-Based Help

The text-based help interface is available in the Command window. To view the help topics, type *help* from the prompt:

```
>> help

HELP topics:
matlab\general    -   General purpose commands.
matlab\ops        -   Operators and special characters.
matlab\lang       -   Programming language constructs.
matlab\elmat      -   Elementary matrices and matrix
                         manipulation.
matlab\elfun      -   Elementary math functions.
matlab\specfun    -   Specialized math functions.
...
...
...
```

To view more specific help, type *help* followed by a topic, command, or function name. The MATLAB function for sine is named *sin*. To learn more about the *sin* function, type

```
>> help sin
 SIN    Sine.
    SIN(X) is the sine of the elements of X.
 Overloaded methods
    help sym/sin.m
```

MATLAB capitalizes the name of the function or command for emphasis. When you use the function, do not capitalize it. The arguments to the function are displayed in parentheses following the function name. The name of function is followed by a short one-line description. In the previous example, the name of the function is *Sine*. "SIN(X) is the sine of the elements of X" is the one-line description.

There may be more than one function with the same name in your search path. We call this an *overloaded method*. MATLAB displays the overloaded methods, if they exist, at the end of the help section.

If the contents of a help section fill more than one screen, you can slow the display by typing the following before you type the *help* command:

```
>>more on
```

This will set the Command window to display one screen at a time. To move forward one line at a time, press any key but the space bar. To move forward a page at a time, press the **space bar**. To quit and return to the command line, type **q**.

Try the following text-based help command:

```
>> help plot
```

You should see several pages of text for this command, some of which are displayed here:

```
PLOT    Linear plot.
    PLOT(X,Y) plots vector Y versus vector X. If X or Y
    is a matrix, then the vector is plotted versus the
    rows or columns of the matrix, whichever line up.
```

(*Note*: Many more lines of text will appear here, ending with the following.)

```
See also SEMILOGX, SEMILOGY, LOGLOG, GRID, CLF, CLC,
TITLE, XLABEL, YLABEL, AXIS, AXES, HOLD, COLORDEF,
LEGEND, SUBPLOT, and STEM.
```

Note that additional related functions are listed near the end of the help text.

To perform a primitive search for a topic or functions, use the *lookfor* function. The *lookfor* function locates all help topics that contain the given argument in the first comment line of the help text—for example,

```
>> lookfor fourier
FFT Discrete Fourier transform.
FFT2 Two-dimensional discrete Fourier Transform.
FFTN N-dimensional discrete Fourier Transform.
IFFT Inverse discrete Fourier transform.
IFFT2 Two-dimensional inverse discrete Fourier
   transform.
```

```
IFFTN N-dimensional inverse discrete Fourier
   transform.
XFOURIER Graphics demo of Fourier series expansion.
FOURIER Fourier integral transform.
IFOURIER Inverse Fourier integral transform.
```

The text-based method of accessing help is useful if you know the name of the command or function and you want to know the syntax and a quick description of the function. For detailed information, you should use the graphical help interface.

2.5.2   The Graphical Help Interface

The graphical help interface is called the Help Browser. You can start the help browser in any of the following three ways:

1.   Choose **Help → MATLAB Help** from the Menu bar of the main MATLAB window.
2.   Choose **MATLAB → Help** from the Launch Pad.
3.   Type **helpbrowser** in the Command window.

Figure 2.20 depicts the Help Browser. Let us explore each of the elements of the Help Browser.

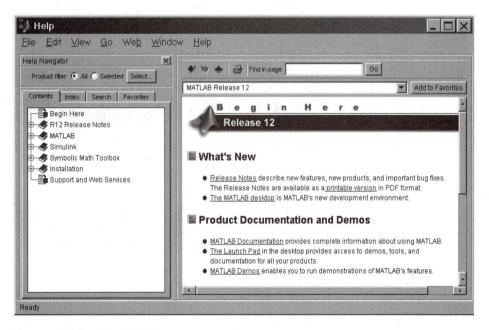

Figure 2.20.   The Help Browser.

Contents

Choosing the **Contents** tab displays the help topics organized as a table of contents. Figure 2.20 shows the opening contents display. Click on the plus (+) sign in front of a topic to expand a selection, and click on the minus (−) sign to shrink the selection. If you have toolboxes installed with your version of MATLAB, their contents appear in the Help Browser. Figure 2.20 shows the help contents for Simulink and the Symbolic Math Toolbox.

Index

The **Index** tab enables the index search feature to appear. Select the **Index** tab. Then type a word or phrase in the window titled "Search index for". The topics that match the search item will appear in the Help Navigator window. Select an item to highlight it. The text for the highlighted item will appear in the right-hand window, which is called the *Display pane*. The example in Figure 2.21 shows the results of looking for the word "sine" in the index. Note that only explicitly indexed keywords can be located in this manner. The Index does not perform a general text search.

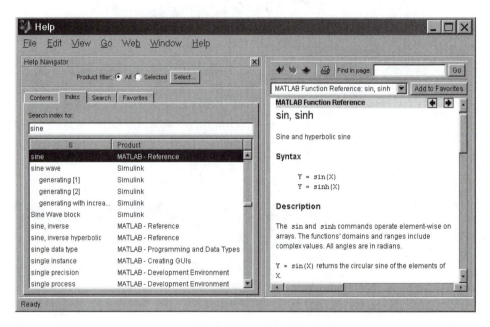

Figure 2.21. The Index feature of the Help Browser.

Search

Choose the Search tab in the Help Browser to search for words or phrases. The Search dialog box will appear as depicted in Figure 2.22. Choose the arrow to the right of the window titled "Search type". Use the pull-down menu to search in

- the full text
- document titles
- function names
- the online knowledge database

A full text search provides the most exhaustive search. For example, try searching for the term "portfolio" in the Index and you will find that there are no matches. Now try using the Search feature and search in Document Titles. You will see that there are eight matches. A full text search produces more than 20 matches on the term "portfolio".

Favorites

If you find that you are frequently revisiting the same help page, you may want to add it to your Favorites list. To add a help page to your Favorites, click on the **Add to Favorites**

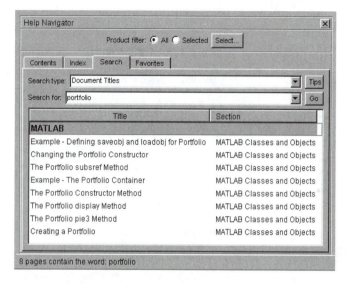

Figure 2.22.   The Search feature of the Help Browser.

button (located over the Display pane near the top right side of the Help window). Choose the **Favorites** tab to view your Favorites list.

You can rename or delete items from the Favorites list by selecting the item and simultaneously clicking the right mouse button. Figure 2.23 shows the resulting pull-down menu.

Help History

The Help History list maintains a list of previously selected help pages. To access the history list, click on the arrow immediately to the left of the **Add to Favorites** button. The history list will appear as a drop-down menu. Select any item on the list to return to its associated help page. Figure 2.24 shows the author's history list.

Help Preferences

You can set several preferences for the Help Browser. To access the Preferences dialog box, either select **File → Preferences** from the Menu bar of the Help Browser or click on the **Select** button to the right of the area titled *Product filter*.

The Preferences dialog box will appear as shown in Figure 2.25. The Help Preferences section will already be chosen for you. From this dialog box, you can select the

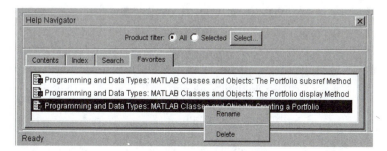

Figure 2.23.   Renaming or deleting items from the Favorites list.

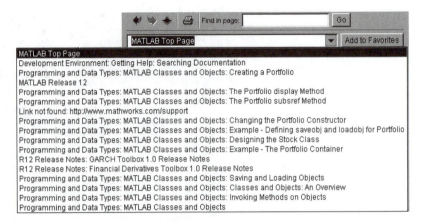

Figure 2.24. The Help History list.

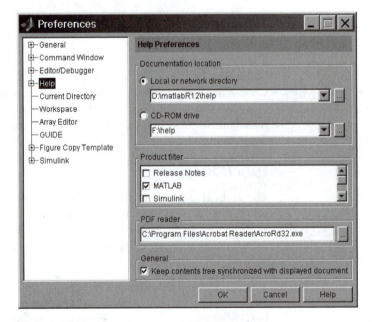

Figure 2.25. The Preferences dialog box.

location of the MATLAB help files and the location of the PDF reader. Some MATLAB documents are stored in PDF format. A PDF reader allows you to view and print these documents. If you do not have a PDF reader installed on your system, you can obtain a free PDF reader from Adobe Systems at

```
http://www.adobe.com
```

You may have noticed that each time you select a new item in the Help Contents tab, the corresponding help page automatically opens in the Display pane. You can turn this feature on or off by checking the selection box titled "Keep contents tree synchronized with displayed document."

You may find that you are getting many irrelevant items when searching for help. For example, when searching for a common term such as *object*, you may get responses in the MATLAB, Simulink, and Symbolic Math Toolbox help sections. Use the product filter menu to select and deselect products in which to search. Then, on the main Help Browser menu, under the selection box titled "Product filter", choose **All** or **Selected** to quickly narrow or broaden your search.

PRACTICE 2.2!

Your best friend for learning MATLAB is the MATLAB Help Browser. Learn to use this tool efficiently by practicing. Suppose that you want to know more about how to print MATLAB help sections. Then follow these steps:

1. Locate information on this topic by using the Contents tab of the Help Browser.
2. Now find the same information by using the Index tab of the Help Browser.
3. Finally, use the Search tab to locate relevant information.

2.5.3   Web-Based MATLAB Help

The main MATLAB Web page is located at

```
http://www.mathworks.com
```

You can view the MATLAB Web pages by using your favorite browser, or you can use the MATLAB window as a Web browser.

To use MATLAB as a Web browser for MATLAB help, choose **Web** from the Menu bar. A drop-down menu will appear, and you can choose to access the MathWorks website, the MATLAB technical support knowledge base, and other related sites.

The address of a website is called a *Uniform Resource Locator* or *URL*. You can access any URL from the MATLAB Command window by typing the keyword *web* followed by the URL. For example, to access the MathWorks site, type the following in the Command window:

```
>> web http://www.mathworks.com
```

The optional argument **–browser** will launch your system default Web browser. For example, the following command will launch the MathWorks site in your default browser:

```
>> web http://www.mathworks.com –browser
```

2.6   SETTING PREFERENCES

To set MATLAB preferences, select **File** → **Preferences** from the Menu bar of any MATLAB window. The Preferences dialog box will appear as depicted in Figure 2.25.

We will discuss preference options throughout the text when introducing each related item. For example, we discuss the preferences for the Array Editor in the section introducing the Array Editor.

For now, select each of the items in turn to see the variety of options available. Clicking on a plus (+) sign in front of an item will expand subitems related to that topic. When you change a preference, it should remain changed across sessions.

PRACTICE 2.3!

Prove to yourself that changes in preferences persist across sessions by doing the following:

1. Open the Preferences dialog box by choosing **File** → **Preferences** from the Menu bar.

2. Open the item labeled "General" by clicking on the plus (+) sign to its left and then select **Fonts & Colors**.
3. In the dialog box titled "Desktop font," choose a different font style and size. Click the **OK** button.

You should see the changes immediately. Now exit MATLAB and then restart. Do your font changes persist?

PRACTICE 2.4!

Become familiar with all of the preferences. Choose **File → Preferences** from the Menu bar. Open each selection and browse. Change the following preferences:

1. Set the number of entries in the "Most recently used file list" to eight.
2. Change the size of a tab in the Command window from four to two spaces.
3. Make sure that your Workspace window preference is set to "Confirm deletion of variables."
4. Open the MATLAB Editor. Pressing the tab key should now produce two spaces.
5. Choose **File** from the Menu bar. As you create and save files, the most recently used list should now keep the eight most recent files.

APPLICATION! COMPOUND INTEREST

The power of compound interest is magic! The best investment strategy is to utilize time, which means that we should start investing while we are young. A friend of mine is a risky investor and has placed $1,000 into an investment that is expected to return 10% annually. I have taken a more conservative strategy and placed $1,000 into an investment that is expected to return 6% annually. Ignoring the risk factor, let us write a MATLAB program that graphs the hypothetical returns of our investments for the next 20 years:

```
% compound_interest.m
% This program computes and plots the principal + interest (P+I)
% for a $1,000 investment over a 20 year period.
% Two interest rates are used: 6% and 10%, compounded annually.

% Create a 1x20 array named 'Years' containing the numbers
% 1,2,...,20.
Years = [1:20];
% Create a 1x20 array named 'Safe' containing P+I at 6%.
Safe = 1000*(1 + 0.06).^Years;
% Create a 1x20 array named 'Risky' containing P+I at 10%.
Risky = 1000*(1 + 0.10).^Years;

% Plot the Safe array.
plot(Safe);
% Tell MATLAB to hold that plot, because we're going to plot
% a second array.
hold on;
% Plot the Risky array.
plot(Risky);
```

```
% The next 6 commands place the labels and title on the graph.
% Create the title. The \bf notation indicates bold font.
title('\bf Rates of Return on $1000 Investment');
% Label the X-axis.
xlabel('\bf Years');
% Label the Y-axis.
ylabel('\bf Dollars');
% Create the graph labels and place a grid on the graph.
text(Years(15),Safe(15),'\bf 6%', 'VerticalAlignment', 'top');
text(Years(16),Risky(16),'\bf 10%', 'VerticalAlignment', 'top');
grid on;
```

Although you have learned very few MATLAB commands, this example should be easy for you to follow. Copy the first part of this program into the MATLAB Editor (down to the first plot command) and then save and run it! Continue to type in code a line at a time, and then press the F5 key to save and run the modified program. Watch the effect on the plot as you add new commands.

Figure 2.26 shows the results of executing the complete program. You can see from the graph that my friend will triple his money in just over 11 years, while it will take 19 years for me to triple mine!

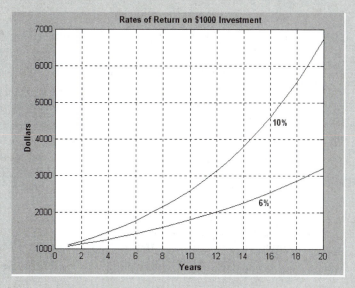

Figure 2.26.   Effect of Compound Interest–6% vs. 10%.

KEY TERMS

Close button
Command History window
command line editing
Command window
Current Directory window
Desktop toolbar
Display pane
focusing the mouse
Launch Pad window

MAT-file
Maximize button
Menu bar
M-book
M-file
Minimize button
overloaded method
Product filter
syntax highlighting

Title bar
tool tip
undocking
Uniform Resource Locator
URL
variable
Workspace window

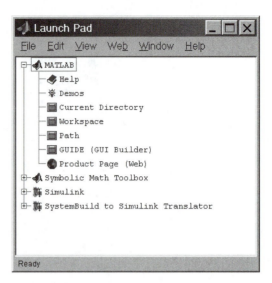

Figure 2.9. The Launch Pad window.

3. If you wish, try executing some of the demos by selecting them from the Demo window menu.

4. When you are finished, click the **Close** button on the Demo window.

The Command Window

The *Command window* is the heart of the MATLAB interactive system. It is from this window that you will access most of the MATLAB commands and functions. Figure 2.10 depicts the Command window.

Type the following statement in the Command window (the $>>$ prompt should already be visible; don't type $>>$):

```
>> Width = 2.3
```

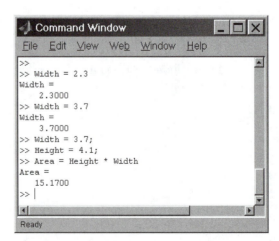

Figure 2.10. The Command window.

NEW MATLAB FUNCTIONS, COMMANDS, AND RESERVED WORDS

ans—the MATLAB default variable name
clear—clear the workspace
exit—exit MATLAB (same as quit)
help—display help text on named topic
helpbrowser—start the MATLAB Help Browser
load—load a data file from disk
lookfor—search all M-files for given keyword
matlab—start MATLAB from the operating system command line
more—turn paging on or off
pi—a function that returns the value of the constant pi
plot—the basic MATLAB plotting command
quit—quit MATLAB (same as exit)
save—save the workspace to a data file
sin—return the trigonometric sine
web—open a Web browser for a given URL

SOLUTIONS TO PRACTICE PROBLEMS

2.2. When using the Contents tab of the Help Browser, choose **MATLAB → Using MATLAB → Development Environment → Getting Help → Printing Documentation**.

When using the Index tab of the Help Browser, type the word *help* in the box titled "Search index for." Scroll down through the topics until you find **Help Browser [2] → printing help**. Note that the index is case sensitive. Typing in *Help* returns nothing.

Finally, when using the Search tab of the Help Browser, type in the phrase "printing help" and click the **Go** button and select **Printing Documentation**. Note that the Search feature is *not* case sensitive, so you could type "PRINTING HELP" and get the same results.

2.3. The font changes should have been saved across sessions. If you are working in a computer lab, you may not have permission to write to the preference file location, and consequently, the changes may not have been saved.

To test this, exit MATLAB and then restart it. Have your newly modified preferences been retained or lost?

Problems

Section 2.1

1. List three ways to undock a window from the main MATLAB desktop. Use the Help Browser if necessary.

2. Does the Command History window keep a history of erroneously typed commands or does it just keep a history of valid commands? Test your answer. Here is an example of a valid command:

```
>> A = 3;
```

Here is an example of an invalid command:

```
>> A = :
```

3. The surface area of a sphere is computed by using the following formula:

$$A = 4\pi r^2$$

In the Command window, write a MATLAB expression that creates a variable *R* and sets its value to 3.2 m. Then write an expression that computes the surface area of a sphere with radius R and places the results in a variable named *SurfaceArea*.

4. MATLAB's symbol for scalar division is "/". The volume of a sphere is computed by using the formula:

$$V = 4/3\,\pi\,r^3$$

Write the MATLAB expressions that compute the volume of sphere with radius 6.13 m. Place the results in a variable named *Volume*.

5. The volume of a cylinder with height *h* and radius of an end *r* (see Figure 2.27) is computed by the following formula:

$$V = \pi r^2 h$$

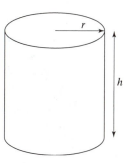

Figure 2.27. A cylinder.

Write the MATLAB expressions that compute the volume of a cylinder with *Radius* = 4.03 m and *Height* = 18.14 m. Place the results in a variable named *Volume*.

Section 2.2

6. Can you start a comment in the middle of a line in an M-file? Create an M-file with the following line of code:

```
Radius = 5   % set the radius to 5
```

What happens when you execute the M-file?

7. Clear your workspace by choosing **Edit → Clear Workspace**. Type the following commands into an M-file:

```
% A = 5;
B = 5; % C = 5;
      % D = 5;
```

Save the M-file and then execute it by pressing the **F5** key. Which variable(s) are created? (*Hint*: View the Workspace window.) Which parts of the M-file are comments?

Section 2.3

8.   Clear your workspace. Create the following variables and assign them the respective values:

```
>> Velocity = 50.3;
>> Altitude = 650.1;
```

Save your workspace to a MAT-file. Now zero both variables as follows:

```
>> Velocity = 0;
>> Altitude = 0;
```

Retrieve that MAT-file by choosing **File → Import Data** from the Menu bar and select your previously saved file. Now, what are the values of *Altitude* and *Velocity*?

9.   You can also import data from a text file. Create the following data by using a text editor such as WordPad, Emacs, or the MATLAB Editor:

```
2   4   6   8
3   5   7   9
0   1   0   1
```

Save the file with the extension **.txt.**

Clear your workspace and then choose **File → Import Data** from the Menu bar of the main MATLAB window. The Open File dialog box will appear. Select your file and open it. Accept the default options in the Import Wizard. Look at your Workspace window. What is the name of the variable that MATLAB created? What is size of the variable?

10.   MATLAB attempts to separate text and data when importing a text file. Create a file containing the following text by using a text editor:

```
NAME        AGE     GPA
Frank       19      3.6
Susan       22      2.5
```

Save and import the file. (Choose **File → Import Data** from the Menu bar.) What happens when you import the file into MATLAB?

11.   When importing text data from an external source, you must type the data regularly and consistently. Missing data can create problems. MATLAB attempts to correct problems by filling in missing data. Use the text editor to create a file containing the following:

```
NAME        AGE     GPA
Frank       19      3.6
Susan       22
Bob         17      2.8
Billy       25      3.1
```

Save the file, and then import the file. What happens when you try to import the file into MATLAB? What does MATLAB assign to Susan's GPA?

12.   MATLAB attempts to determine the character that delimits data in a file. Common delimiters are a blank space, a tab, or a comma. Problem occurs with each of these delimiters. Create and import the following comma-delimited data into MATLAB:

```
NAME,WEIGHT
John,220
Barbara,95
Adam, Jr.,158
```

You will notice that MATLAB will guess that the delimiter used is a comma. The problem is that the data "Adam, Jr." contains a comma. This confuses MATLAB. Select the *data* tab from the Import Wizard. Does it show the correct value? Why or why not?

Section 2.4

Use the example in Section 2.4.3 to guide you with Problems 13 and 14.

13.   The MATLAB function for the trigonometric tangent is *tan*. Plot the tangent function from $-\pi$ to π in increments of 0.1.

14.   The MATLAB function for trigonometric cosine is *cos*. Plot the cosine function from $-\pi$ to π in increments of 0.1.

15.   Print the plot for Problem 14.

16.   Create an M-file that shows the solution for Problem 14. Print the contents of the M-file.

Section 2.5

Use the MATLAB Help Browser to find the answers to the following questions:

17.   What command can you type in the Command window that will invoke the Workspace Browser?

18.   What commands can you type that display the same information as the Workspace Browser, but displays the information in the Command window?

19.   The name "foo" appears frequently in the MATLAB documentation. What is "foo"?

20.   What commands can you type in the Command window to find the license number and version of MATLAB?

3

The Programming Elements of MATLAB

3.1 INTRODUCTION

This chapter introduces you to the basic elements of the MATLAB programming language. Please note that even though we are using MATLAB as the language in this text, other programming languages also use many of the concepts presented in the chapter.

This is somewhat analogous to learning a Romance language such as Italian. If you learn Italian, the fundamental structures of other Romance languages such as French and Spanish will be familiar to you, and those languages will be easier to learn. After learning MATLAB, you will find it easier to learn other programming languages such as C, C++, or Java.

First, let us make a few definitions. These may seem tedious to you. However, a programming language such as MATLAB demands precision. In later discussions, we must be able to state ideas precisely and clearly. This requires common understanding of a few terms.

3.1.1 Lexical Elements

A computer program is built from basic components called *lexical elements*. The lexical elements of a language are the building blocks or alphabet from which the language is written. The lexical elements of a human language consist of words, symbols, and punctuation marks. Different human languages have different punctuation marks. For example, Spanish uses accent marks within written text. Languages such as Chinese have a completely different alphabet than Western languages. Likewise, different programming languages have different lexical elements. The lexical elements of the MATLAB programming language consist of

OBJECTIVES

After reading this chapter, you should be able to

- Describe the difference between a language's syntax and its semantics.
- Create and access floating-point and character arrays.
- Create and access cell arrays.
- Use MATLAB's scalar, logical, and relational operators.
- Correctly evaluate numeric and logical expressions.
- Identify MATLAB's reserved words.
- Create legitimate MATLAB variable and function names.
- Modify your search path.

- *operators*: *Operators* are symbols that are used to denote mathematical or logical operations such as the plus sign (+). We will introduce some of MATLAB's operators later in this chapter.

- *special characters*: *Special characters* are keyboard characters that have a special meaning in MATLAB. Special characters are the punctuation marks of the language, and they include parentheses, curly braces, commas, and semicolons. A *continuation* is a special character that allows a programmer to continue a statement on the next line. The MATLAB continuation character is the ellipsis (three or more contiguous periods). The following section of code uses a continuation:

```
>> A = [1 3 5; 2 4 8] + ...
      [2 4 8; 3 5 7]
A =
     3      7     13
     5      9     15
```

- *names*: *Names* consist of reserved words, function names, and variable names. A *reserved word* is a predefined word. You cannot change the meaning of a reserved word in MATLAB, unless you recreate the MATLAB program. *Function names* and *variable names* can be reassigned. We will discuss reserved words and the rules for creating legitimate names later in the chapter.

3.1.2   Syntax and Semantics

The *syntax* of a language is the set of rules used to combine the lexical elements into legitimate constructs. In a human language, the syntax is concerned with building legitimate sentences and paragraphs. In a programming language, the syntax describes how to build expressions, statements, functions, and programs from lexical elements.

An important difference between human and computer languages is that humans are very tolerant of incorrect syntax. The following sentence has numerous spelling and punctuation errors, but most humans can still decipher its meaning:

```
eye wint tu thee - fare and road the; fare is weel
```

A programming language compiler or interpreter, however, is very strict about syntax. A single misplaced comma or parenthesis may cause the whole program to crash.

The syntax of a language is concerned only with its proper structure or grammar. The *semantics* of a language is the meaning given to its elements. For example, the syntax of the *sin* function is

```
Y = sin(X)
```

The *sin* function expects a single argument enclosed in parentheses. If you leave out one of the parentheses, you'll get a syntax error. The MATLAB interpreter will catch this error and return an error message. Here's an example:

```
>> Y = sin(X
??? Y = sin(X
             |
Error: ")" expected, "end of line" found.
```

The meaning or semantics of the *sin* function is to return an approximation of the trigonometric sine. If a programmer improperly writes the *sin* function to return the tangent instead of the sine, it is called a semantics error. In the rest of this text, we will discuss both the syntax and semantics of various MATLAB commands.

3.2   DATA STORAGE

3.2.1   Introduction

Another key concept for programming languages is the storage of data. *Data structures* are the mechanisms that a programming language provides for storing and organizing data. You have already used some data structures. In the previous chapter, you created a few variables and performed computations with them. In this chapter, we will define more precisely how MATLAB stores data.

MATLAB provides a number of primitive built-in data structures such as floating-point arrays and character strings. The *primitive data structures* are the basic elements and can be used to build complex data structures. MATLAB provides means for constructing complex data structures.

MATLAB was originally written in the programming language FORTRAN. The FORTRAN language was designed for use by scientists and engineers. FORTRAN's primitive data structures at that time consisted of scalars such as integers and floating-point numbers. These were used to build complex data structures such as arrays.

One thing that distinguishes MATLAB as a programming language is that the primitive data structure is the array. You can think of an *array* as a group of cells or boxes, and each cell or box in the group contains the same type of object. For example, the following boxes contain letters:

E	R	W	F	G	G	H	G
1	2	3	4	5	6	7	8

Each box in the array is numbered from one to eight, left to right. One feature of an array is that the elements can be accessed by using subscripts. For example, if our array is named A, then the third element of A can be accessed by using the notation $A(3)$. Hence, the cell $A(3)$ contains the letter W.

The *data types* that MATLAB supports are all built by using an array structure. MATLAB even stores a scalar such as the number 5.23 as a 1×1 array. All other primitive and constructed data types are derived from the array structure.

The designers of MATLAB have highly optimized the computations on arrays. This has simplified the programmer's optimization task.

In this text, most of the examples and problems use only a few data types: characters, strings, double precision floating-point numbers, and cell arrays. We will explain these types in the next sections. If you want to learn more about other MATLAB data types, see Appendix C.

3.2.2   Data Declaration

Before you can use a variable in a MATLAB program, you must declare it. In MATLAB, this is easy. You declare a variable dynamically by assigning a value to the variable. Clear your workspace and then type the following statement:

```
>> A = 'foo';
```

In a clear workspace, the preceding statement results in the creation of the variable A, and it assigns the character string *foo* to the variable.

You can create a variable with an empty value by assigning it an empty array. For example, type

```
>> B = [ ];
```

This results in the variable B being declared as a double array with size 0×0.

Arrays can have more than one dimension. To enter a two-dimensional array, you should separate elements in the same row with commas or spaces. You can create a new row by using a semicolon or a new line. Square braces should bracket the whole array. The array:

$$\begin{bmatrix} 1 & 3 & 5 \\ 2 & 4 & 6 \end{bmatrix}$$

can be entered and assigned to the variable A by typing

```
>> A = [1, 3, 5; 2, 4, 6]
A =
        1    3    5
        2    4    6
```

All the rows in an array must have the same length. However, entering the following array results in an error because the two rows have different lengths:

```
>> A = [1, 3, 5; 2, 4]
??? Error using ==> vertcat
All rows in the bracketed expression must have the same
number of columns.
```

You can see the size, type (or class), and number of bytes required to store the array by typing *whos*. A *byte* is a unit of storage on a computer. Here's an example:

```
>> whos
    Name         Size             Bytes  Class
    A            2x3                 48  double array
```

Elements in a two-dimensional array can be accessed by using subscripts. The first subscript refers to the row and the second subscript refers to the column. A comma is used to separate subscripts. For example, you access the element in the first row and third column of array A as follows:

```
>> A(1,3)
ans =
        5
```

Another way to declare a variable in a program is to use the *input* statement. The *input* statement displays a prompt in the command window and waits for the user to type a response. The following *input* statement prompts the user to type a number and then assigns the result to variable C:

```
>> C = input('Type a number:')
Type a number:
```

Of course, there is nothing to prevent you from typing a nonnumber. Practice using the *input* statement. View the Workspace window afterwards to see the result.

PRACTICE 3.1!

Test your understanding of creating and accessing arrays in MATLAB.

1. Create the following two-dimensional array and assign it to the variable A:

$$\begin{bmatrix} -4 & 0 & 12 & 2 \\ 1 & 22 & 3 & 81 \\ 85 & 2 & 12 & -6 \end{bmatrix}$$

2. Verify the dimensions of A by using the *whos* command.
3. Access the number in the 2nd row and 3rd column. What did you type?
4. Access the cell containing the number 85. What did you type?

3.2.3   Characters and Strings

Characters are entered by using single quotes as delimiters—for example,

```
>> C = 'W'
C =
W
```

If you do not use the single quotes, MATLAB will try to assign the contents of the variable named W to C. If quotes are used, MATLAB assigns the literal character W to the variable C.

Characters are stored internally as 16-bit unsigned integers. They are stored by using a code called 16-bit ASCII Unicode. For example, the character W is stored by using the code 87. Usually, you do not need to know how MATLAB stores characters. Sometimes, knowing the internal representation will help you to understand what is happening. For example, type the following in the Command window:

```
>> 'W' + 1
ans =
    88
```

This result does not make much sense, unless you know that MATLAB stores the letter W as 87. See Appendix A for a table of the ASCII character codes.

Strings are groups of characters and are entered by using single quotes as delimiters. A string is stored as an array of characters, starting with the index one. You can access characters within strings by using the array name followed by the index in parentheses. For example, the second character in the following string can be accessed by using the notation $C(2)$:

```
>>C = 'New Orleans';
>> C(2)
ans =
e
```

PRACTICE 3.2!

Test your understanding of creating and accessing strings in MATLAB.
1. Create the string "America the Beautiful" and store the results in a variable named S.
2. Type *whos*. What is the size and type of S.
3. How do you access the letter 'B' in S?

Internally, MATLAB associates characters and strings with a certain type called *char*. Why is this important for you to know? Certain MATLAB functions will only work with characters or strings.

For example, the *strcat* function concatenates two or more strings together and returns the following result:

```
>> strcat('Anta', 'rctica')
ans =
Antarctica
```

However, the function does not know what to do with nonstring arguments. If we use two numbers as inputs, MATLAB returns a warning, as it is shown here:

```
>> strcat(45, 12)
Warning: Input must be a string.
```

To verify that a variable name is associated with type *char*, use the *ischar* function. The *ischar* function returns true (1) if the variable is of type *char*, otherwise it returns false (0). Here's an example:

```
>> ischar(A)
ans =
      1
```

3.2.4   Double-Precision Floating-Point Numbers

The most common type of numbers that you will use with MATLAB are *double-precision floating-point* numbers. In MATLAB, this is called the *double* type, which, by the way, is MATLAB's default data type. Internally all calculations are performed by using arrays of double-precision numbers.

There are four components to a floating-point number:

- a sign
- a mantissa
- a base
- an exponent

The following is an example of a floating-point number:

```
-5.23 x 10^3
```

In this example, the sign is negative, the mantissa is 5.23, the base is 10, and the exponent is three.

Type the following at the Command window prompt:

```
>> A = 5
A =
      5
```

Note that, although we have entered an integer, MATLAB converts the number five to a 1×1 array containing a double floating-point value. A number of type double requires 8 bytes of storage. We use the *whos* command to verify this:

```
>> whos A
  Name         Size           Bytes  Class

    A           1x1                8  double array
  Grand total is 1 elements using 8 bytes
```

3.2.5   Cell Array Type

The arrays that we have mentioned so far contain elements that are all the same type. You cannot define a standard numeric array that contains some characters and some floating-point numbers. You cannot convert a single entry in an array from character to double or vice versa. However, you can convert the type of an entire array at once.

A *cell array* is an array type for which each entry may be of a different type. Some cells may hold integers and others may hold double numbers. A cell may even hold strings or other arrays, including other cell arrays.

To avoid confusion with the accessing methods of regular arrays, the brackets for cell arrays are curly braces, {}. To assign elements to a cell array, enclose the elements in curly braces. For example, to create the cell array *A*, which contains the three elements

- the string 'foo'
- the number 3.4
- the array [3, 5, 7]

type

```
>> A = { 'foo', 3.4, [3, 5, 7]}
A =
     'foo'    [3.4000]    [1x3 double]
```

Note that MATLAB does not display the contents of nonscalar elements when a whole cell array is printed. In order to save space, MATLAB only displays the size and type of nonscalar numeric arrays.

You can access the contents of a cell array element by using subscripts enclosed by curly braces. To copy the contents of the third element of *A* into *B*, type

```
>> B = A{3}
B =
     3    5    7
```

To make a copy of a cell, use subscripts enclosed by parentheses. For example, to copy the third cell of *A* into *B*, type

```
>> B = A(3)
B =
     [1x3 double]
```

What is the difference? In the first example, we copied a 3-element array into *B*. In the second example, we copied *a cell* containing a 3-element array into *B*. Cell arrays are important for programming with MATLAB, because input and output arguments are stored in cell arrays.

How can we access a single element of an array stored in a cell array? For example, we might want to access the second element of the array that resided in the third cell of *A*. To access an element within a cell, use parentheses after the curly braces, as in this example:

```
>> C = A{3}(2)
C =
     5
```

Read this statement as "take the third cell of *A*, and then take the second element of the results."

PRACTICE 3.3!

Test your understanding of cell arrays.
1.   Create a cell array named *Cell* that contains
     - the string 'King Kong'
     - the scalar 25
     - the array [2, 4, 6; 1, 3, 5]

2.   Copy the contents of the first element of *Cell* to a variable named *String*.
3.   Copy the contents of the third element of *Cell* to a variable *A*.
4.   Copy the third cell of *Cell* to a variable *A_Cell*.
5.   Copy the element in the first row and second column of the third cell of *Cell* to a variable *An_Element*.

3.3   OPERATORS AND EXPRESSIONS

As we discussed earlier, operators are symbols used to denote arithmetic, logical, or relational operations. A unary operator takes one argument. A binary operator joins two arguments.

For example, the plus sign (+) usually denotes addition. We may think that we know what addition means, but MATLAB defines addition very precisely. The use of the plus sign as a binary operator in MATLAB denotes the element-by-element addition of two arrays of floating-point numbers. The arrays must have the same size, unless one is a scalar, in which case each element of the nonscalar array is added to the scalar.

An *expression* is a syntactic unit that evaluates to a value. A variable alone is a simple example of an expression. You can build expressions that are more complex by using mathematical operators, logical operators, and function calls. When you type a legitimate expression into the MATLAB interpreter, the value of that expression (or an error message) is returned. The following is an example of a legitimate MATLAB expression:

```
>> (3 + 4) - (5^2 + 2)
ans =
    -20
```

Note that MATLAB evaluates the expression and returns the resulting value.

3.3.1   Scalar Operators

The scalar arithmetic operators and their symbols are

- addition (+)
- subtraction (−)
- multiplication (*)
- division (/)
- exponentiation [raising a scalar to a power (^)]

MATLAB uses the standard arithmetic symbols to denote arithmetic operators with the exception of the multiplication and the power operators. The MATLAB multiplication symbol is the asterisk (*). For example, MATLAB denotes two multiplied by three as 2*3. The power operator is the caret (^) symbol. For example, x^2 is written as x^2.

Here are some examples of the use of scalar operators:

```
>> A = 5;
>> B = 12;
>> C = 2;
>> A - B
ans =
     -7
>> A * B
ans =
     60
>> A^C
ans =
       25
```

3.3.2   The Colon Operator

The colon operator is a very important MATLAB operator. One way we use the colon operator is to generate sequences and vectors.

Let us use the colon operator to generate several sequences. There are two variants of the colon operator syntax. The first variant is

begin_value : *end_value*

MATLAB makes it easy to create sequential arrays with the use of the colon operator. To create the sequence from −5 to 5, type

```
>> -5 : 5
ans =
    -5  -4  -3  -2  -1   0   1   2   3   4   5
```

The default increment value is one (1). The second variant of the colon operator allows you to specify the increment value:

begin_value : *increment* : *end_value*

To create the numbers from 15 to 16 in increments of 0.2, type

```
>> 15 : 0.2 : 16
ans =
    15.0000  15.2000  15.4000  15.6000  15.8000  16.0000
```

You can create decrementing sequences by using a negative increment value—for example,

```
>> 50 : -10: 0
ans =
    50    40    30    20    10     0
```

PRACTICE 3.4!

Create the following sequences by using the colon operator:
1. 1 3 5 7 9 11 13
2. −10 −5 0 5 10
3. −4 −8 −12 −16 −20

3.3.3 Numeric Expressions

Numeric expressions are expressions that evaluate to a numeric value. The following are examples of numeric expressions, assuming that *A*, *X*, and *Y* are defined:

```
15
A * 5^2
sin(2 * pi)
(X - 5) * (Y + 2)
```

If you attempt to evaluate an expression for which any part is undefined, you will get an error. To test this, first clear your workspace. Now type the following expression in the Command window and notice that MATLAB returns an error because *X* is undefined:

```
>> (3 - X) + 5
??? Undefined function or variable 'X'.
```

Define *X* and the error will disappear:

```
>> X = 2;
>> (3 - X) + 5
```

```
ans =
      6
```

Invalid operators may not appear in a numeric expression. For example, the assignment operator (=) may not be used in a numeric expression. Some other languages, such as C, do allow assignment within an expression. Type the following expression and note the error message:

```
>> 3 + (A = 5)
??? 3 + (A = 5)
              |
Error: MATLAB assignment cannot be nested.
```

The error message in this example may seem cryptic. Recall that, by default, MATLAB assigns the results of an expression to the variable *ans*. Thus, in this case, we are trying to make two assignments (or nested assignments) in the same expression.

3.3.4   Relational Operators

A *relational operator* is a binary operator used to make a comparison and it returns true or false. The relational operators include the following comparisons:

- less than ($<$)
- less than, or equal to ($<=$)
- greater than ($>$)
- greater than or equal to ($>=$)
- equality ($==$)
- inequality ($\sim=$)

A *Boolean expression* or *conditional expression* is an expression that evaluates to true or false. Conditional expressions often use one or more of the relational operators.

MATLAB does not support a true Boolean type, but treats nonzero scalars as true and the scalar zero as false. For example, the following expression tests if five is less than three:

```
>> 5 < 3
ans =
      0
```

As you can see, MATLAB returns false (0).

The Boolean evaluation of nonscalar arrays is slightly more complex. If a scalar and array are compared, then the scalar is compared with each element of the array. For the expression to be true, the scalar must evaluate to true when compared with each and every member of the array. For example, the following expression evaluates to false because three is not less than each element of A:

```
>> A = [3, 4, 5]
>> 3 < A
ans =
      0      1      1
```

In the following example, the logical expression evaluates to true, because five is greater than or equal to every element of A:

```
>> 5 >= A
ans =
      1      1      1
```

If we compare two nonscalar arrays, the logical operation must evaluate to true for each pairwise comparison. The two arrays must be the same size. In the following example, the expression $A < B$ evaluates to true because each element of A is less than its corresponding element in B:

```
A = [3, 4, 5]
B = [4, 5, 6]
>> A < B
ans =
        1    1    1
```

The relational operators are of equal precedence to one another. (See Table 3.1.) This means that MATLAB interprets relational operators from left to right, unless parentheses are used. Hence, the following example returns true:

```
>> 5 < 3 < 1
ans =
        1
```

TABLE 3.1   Operator order of precedence.

Symbol	Operation
( )	parentheses, groups items
.'	transpose
.^	power
'	complex conjugate transpose
^	matrix power
+	unary plus
−	unary minus
~	logical negation
.*	multiplication
./	right division
.\	left division
*	matrix multiplication
/	matrix right division
\	matrix left division
+	binary addition
−	binary subtraction
:	colon operator
<	less than
<=	less than or equal
>	greater than
>=	greater than or equal
==	equal
~=	not equal
&	logical AND
|	logical OR

MATLAB first evaluates $5 < 3$, which is false (0), and then $0 < 1$ returns true (1). You can use parentheses to force the order of evaluation as in the following example:

```
>> 5 < (3 < 1)
ans =
        0
```

The equality operator compares the equality of elements on an element-by-element basis. Here's an example:

```
>> A = [1 3 5];
>> B = [5 3 1];
>> A == B
ans =
        0     1     0
```

The equality operator is frequently confused with the assignment operator (=). This is a common source of programming errors. Fortunately, MATLAB will catch the misuse of the assignment operator. In the following example, $(7 = = 8)$ evaluates to false or zero and then $(5 < 0)$ evaluates to false or zero:

```
>> 5 < (7 = = 8)
ans =
        0
```

If we intentionally misuse the assignment operator, MATLAB recognizes that an assignment statement cannot result in a value, and produces an error:

```
>> 5 < (7 = 8)
??? 5 < (7 = 8)
              |
Error: ")" expected, "=" found.
```

PRACTICE 3.5!

Test your understanding of relational operators and conditional expressions in MATLAB.

Type the following statement in the Command window:

```
A = [1 0 0 0]
```

What should the next expressions return? Predict the results by hand then verify your answers by using MATLAB.

```
1.  5 < 1
2.  0 <= A
3.  1 == A
4.  A == [0 1 1 1]
```

PROGRAMMING TIP 3.1!

An alternate method for testing equality is the function *isequal*. The *isequal* function compares each element of its arguments, but returns a single truth value, instead of an array of values. Note the difference in this example:

```
> A = [4,5,6]
> B = [4,5,6]
```

```
> A == B
ans =
        1     1     1
> isequal(A,B)
ans =
        1
```

3.3.5 Logical Operators

The following are MATLAB's logical operators:

- logical AND (&)
- logical OR (|)
- logical negation (~)

The logical operators act on an element-by-element basis for their arguments, returning true or false for each element.

MATLAB does not have an operator for the exclusive OR, but does have a built-in function, called *xor*, that performs the exclusive OR operation. In this section, we will explain the meaning of the three logical operators, as well as the *xor* function. Table 3.2 summarizes their truth values.

TABLE 3.2 Truth values of the logical operations.

A	B	(~A)	A & B	A|B	XOR(A,B)
0	0	1	0	0	0
1	0	0	0	1	1
0	1	1	0	1	1
1	1	0	1	1	0

Do not forget that MATLAB treats any nonzero number as true and treats zero as false. For example, the number five is logically true, so the negation of five is zero or false. Here's an example:

```
>> ~5
ans =
     0
```

If the argument is an array, the negation operator returns an array that contains the opposite truth value for each element of the input array—for example,

```
>> A = [1 0 0 -3];
>> ~A
ans =
     0     1     1     0
```

The AND operation returns true if both arguments are true and returns false otherwise. The ampersand symbol (&) denotes the AND operation—for example,

```
>> 0 & 0
ans =
     0
>> 1 & 0
ans =
     0
>> 1 & 1
ans =
     1
```

If the arguments to the AND operator are arrays, then an array is returned that contains the AND of each respective pair of arguments. Both input arrays must be the same size. Here's an example:

```
>> A = [1 0 0 1];
>> B = [1 1 0 0];
>> A & B
ans =
     1     0     0     0
```

The logical OR operator returns true if the OR of any of its respective arguments are true; it returns false otherwise. The vertical bar (|) is used to denote the OR operation—for example,

```
>> 0 | 0
ans =
     0
>> 1 | 0
ans =
     1
>> 1 | 1
ans =
     1
```

If the arguments to the OR operator are arrays, then an array is returned that contains the OR of each respective pair of arguments. Both input arrays must be the same size—for instance,

```
>> A = [1 0 0 1];
>> B = [1 1 0 0];
>> A | B
ans =
     1     1     0     1
```

The *xor* function returns true if one element is true and the other is false and returns false otherwise. In other words, *xor* returns true if the truth values of the elements are different. Here's an example:

```
>> A = [1 0 0 1];
>> B = [1 1 0 0];
>> xor(A, B)
ans =
     0     1     0     1
```

Two other useful logical MATLAB functions are the *all* function and the *any* function. The *all* function returns true if all elements of its argument are true. The *any* function returns true if any of its elements are true. The following examples demonstrate the use of these functions:

```
>> A = [3 -4 8.2 0];
>> any(A)
ans =
     1
>> all(A)
ans =
     0
```

Note: We have been using one (1) and zero (0) for the examples so far, but remember that MATLAB evaluates any nonzero value as true.

PRACTICE 3.6!

Test your understanding of logical operators in MATLAB. Clear your workspace and create the following array *A*:

```
A = [5 0 0 -2]
```

What should the next expressions return? Predict the results by hand and then test your answers by using MATLAB.

```
1. ~A
2. A & 1
3. A | 1
4. xor(A, [1 0 1 0])
5. any(A)
6. all(A)
```

3.3.6   Order of Precedence

The order in which operators are evaluated is important. For example, does the expression

$$3 / 4 + 2$$

evaluate to 2.75 or 0.5? In other words, which operation is performed first, division or addition?

The default order in which operators are evaluated is called the *order of precedence*. Table 3.2 lists the order of precedence for MATLAB operators. You have not yet been introduced to some of these operators, especially the matrix operations. As you proceed through the text and learn to use all of the operators, refer back to Table 3.2 as necessary, as it shows the precedence levels from highest to lowest. Please note that operators in each box are at the same level of precedence.

If there are no parentheses, operators within the same precedence level are evaluated left to right. For example, the following expression evaluates to 1.5, not 6, since the operators are of equal precedence:

```
>> 12 / 4 / 2
ans =
    1.5000
```

Recall that logical operators are of the same precedence and are therefore evaluated left to right. The following expression evaluates to false (0):

```
>> 12 > 4 < -1
ans =
     0
```

To see why, perform the operations one at a time, from left to right:

```
>> 12 > 4
ans =
     1
>> 1 < -1
ans =
     0
```

If operators are of unequal precedence, then MATLAB evaluates the higher precedence operators first. For example, the expression

```
3 * 5 ^ 2
```

is evaluated as `3*25=75`, rather than `15^2 = 225`, since the power operator takes precedence over the multiplication operator.

The following expression evaluates to `[3  4  5]`, since subtraction and addition take precedence over the colon operator:

```
>> 3 : 6 - 5 : 4 + 1
ans =
     3      4      5
```

You can use parentheses to change the order or precedence. For example, the following use of parentheses changes the value of previous expression:

```
>> (3 : 6) - (5 : 4 + 1)
ans =
    -2     -1      0      1
```

In this case, an array and a scalar are created and the scalar is subtracted from each element of the array. Verify this by executing pieces of the following expression separately:

```
>> (3 : 6)
ans =
     3      4      5      6
>> (5 : 4 + 1)
ans =
     5
```

Subtracting 5 from `[ 3 4 5 6 ]` results in `[-2 -1 0 1]`.

PROGRAMMING TIP 3.2!

If you are unsure of the order of precedence, it is acceptable to use parentheses even when they are not needed. The use of parentheses and spacing can make your code easier to understand.

The following two expressions produce the same result (4.5), but the second is fully parenthesized to make the meaning clearer:

$$5 * 3 / 6 + 2$$
$$((5 * 3) / 6) + 2$$

3.4   NAMES

3.4.1   Introduction

There are three types of names in MATLAB:

- reserved words
- variable names
- function names

3.4.2   Reserved Words

A reserved word is an immutable name, means that it has a special meaning that cannot be changed. An example of a reserved word is *break*. A *break* statement is used to terminate a control loop. We will fully discuss the meaning of the *break* statement later in the text.

The meaning of *break* was determined during the design of the MATLAB language. This is different from a function name or a variable name. For example, you can overload the name of a function such as *sin*. *Overloading* a name signifies that a name can have two or more simultaneous meanings. Try the following:

```
>> sin = 6
sin =
     6
```

The effect of the previous statement was to create a variable named *sin*. This hides the other meaning of *sin*, which is the trigonometric sine function.

You cannot overload a reserved word

Prove to yourself that *break* is a reserved word. Type the following in the Command window:

```
>> break = 6
??? break = 6
           |
Error: Missing operator, comma, or semicolon.
```

MATLAB returns an error, but does not explicitly tell you that you have misused a reserved word. To determine whether a word is reserved, use the *iskeyword* function. Here's an example:

```
>> iskeyword('break')
ans =
     1
```

Reserved words are case sensitive. The word "Break" is not a reserved word. You can assign a value to *Break*. Verify this by typing the following:

```
>> iskeyword('Break')
ans =
     0
>> Break = 6
Break =
     6
```

To get a list of all of MATLAB's reserved words, use the *iskeyword* function without an argument:

```
>> iskeyword
ans =
    'break'
    'case'
    'catch'
    ...
    ...
    'while'
```

3.4.3 Variable Names

MATLAB has several rules for creating variable names. A variable name must start with a letter. Any number of letters, digits, or underscores may follow the first letter. MATLAB uses the first 31 characters of a variable name and truncates the rest. In MATLAB 6.5

Release 13, this length has been increased to 63 characters. Also, variable names in MATLAB are *case sensitive*.

Examples of legitimate variable names are as follows:

A_123

X

x

The variable

A_Matrix_Representing_A_System_Of_Equations

is legitimate, but will be truncated to 31 characters as follows:

*A_Matrix_Representing_A_System_*

As we explained earlier, after the 31st character, MATLAB discards the rest of the characters in the variable name. You should have no problem finding names of less than 31 characters for all of your variables.

Some invalid variables names are as follows:

5X—A variable name must begin with a letter.

WordDict_##—The # character is not a legitimate character for a variable name. The only special character allowed in a variable name is the underscore character.

_class14—A variable name must begin with a letter.

otherwise—The word "otherwise" is a reserved word.

PRACTICE 3.7!

Create variable names until you feel comfortable with the naming rules. For example, the following produces a correct result.

```
> My_Variable_Name = 5
My_Variable_Name =
      5
```

Here MATLAB assigns the value five to the variable name *My_Variable_Name*, and the new variable will appear in the Workspace window.

The following name is incorrect, resulting in an error message:

```
> _foo = 5
??? _foo = 5
     |
Error: Missing variable or function.
```

As you see, the variable name will not appear in the Workspace window.

3.4.4 Function Names

The naming rules for functions are similar to the naming rules for variables. A function name must start with a letter, and any number of letters, digits, or underscores may follow the initial letter. As with variable names, the first 31 characters of a function name are used by MATLAB and the remaining characters are truncated. In MATLAB 6.5 Release 13, this length has been increased to 63 characters.

Functions are stored as files with the same name as the function and the M extension. If the operating system you are using has file-naming conventions that are more restrictive than MATLAB's rules, the operating system rules take precedence. This is not a problem for Microsoft Windows 98, NT, 2000, and XP or most UNIX operating systems.

For functions, the case sensitivity of the name is more complex than with variables. User-defined functions are case insensitive. A user-defined function is a function that you create. We will show you how to create user-defined functions in Chapter 7.

Built-in MATLAB functions are case sensitive, and in order to execute functions, MATLAB requires you to type the function's name in lowercase letters. This is confusing, as MATLAB presents the definition of functions in uppercase letters. For example, MATLAB's command-line *help* displays function names in uppercase letters. The following steps will verify this:

```
>> help sin
 SIN    Sine.
      SIN(X) is the sine of the elements of X.
```

If you try to execute the built-in *sin* function by using all caps (or any capitalized letters), the following error message results:

```
>> SIN(5)
??? Capitalized internal function SIN; Caps Lock may
 be on.
```

Many programming languages contain the concept of a user-defined constant (i.e., a name association that, once made, does not change for the duration of the program execution). MATLAB has a number of functions that you may come to rely on as constants e.g., the function pi:

```
>> pi
ans =
    3.1416
```

These are not constants, but they are function names that can be modified!

PROGRAMMING TIP 3.3!

Resist the temptation to assume that the value associated with the word pi is constant. Any function name, including MATLAB pre-defined functions may be reassociated with another value or function. This includes functions that you may assume to be constant. For example, the following command associates the name pi with a new value.

```
>> pi = 555.5
pi =
  555.5000
```

If you now run a script that uses the name pi, it will produce the wrong result. The following session demonstrates how such an error might occur:

```
>> diameter = 16
diameter =
   16
>> circumference = diameter * pi
circumference =
     8888
```

3.5 PROGRAM ORGANIZATION

3.5.1 Search Paths

The source code for a MATLAB program is organized into one or more files called M-files. The location of M-files has a meaning in MATLAB. First, for MATLAB to find an M-file, it must be in your MATLAB search path. In addition, any file that you want to execute or edit in MATLAB must reside in the current directory or in a directory that is on your search path.

To view your current search path, choose **File → Set Path** from the Menu bar. The Set Path dialog box will appear as depicted in Figure 3.1. MATLAB set many default paths for you when MATLAB was installed.

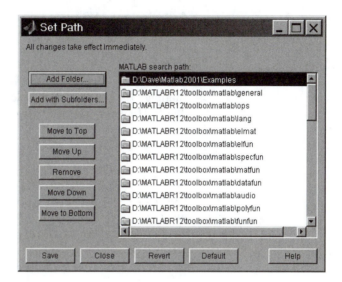

Figure 3.1. The Set Path dialog box.

It is not advisable to store your personal M-files under any of the MATLAB default directories, since your files could be destroyed when a new version of MATLAB is installed. In Figure 3.1, you can see the paths some of the default directories in the author's installation file. The default paths allow you to access MATLAB's built-in functions. Moreover, the author also added a path for his example files:

D:\Dave\MATLAB 2001\Examples.

MATLAB reads the search path by starting at the top and trying each location in turn. The *Move* buttons in the Set Path dialog box allow you to change the search order. (See Figure 3.1.) Note that when you add a new path, it takes effect immediately, but it will not be persistent across sessions, unless you save the path by clicking the **Save** button.

3.5.2 Types of M-files

An M-file is a text file that contains MATLAB code. There are two types of M-files, scripts and functions. In previous examples, you saved MATLAB commands to an M-file. The type of M-file that you created is called a *script*.

Scripts

A script is an M-file that contains a series of MATLAB commands. When you execute the script, the MATLAB interpreter executes the lines of code in the script one at a time. If you change the value of a variable in a script, the value will also change in your workspace. Conversely, if you change the value of a variable in your workspace and then run a script, the value is changed in the script.

Another way of thinking about this is to know that a variable name in a script and in the workspace point to the same memory location. Any variable that is created or modified in the script will be visible in the general workspace. In addition, any variable that is created or modified in the general workspace will be visible in the script.

Let us test the validity of these statements with an example. To setup the environment for the test, perform the following commands:

1. First, create an M-file that contains the lines of code

    ```
    A = 5.24
    B = 2 * C
    ```

    The first line of code assigns the value 5.24 to the variable *A*. The second line multiplies the contents of variable *C* by 2 and then assigns the results to variable *B*. However, we have not yet defined *C*, so this command should produce an error.

2. Save the file in your personal M-file folder and name it *test_script.m*.

3. Clear the Command window by choosing **Edit → Clear Command Window** from the Menu bar. Open the Workspace window by clicking the **Workspace** tab. Clear the Workspace by choosing **Edit → Clear Workspace** from the Menu bar.

    An alternate method for clearing your workspace is to use the *clear* command. Type *clear* in your Command window. Note that this clears all of the variables in your Workspace window.

Now we are ready to perform our test. Our first claim says that a variable created in the script will become visible in the workspace. Run the script by typing

```
>> test_script
A =
    5.2400
??? Undefined function or variable 'C'.
```

Note that the variable *A* immediately appears in the Workspace window. Our first claim is valid.

Now let us test the second claim, which states that a variable created in the workspace will be visible in the script. The first time you executed the script, an error occurred because *C* did not exist. In the Command window, type the following:

```
>> C = 3
C =
    3
```

The variable *C* will appear in your Workspace window. Now, run the script again and note that the error does not occur this time:

```
>> test_script
A =
    5.2400
B =
    6
```

This test demonstrates that the names in a script and the general workspace share the same visibility. The area of visibility of a name is called its *scope*. Names in the general workspace and a MATLAB script share the same scope.

Except in the simplest of programs, this is not a good thing. As programmers, we want to have more control over the scope of variables and other named objects. If you have 50 M-files each using the variable named *Sum*, you may want to control whether or not *Sum* is the same variable in all of the scripts. A change in the variable *Sum* in one script may inadvertently change the value of *Sum* in another script. The use of user-defined functions gives you a way to exert more control over the scope of variables.

PROGRAMMING TIP 3.4!

A script shares the same workspace as your interactive Command window. It is a good practice to clear your workspace at the beginning a script. This will start the script from the same starting point each time you execute it and will reduce unexpected errors. You can do so by placing the *clear* command as the first command in every script you write.

Functions

A function is a more structured form of M-file. An example of a MATLAB function is the *log* function, which returns the natural logarithm of a number:

```
>> A = log(1.0)
A =
        0
```

The *log* function expects an input. In the example, the input is 1.0. The inputs to a function are called its *input arguments* or *input parameters*. A function also can return nothing, a single value, or multiple values. In the example, the log function with an input argument of one returns zero. In Chapter 7, we will show you how to write your own functions. In Chapter 7, we will also discuss the structural components of a function, the syntax and scope of function names, variables within a function, and a function's parameters.

As we shall see, a function allows you to have more control over the scope of names and allows you to bundle the code for a particular algorithm into a localized module.

KEY TERMS

array	double precision	relational operator
Boolean expression	expression	reserved words
byte	floating point	scope
case sensitive	function	script
cell array	function names	semantics
char	input arguments	special characters
characters	input parameters	strings
conditional expression	lexical elements	syntax
continuation	operators	type
data structures	order of precedence	variable names
data types	overloading	
double	primitive data structures	

NEW MATLAB FUNCTIONS, COMMANDS, AND RESERVED WORDS

all—returns true if all elements of an array are non-zero
any—returns true if any element of an array is non-zero

break—terminate a while or for loop

clear—clears the workspace

input—prompts for user input and returns what is typed

ischar—returns true if its argument is a character type

isequal—returns true if two arrays are the same size and contain the same values

iskeyword—returns true if its argument is a keyword; and also returns true if its argument is a reserved word. With no argument returns a list of reserved words

log—returns the natural logarithm of its argument

strcat—concatenates its string arguments

whos—lists types and sizes of variables

xor—returns the logical XOR of its arguments

SOLUTIONS TO PRACTICE PROBLEMS

3.1.
```
1. >> A = [-4 0 12 2; 1 22 3 81; 85 2 12 -6];
2. >> A(2,3)
3. >> A(3,1)
```

3.2.
```
1. S = 'America the Beautiful';
2. size = 1×21, type = char array
3. S(13)
```

3.3.
```
1.  >> Cell = { 'King Kong', 25, [ 2, 4, 6; 1, 3, 5] }
    Cell =
            'King Kong'    [25]     [2x3 double]
2.  >> String = Cell {1}
    String =
    King Kong
3.  >> A = Cell{3}        %Note: curly braces
       A =
          2      4      6
          1      3      5
4.  >> A_cell = Cell(3) % Note: parentheses
    A_cell =
                   [2x3 double]
5.  >> An_Element = Cell{3}(1,2)
       An_Element =
                    4
```

3.4.
```
1.    1 :  2:  13
2.  -10 :  5:  10
3.   -4 : -4 :-20
```

3.5.
```
1.  0
2.  1  1  1  1
3.  1  0  0  0
4.  A =  0  0  0  0
```

3.6.
```
1.  0  1   1   0
2.  1  0   0   1
3.  1  1   1   1
```

```
4.  0     0     1     1
5.  1
6.  0
```

Problems

Section 3.1

1. Suppose that the programmer who wrote the log function for MATLAB misunderstood and wrote it to return the base 2 logarithm, instead of the base e logarithm. Is the programmer's mistake an example of a syntax error or a semantics error?

2. Is the MATLAB interpreter more likely to catch a syntax error or a semantics error?

Section 3.2

3. Create a two-dimensional array of strings called "Names," with each of the following names in a separate row: "Ralph", "Susan", and "Frank". The results should look like this:

    ```
    Names =
    Ralph
    Susan
    Frank
    ```

    What happens if you use a similar command to create a two-dimensional array of strings with each of the following names: "Ralph", "Rebecca", and "Frank"?

4. Create the following two-dimensional array A.

    $$\begin{bmatrix} 1 & 3 & 5 \\ 2 & 4 & 6 \end{bmatrix}$$

    How many bytes does MATLAB use to store A?

5. Create the following two-dimensional array B:

    $$\begin{bmatrix} 1.45 & 3.23 & 5.54 \\ 2.66 & 4.16 & 6.87 \end{bmatrix}$$

    How many bytes does MATLAB use to store B?

6. Create a cell array named "CellArray" that contains

    - the scalar 45
    - the array [45]
    - the string "45"

7. Are the first and second cells of CellArray equal? Why or why not? Use the *isequal* function to test your answer.

Section 3.3

8.　Evaluate the following numeric expressions:

```
3/5*3
3/5+3
3^2*2
8-1-1-1*6
```

9.　Evaluate the following conditional expressions:

```
[2 3 4] <= [3 3 5]
5 > 3 * 2
6 + 3 ~= 3 ^ 2
```

10.　Evaluate the following logical expressions:

```
1 & 1
0 | 1
0 | ~1
[0 0 1] | [0 0 1]
[~0 0 ~1] & [1 1 1]
```

Section 3.4

For the next three problems, use the *iskeyword* and *which* functions to help you.

11.　Which of the following are reserved words?

global
foo
try
catch
help
input

12.　Which of the following are legitimate variable names?

global
foo
try
catch
help
input

13.　Which of the following are legitimate function names?

MyFunction
sin
sin#2
Sin
12sin
MySin

Section 3.5

14.　Write a script that asks for user input and displays the negation of the input. An example of the output from the script is

```
Type an expression: [5 0 1]
ans =
      0     1     0
```

15. Write a script that prompts a user for the height and end radius of a cylinder and returns the volume of the cylinder. An example of the output from the script is

```
Radius (meters): 5
Height (meters): 12
Volume =
   942.4778
```

16. Write a script that prompts a user for a beginning value, an ending value, and an increment. The program then should generate a sequence by using the inputs. *Hint*: Use the colon operator. An example of the output from the script is

```
Beginning value: -12
Ending value: 10
Increment: 5
ans =
   -12    -7    -2     3     8
```

4

Control Structures

4.1 INTRODUCTION

The simplest way to control the flow of a program is to execute a series of statements one at a time. The scripts that you have written so far in this text have used such a method, which is rarely satisfactory for programs of any complexity. Usually, you will want more control over the flow of a program's execution.

One way to control the flow of a program is to make a decision. The direction the program takes will branch depending on the results of the decision. We call this type of program statement a *selection statement* because it *selects* the direction of the program. Another method for controlling the flow of execution in a program is to make a loop. We call this type of program statement a *repetition statement*. A loop may continue a definite or indefinite number of times.

Another method of changing the flow of a program is to call a function. A function call results in passing the flow of control to another body of code. When the function is finished, control typically passes back to the next line of code following the function call. A special case of a function call in which a function calls itself is called *recursion*.

We will discuss selection and repetition statements in this chapter. Chapter 6 covers the creation and use of functions. Chapter 7 discusses the special case of recursion. Before doing so, however, we will describe several methods for depicting the flow of a program. These methods—the use of pseudocode and flowcharts—have proven useful to programmers for describing a program segment in abstract terms. It is usually easier to describe the logic of an algorithm by using pseudocode or a flowchart before writing any code. Once the algorithm is well defined, writing the code is a much easier task.

OBJECTIVES

After reading this chapter, you should be able to

- Write pseudocode that describes an algorithm.
- Create a flow chart that depicts an algorithm.
- Correctly write program segments that use *if* and *switch* statements.
- Correctly write program segments that use *for* and *while* loops.

4.2   PSEUDOCODE

Pseudocode is a verbal description of a segment of code. It is Englishlike, but does not use the syntax of a particular language. A programmer could translate a segment of pseudocode into MATLAB, C, FORTRAN, or Pascal.

The text in Figure 4.1 describes an algorithm for assigning letter grades based on a test score to students. You do not have to understand any programming language to understand this algorithm. The pseudocode is written in precise and unambiguous terms. Later in this section, you will see how to translate the pseudocode into MATLAB code.

```
If the student's grade is between 90 and 100 (inclusive)
  then assign an A.
If the student's grade is between 80 and 89 (inclusive)
  then assign a B.
If the student's grade is below 80 then
  assign a C.
```

Figure 4.1. An example of pseudocode.

4.3   FLOWCHARTS

A *flowchart* is a graphical representation of a code segment. A flowchart makes it easy to visualize the flow of a program's logic. A directed arc, or line with an arrow, denotes the direction of the logic in the flowchart.

We use several special symbols to create flowcharts. Table 4.1 summarizes these symbols.

TABLE 4.1. Flowcharting symbols.

Name	Meaning	Symbol
	stop or start	
diamond	decision	
rectangle	computation	
hexagon	loop	
parallelogram	input/output	
line	flow of logic	$\longrightarrow$

The *terminator symbol* denotes the start or end of a program. If the terminator is labeled *Start*, a single arc may emanate from it, and no arcs may enter it. If the terminator is labeled *Stop*, no arcs may exit it.

The *diamond* denotes that a choice or decision is being made. The program may branch in one of several directions following that decision. A decision usually has two arcs exiting it, one for true and one for false. Occasionally, a decision may have more than two exits (e.g., less than, greater than, and equal to).

A *rectangle* denotes a computation. The computation is placed inside the rectangle. The computation is written by using either pseudocode or mathematical notation.

Programming language notation is not used, since a flowchart is a generic depiction. That is, it is not specific to any single programming language.

The *hexagon* denotes a loop in the program. A loop is used to make repetitive computations. We will explain program loops later in this chapter.

The *parallelogram* denotes that input or output (I/O) is to be performed. An example of input is typing a number at the keyboard. An example of output is directing a result to the screen or printer.

A simple example of the use of a flowchart is the computation of the volume of a cylinder. Recall that the formula for calculating volume of a cylinder is

$$V = \pi r^2 h$$

All flowcharts should begin with a start symbol and end with a stop symbol. Suppose that we want to write a program that asks the user for a radius and height, computes the volume, and displays the results. The pseudocode for this program might read as follows:

```
Input r and h.
Compute V = πr²h.
Output V.
```

Figure 4.2 shows a flowchart that describes the same algorithm.

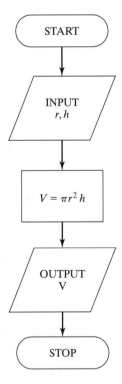

Figure 4.2. Flowchart for computing the volume of a cylinder.

Note the several conventions that are present in this example. Normally, the direction of the flow of logic is from left to right or from top to bottom. A start symbol may have a single flow line, and it must exit the symbol. A stop symbol may have a single flow line, and it must enter the symbol. A computation symbol (rectangle) has two flow lines, one that enters and one that exits.

A flowchart can be a helpful aid in every phase of program development. In the analysis phase, a flowchart is a means of communicating with the customer (or your instructor) to make sure that everyone understands the problem's solution.

In the design phase, the flowchart can be successively broken into smaller pieces—this is the top-down design method. For example, in Figure 4.2, the computation box could have represented a large and complex computation (e.g., find the predicted temperature in Miami for tomorrow). During the design phase, that single box might be represented by another flowchart which computes that predicted temperature.

During the coding phase, we use the flowchart like a blueprint. With well-written flowcharts at hand, the coding task becomes much easier. The flowchart serves as one form of program documentation—a visual document or map of the program's logic.

The use of the flowchart can assist in debugging and maintenance of large bodies of code. In real-world applications, programming code is passed from programmer to programmer as employees get promotions or change jobs. The flowchart serves as a quick way for a new programmer to get an understanding of the code.

4.4 SELECTION STATEMENTS

A simple form of flow control is the *branch* or *selection statement*. A selection statement passes the flow of control in one direction or another depending on the value of a conditional expression. In other words, we use a selection statement to make a choice.

MATLAB has two selection statements, the *if* statement and the *switch* statement. There are three variants of the *if* statement.

4.4.1 The *if* Statement

The syntax of the *if* statement is shown in Figure 4.3.

```
if conditional_expression
   ...
   ...
   ...
end
```

Figure 4.3. The syntax of the *if* statement.

The *end* reserved word is a type of bracket. It signifies the end of a block of code, in this case the end of the *if* statement. Inside the block, many statements of code may exist, including other conditional statements.

The meaning or semantics of the *if* statement is as follows:

> **If the *conditional_expression* is true, execute the code within the block; otherwise, pass control to the next statement after the end of the block.**

For example, we may want to get a person's age, store the age in the variable *Age*, and print *No alcohol* if the variable *Age* is less than 21. The pseudocode for this algorithm is

```
Input Age.
If Age < 21 print 'No alcohol'.
```

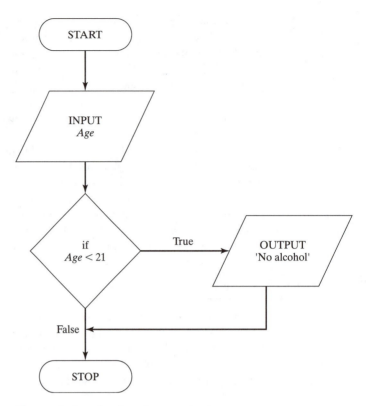

Figure 4.4. Flowchart for example *if* statement.

A flowchart that describes the same algorithm is shown in Figure 4.4. A common convention for a decision symbol (diamond) is to have the arrow denoting *True* to emanate from the right side of the diamond. The arrow denoting *False* should emanate from the bottom of the diamond. Note that a decision symbol has a single flow line that enters it and has usually two exit lines.

An example of MATLAB code that implements this algorithm is this:

```
Age = input('Age: ');
if Age < 21
    disp('No alcohol')
end
```

The effect of the first statement is to create the variable *Age* and store the results of the input statement in *Age*. The *if* statement tests the value of *Age* and compares it with 21. If it is less than 21, the *disp* or display statement prints its argument to the screen.

PRACTICE 4.1!

Create an M-file. Copy the following code into the M-file, save it, and execute the code by choosing **Debug** → **Run** from the Menu bar of the MATLAB Editor or use the shortcut key **F5**:

```
Age = input('Age: ');
if Age < 21
    disp('No alcohol')
end
```

4.4.2   The *if-else* statement

An extension of the *if* statement is the *if-else* statement. Figure 4.5 shows the syntax of the *if-else* statement.

```
if conditional_expression
  ...
  ...
else
  ...
  ...
end
```

Figure 4.5.   The syntax of the *if-else* statement.

The meaning of the *if-else* construct is as follows:

> **If the *conditional_expression* is true, execute the code between the *if* and the *else*; otherwise, execute the code between the *else* and the *end*.**

The *if-else* statement allows us to specify the code to execute if the conditional expression is false. For example, suppose we want to extend our previous age-checking algorithm to print "Alcohol allowed in moderation" if the person's age is greater than or equal to 21. The pseudocode for this algorithm is this:

```
Input Age.
If Age < 21 print 'No alcohol'
Otherwise, print 'Alcohol allowed in moderation'
```

Figure 4.6 shows a flowchart that describes the same algorithm. The MATLAB code that implements this algorithm is

```
Age = input('Age: ');
if Age < 21
    disp('No alcohol')
else
    disp('Alcohol allowed in moderation')
end
```

4.4.3   The *if-elseif* statement

The third form of the *if* statement is the *if-elseif* statement. Figure 4.7 shows the syntax of this extension.

The meaning of the *if-elseif* construct is as follows:

> **If *conditional_expression_1* is true, execute the code between the *if* and the next *elseif*. If *conditional_expression_1* is false, proceed to test the next *elseif*. Test each of the *elseif* statements in turn until either one of them is found to be true or the *end* is reached.**

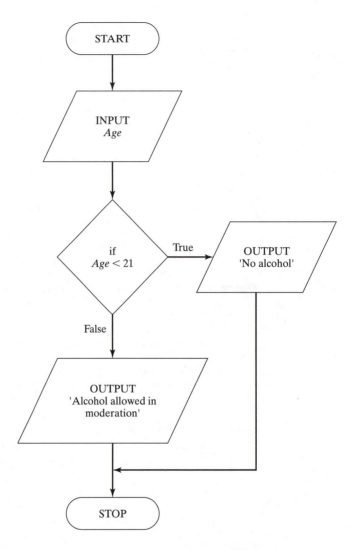

Figure 4.6. Flowchart for example *if-else* statement.

If the conditional expression for any *elseif* is true, execute the code between that *elseif* and the next *elseif*, *else*, or *end*, which ever occurs first. Then proceed to the next statement after the *end*.

The *else* statement is a catchall and is optional. Note that only one of the blocks of code is executed. If more than one conditional expression is true, the first one's block is executed and the others are ignored.

The *if-elseif* statement allows you to test two or more conditions in the same construct. For example, suppose we want to extend our preceding age-checking algorithm to print *Senior discount* if the person's age is greater than or equal to 65. In this case, we do not want to print "Alcohol allowed in moderation". We will assume that the seniors will use alcohol moderately. The pseudocode for this algorithm is

```
Input Age.
If Age < 21 print 'No alcohol'
```

```
elseif Age > 65 print 'Senior discount'
else print 'Alcohol allowed in moderation'
```

Figure 4.8 shows a flowchart that describes this algorithm.

```
if conditional_expression_1

  ...

  ...

elseif conditional_expression_2

  ...

  ...

  ...

  ...

elseif conditional_expression_n

  ...

  ...

else

  ...

  ...

end
```

Figure 4.7. The syntax of the *if-elseif* statement.

In the previous examples of MATLAB code, the comments have been omitted to save space and because the code is explained in the text. It is important to document your code with comments. The following section of MATLAB code implements the previous algorithm and contains comments that explain the purpose of the M-file and each MATLAB statement within the M-file:

```
% This code requests the user to input an age in
% years and displays relevant output pertaining
% to alcohol use depending on the user's age.

% Display prompt and input age
Age = input('Age: ');

% Minimum age for drinking alcohol is 21
if Age < 21
    disp('No alcohol')
% Folks 65 or older get a discount
elseif Age >= 65
    disp('Senior discount')
% People between 21 and 65 are allowed to drink
else
    disp('Alcohol allowed in moderation')
end
```

Create an M-file with this code and execute it.

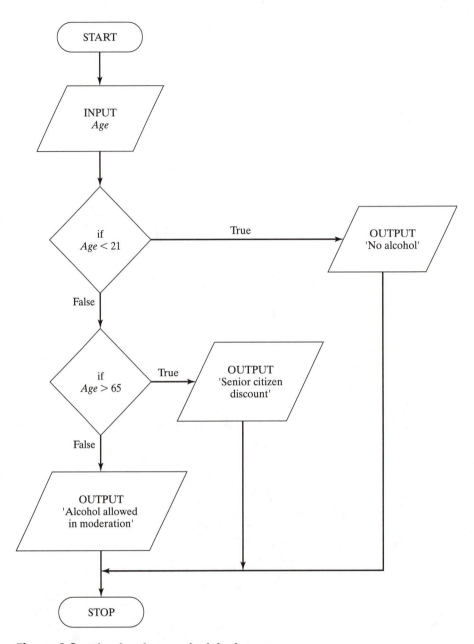

Figure 4.8. Flowchart for example *if-elseif* statement.

PRACTICE 4.2!

Suppose we want to sort numbers into three partitions in the following manner: If the number is less than 15, the string "too small" is printed. If the number is between 15 and 25, inclusively, the string "just right" is printed. If the number is greater than 25, the string "too large" is printed.

Create a MATLAB program that inputs a number and implements the preceding algorithm. Save your work as an M-file. Make sure that you comment your code. At the beginning of the M-file, explain the purpose of the code. Place a comment on a separate line before each MATLAB statement explaining what the statement does.

Check your solution by executing the script, using various inputs.

PROGRAMMING TIP 4.1!

Use indentation to clarify your code. Indentation is not part of MATLAB syntax—it is not required. Indentation serves to make the code easier to read. It is common practice to indent the statements within a block. This is especially true if statements are nested several layers deep.

Here is an example of code that is not indented:

```
if a > 0
if b > 0
c = 5
else
c = 6
end
end
```

Here is the same code with indentation:

```
if a > 0
    if b > 0
        c = 5
    else
        c = 6
    end
end
```

The indentation helps clarify to which *if* the *else* belongs. The rule is that an *else* or *elseif* statement belongs to the nearest preceding *if* statement at the same level of nesting. It does make a difference!

In the preceding code, the *else* belongs to the second *if* statement. In the following code, the *else* belongs to the first *if* statement:

```
if a > 0
    if b > 0
        c = 5
    end
else
    c = 6
end
```

PRACTICE 4.3!

Create an M-File for both of the nested *if-else* statements that follows. What do you think the value of *c* will be if a, b, and c are initially $a = 4, b = 0$, and $c = 2$? Check your answers by setting the initial values of a, b, and c then execute the scripts.

Statement 1:

```
if a > 0
    if b > 0
        c = 5;
    else
        c = 6;
    end
end
disp(c)
```

Statement 2:

```
if a > 0
    if b > 0
        c = 5;
    end
else
    c = 6;
end
disp(c)
```

4.4.4 The *switch* Statement

Another type of selection statement in MATLAB is called the *switch* statement. We use the *switch* statement to make a choice from among several alternatives. Figure 4.9 shows the syntax of the *switch* statement.

```
switch expression
    case value_1
        ...
    case value_2
        ...
    .
    .
    .
    case value_n
        ...
    otherwise
        ...
end
```

Figure 4.9. The syntax of the *switch* statement.

The meaning of the switch statement is as follows:

If the value of the expression is *value_1*, execute the statements between the first and second *case* statements. If the value of the expression is *value_2*, execute the statements between the second and third *case* keywords. Repeat this process for all *case* keywords.

An optional *otherwise* clause may be used.

If an *otherwise* clause is used and none of the *case* statements are matched, execute the code between the *otherwise* and the *end* keywords.

If an *otherwise* clause is not used and none of the *case* statements are matched, control passes to the first line of code after the matching *end* statement.

Only the first matching *case* statement's code is executed. Once the code after a *case* statement is executed, control passes to the first line of code after the matching end statement.

Note that the test expression in a switch statement does not have to be a conditional expression. That is, it does not have to evaluate to true or false. The *switch* expression may evaluate to a scalar numeric value or a string. The example in Figure 4.10 matches a single character grade and displays various messages depending on the outcome. You can test multiple values in a single *case* statement by separating values with commas and placing them in a cell array as shown in line 8.

4.5 REPETITION STATEMENTS

Many algorithms perform some operation over a list or sequence of elements. For example, we may want to add 10 points to all of the student grades in a list that meet a certain condition. As you can see, this would be very tedious if there is a large number of students:

```
if student 1 was not absent add 10 points to final
   grade
if student 2 was not absent add 10 points to final
   grade
if student 3 was not absent add 10 points to final
   grade
if student 4 was not absent add 10 points to final
   grade
...
...
if student n was not absent add 10 points to final
   grade
```

A programming construct that simplifies this type of coding task is called a loop. We also call this type of statement a *repetition* statement.

```
 1 switch grade
 2 case 'A'
 3   disp('Excellent')
 4 case 'B'
 5   disp('Very good')
 6 case 'C'
 7   disp('Good')
 8 case {'D', 'E', 'F'}
 9   disp('Better luck next time')
10 otherwise
11   disp('Invalid input')
12 end
```

Figure 4.10. Example MATLAB code for a *switch* statement.

The use of a loop to walk through a sequence is called *iteration*. The notion of iteration is an important one for computer programming because so many algorithms involve some form of stepping through a sequence. MATLAB supports the two most common forms of loop structures in programming languages—the *for* loop and the *while* loop.

4.5.1   The *for* Loop

The *for* loop is typically used when the programmer knows the number of iterations to be performed. We call this type of loop a *definite iterator*. Figure 4.11 shows the syntax of the *for* statement.

```
for variable = sequence_expression

   ...

   ...

end
```

Figure 4.11. The syntax of the *for* statement.

The meaning of the for statement is as follows:

> **The *sequence_expression* is evaluated and the initial value of the sequence is assigned to the *variable*. The body of the loop is then executed repeatedly, using each value of the *sequence_expression* in turn. After the last value in the *sequence_expression* is assigned to the *variable*, the body is executed one last time and then control is passed to the statement following the *end* statement.**

As an example, the following code calculates the sum of squares from 1 to 5:

```
A = 0;
for Index = 1:5
    A = A + Index^2;
end
```

The third line of code

```
A = A + Index^2;
```

may be confusing at first. It is not an equation, but an assignment statement. The meaning of this line of code is

> Take the value of *Index* and square it. Add the result to the current value of *A*. Assign the results to the variable *A*.

Each time the loop is executed, the variables *A* and *Index* have new values. The values 1, 2, 3, 4, and 5 are sequentially assigned to the variable *Index*. For each value of *Index*, the statements between the *for* reserved word and the *end* reserved word are executed. Figure 4.12 shows a flowchart of this algorithm. In the flowchart, we have explicitly set

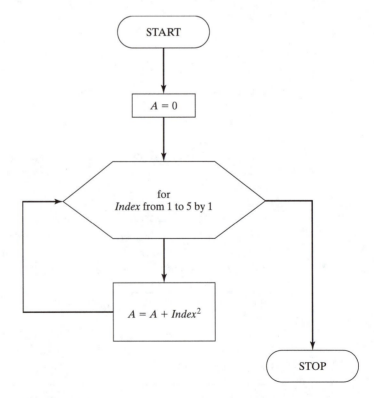

Figure 4.12. Flowchart of example *for* loop.

the increment to be one (1), since the flowchart is using pseudocode. When using MAT-LAB code, the default increment is one (1).

Table 4.2 tracks the values of A and *Index* at each step of the *for* loop. Follow the flowchart and track the values of both variables in Table 4.2. Now, follow the MATLAB code and track the values of both variables in Table 4.2.

TABLE 4.2. Variable tracking table.

Step # of loop	Index	A
before loop		0
1	1	1
2	2	5
3	3	14
4	4	30
5	5	55

Another method for tracking the intermediate results is to remove the semicolon from selected statements in your code. Note that the semicolon has been removed from the third line of the following code:

```
A = 0;
for Index = 1:5
    A = A + Index^2
end
```

Execute the code and you will see that the value of A is displayed each time the third line is executed:

```
A =
    1
A =
    5
A =
    14
A =
    30
A =
    55
```

Obviously, this method is less helpful if the number of iterations is very large, since the results will rapidly scroll off the screen.

The *colon* operator is commonly used for the sequence expression in a *for* loop. Recall that the *colon* operator allows noninteger sequences. The following loop computes the sum of the sines of the numbers from π to 2π incremented by 0.2:

```
A = 0;
for Index = pi: 0.2: pi*2
    A = A + sin(Index);
end
```

The sequence does not have to progress in a positive direction. For example, the following code loops from 10 to 1, decrementing by 1 in each step:

```
A = 0;
for Index = 10: -1: 1
    A = A + Index^2;
end
```

In the preceding examples, the sequence expression is evaluated before the loop begins executing. The sequence expression cannot be modified once the loop has started. If this were allowed, can you see where a programmer might get into trouble? It is dangerous to modify a sequence expression variable inside the loop once the loop has started execution. The bodies of code in the loop foregoing examples are very small, but imagine a *for* loop in which the body of the loop is 30 or 40 lines long. It is possible that you will inadvertently modify the value of the sequence expression variable inside the body of the loop. For this reason, MATLAB evaluates the sequence expression before the loop executes and does not allow you to change its value within the body of the loop.

PRACTICE 4.4!

Prove to yourself that a sequence expression is evaluated before the *for* loop starts and cannot be modified once the loop has started. Execute the following code:

```
A = 0;
N = 5;
for Index = 1:N
    A = A + Index^2;
    N = 20;
end
disp(A);
```

What is the value of *A* at the end of the loop if the expression 1:*N* can be changed after the loop has started? What is the value if it cannot be changed? What does MATLAB produce?

Another type of sequence expression is simply a vector (or one-dimensional array). The *for* loop will walk through the array, assigning each element in turn to the loop variable. For example, the following loop will print, in turn, each of the three numbers in the array [3.4, 85, -2.8]:

```
for Index = [3.4, 85, -2.8]
    disp(Index)
end
```

The output is

```
 3.4000
 85
-2.8000
```

Since a string is an array of characters, you can use a loop to walk through each letter of a string. For example, the following loop prints "Found an a" each time the letter A is identified:

```
for Index = 'This is the way to Tallahassee.'
  if lower(Index) == 'a'
    disp 'Found an a'
  end
end
```

The *lower* function converts each letter to lowercase, so that both upper- and lowercase A's are found.

The output is

```
Found an a
Found an a
Found an a
Found an a
```

Later, we will show you that many of the typical uses of loops are not necessary in MATLAB because of MATLAB's powerful array operations. For example, the previous example that computes the sum of squares from 1 to 5 may be calculated by using the following statement:

```
>> A = sum((1:5).^2)
A =
    55
```

Here's how it works: The expression (1:5) uses the colon operator to create the array.

```
[1, 2, 3, 4, 5]
```

The array exponentiation operator (.^) computes the square of each element in the array, resulting in

```
[1, 4, 9, 16, 25]
```

The *sum* function adds the elements of the array, resulting in 55.

Should you use a *for* loop or MATLAB array operations? MATLAB has optimized its built-in array functions, so its array operations are usually much faster. Thus, if you are using a large array, the MATLAB array operation is preferable.

On the other hand, some algorithms involving sequential operations are difficult to understand. If speed is not an issue, using a *for* loop sometimes makes your code easier to read. More complex array operations are presented in Chapter 10 under the section titled *Array Optimization Techniques*.

PROGRAMMING TIP 4.2!

One of the most common syntax errors that you will incur will be missing *end* statements. The following code segment is intended to count the number of occurrences of digits in a string:

```
1 Count = 0;
2 for Index = 'There are 15 minutes in 0.25 hours.'
3    if any(Index == '0123456789')
4      Count = Count + 1;
5
6 end
7 disp(['Number of digits = ', int2str(Count)]);
```

Note the extended syntax for the *disp* statement in line 7. The *disp* function can take an array as an *input* argument. However, all elements in the array must be the same type. The *int2str* function rounds the numerical variable "Count" to an integer and then converts the integer to a string.

When executed, MATLAB produces the following syntax error:

```
??? Error: File:
D:\Dave\Matlab2001\Examples\ProgrammingTip_4_2.m
Line: 7 Column: 47
"end" expected, "End of Input" found.
```

Note that we forgot to use an *end* statement corresponding to the *if* statement. There are several ways to help prevent this type of error. One method is to use indentation. Then you can check if an *end* reserved word is needed each time the indentation moves left.

Modify the preceding code above by placing an *end* on line 5, save, and execute the code.

The MATLAB editor will attempt to indent your code for you. To use this feature, choose **Edit →
Select All** from the Menu bar. Then choose **Text → Smart Indent** from the Menu bar.

Another helpful feature is called syntax highlighting. The MATLAB Editor colors syntactic elements differently. By default, reserved words are colored blue. The coloring should help you match up other reserved words with their respective *end* keywords.

The indentation parameters as well as the syntax highlighting features may be modified by choosing **File → Preferences** from the Menu bar.

4.5.2   The *while* Loop

There are occasions when we do not know ahead of time how many iterations a loop should make. This type of loop is called an *indefinite iterator* and one implementation is called a *while* loop. The *while* statement continues to loop as long as some condition is true. The syntax of the *while* statement is shown in Figure 4.13.

```
while conditional_expression

   ...

   ...

end
```

Figure 4.13.   The syntax of the *while* statement.

The meaning of the while statement is as follows:

> The *conditional_expression* is evaluated as true or false. If the expression is true, the body of the loop is executed and then the *conditional_expression* is evaluated again. If the *conditional_expression* evaluates to false, control is passed to the next statement following the *end* statement. If the *conditional_expression* is never false, the while statement will loop indefinitely.

The following section of code repeatedly asks the user for input and computes the sum of squares of the numbers until the user presses the **Enter** key (without typing a number):

```
SumSquare = 0;
In = 0;
while ~isempty(In)
   SumSquare = SumSquare + In^2;
   In = input('Type a number (press Enter alone to quit):');
end
disp(['The sum of squares = ', num2str(SumSquare)])
```

A *for* loop is not appropriate in this example because we do not know ahead of time how many times the loop will iterate. Note the use of the *isempty* function. This function returns true if its argument is the empty array [ ]. The *num2str* function converts *SumSquare* to a string so that all of the arguments to the *disp* statement are of the same type. The *input* statement returns the empty array if nothing is typed before pressing the **Enter** key.

Here's an example of the execution of this section of code:

```
Type a number (press Enter alone to quit): -1
Type a number (press Enter alone to quit): 2
Type a number (press Enter alone to quit): 3
Type a number (press Enter alone to quit):
The sum of squares = 14
```

A second example of a *while* loop is shown in Figure 4.14. Create and save an M-file that contains this code. The code counts the number of characters in a string up to the first occurrence of an uppercase or lowercase letter "X". If no "X" occurs, all characters are counted. Blanks are included as characters.

```
 1 Count = 0;
 2 Index = 1;
 3 Str = input('Type a string: ');
 4 while Index <= length(Str) & upper(Str(Index)) ~= 'X'
 5    Count = Count + 1;
 6    Index = Index + 1;
 7 end
 8 disp(['There are ', int2str(Count), ' characters in']);
 9 disp([' ',Str])
10 disp('before the first X.');
```

Figure 4.14. A *while* loop that counts the characters in a string up to the first "X".

If we were simply counting all of the characters in a string, a *for* loop would suffice. However, since we do not know ahead of time if an "X" will occur, a while *loop* is a better choice. The following is a sample output for this section of code:

```
Type a string: 'He is an example of an actor.'
There are 10 characters in
    He is an example of an actor.
before the first X.
```

The most complex part of the example is the conditional expression in the *while* statement (line 4). The first part of the conditional expression is

```
Index <= length(Str)
```

This part of the expression returns true as long as the variable "Index" is less than or equal to the length of the string. This is the stopping condition for the loop if there is not an X in the string.

The second part of the conditional expression is

```
upper(Str(Index)) ~= 'X'
```

This part of the expression takes a single character from the string and compares the uppercase of the character to 'X'. The expression returns true if there is not a match. This is the stopping condition if there is an 'X' or 'x' in the string.

Both parts of the expression are combined with a logical AND operation (&), which means that both parts must be true for the loop to continue. The meaning of the whole conditional expression in English is as follows:

> Loop while the end of the string has not been reached AND an 'X' or 'x' has not been found. Otherwise, pass control to the first line after the matching *end* statement.

PROGRAMMING TIP 4.3!

A common programming error is to entirely forget to modify the loop variable within a *while* loop or to incorrectly modify the loop variable. In the following section of code, the intention of the programmer is to compute the sum of the squares (SS) of the odd numbered elements of an array:

```
A = input('Input an array of numbers: ');
SumSquare = 0;
Index = 1;
while Index ~= length(A)
    SumSquare = SumSquare + A(Index)^2;
    Index = Index + 2;
end
disp(['The SS of the odd elements is ',num2str(SumSquare)])
```

However, the code does not perform correctly. In the following example, the wrong answer is produced because the last element in the array is missed:

```
Input an array of numbers: [ 1 3 5 ]
The sum of squares of the odd elements is 1
```

In the following example, the loop variable increments past the end of the array:

```
Input an array of numbers: [ 1 3 5 7 ]
??? Index exceeds matrix dimensions.
```

Using the <= operator instead of ~= in the *while* statement would solve both problems.

Can the *conditional_expression* be modified once a *while* loop has started? The answer is yes. Because the *while* statement is specifically meant to be used for indefinite iteration, the *conditional_expression* is reevaluated in each iteration.

PRACTICE 4.5!

In the following code, the conditional expression

    Index <= N

is reevaluated each time the loop is iterated:

```
1  Index=1; N=5; SumSquare=0;
2  while Index <= N
3    SumSquare = SumSquare + Index^2;
4    Index = Index + 1;
5    N = 2;
6  end
7  disp(SumSquare)
```

How many iterations will this *while* loop make? What is the value of *SumSquare* when it is displayed in line 7? Test your answer by creating an M-file with this code and executing it.

PRACTICE 4.6!

The evaluation of conditional expressions that contain nonscalar variables can be confusing. Review the section on conditional expressions. Then explain why the following section of code results in *SumSquare* = 50 (if necessary, add a display statement to the code to see the value of the expression

```
Index <= A
```

during each iteration):

```
Index = 1;
A = [3,4,5,6,7];
SumSquare = 0;
while Index <= A
    SumSquare = SumSquare + A(Index)^2;
    Index = Index + 1;
end
disp(SumSquare)
```

APPLICATION! TIME IN FLIGHT

Assuming no air resistance, we can calculate the time of flight for a cannon ball by using the following closed-form equation:

$$t = \frac{2V \sin \theta}{g}$$

In the equation, t is the time in seconds, V is the muzzle velocity when the cannon ball leaves the cannon, and θ (theta) is the angle from horizontal of the initial flight path.

Assume that the gravitational constant

$$g = 9.81 \ m/s^2.$$

The program accepts V and θ from the user and prints the time of flight. Then it exits when V or θ equal zero. Create a new M-file, type in the following code, and execute it (recall that the *num2str* function converts a number to a string):

```
% Application_Ch4.m
%
% This program requests the user to input an initial
% velocity (V) and the angle from horizontal (Theta)
% for a projectile.
%
% The program then computes and displays the time in
% flight for the projectile.
%    - Air resistance is assumed to be zero.
%    - The program exits when either input value = 0

G = 9.81;    % gravitational constant = 9.81 m/s^2
Theta = -1;  % set initial Theta to dummy value
V = -1;      % set initial V to dummy value

% loop while V and Theta are both nonzero
while V ~= 0 Theta ~= 0
  V = input('Initial velocity (m/s): ');
  Theta = input('Initial angle (degrees): ');
  % if V and Theta are nonzero, then compute results
  if V ~= 0 Theta ~= 0
```

```
      % convert degrees to radians
      Radians = Theta * pi/180;
      % calculate flight time in seconds
      Time = (2 * V * sin(Radians))/9.81;
      % display results
      disp(['Flight time = ', num2str(Time), ' seconds.'])
   end
end
```

KEY TERMS

branch	hexagon (loop symbol)	rectangle (computation symbol)
colon operator	indefinite iterator	recursion
definite iterator	iteration	repetition statement
diamond (decision symbol)	parallelogram (I/O symbol)	selection statement
flowchart	pseudocode	terminator (stop/start symbol)

NEW MATLAB FUNCTIONS, COMMANDS, AND RESERVED WORDS

case—reserved word for each case in a switch statement
disp—displays an array to the screen
else—part of the *if* statement syntax
elseif—part of the *if* statement syntax
end—mark the end of a block of code
for—a definite iterative loop statement
if—a selection statement, used to branch execution
int2str—converts an integer value to a string, rounds non-integers
isempty—returns true if argument is the empty array, false otherwise
length—returns the length of a vector
lower—returns the lower case of a character
num2str—converts a number to a string including fractional part
otherwise—catch all in a switch statement, used if no cases match
rem—returns remainder of division of its two arguments
round—returns the rounded integer portion of its argument
sum—sums the elements of an array
switch—a selection statement that allow a choice among several cases
upper—returns the upper case of a character string
while—an indefinite loop statement

SOLUTIONS TO PRACTICE PROBLEMS

4.2.

```
1 % Example_4_2.m
2 % Tests for numbers between 15 and 25, inclusive.
3 % Prints appropriate message.
4 X = input('Number: ');
5 if X < 15
6    disp('too small')
7 elseif X <= 25
8    disp('just right')
9 else
10   disp('too large')
11 end
```

4.3.   6, 2

4.4.   The resulting value is $A = 1$ if the expression 1:N can be changed. $A = 55$ if the sequence expression cannot be changed. MATLAB returns 55.

4.5.   The outcome is that the loop is terminated after two iterations, resulting in SumSquare = 5.

4.6.   The *while* loop terminates when *Index* = 4 because *Index* must be less than or equal to every element of *A*.

Problems

Write pseudocode, a flowchart, and MATLAB code for Problems 1–7. Document your code!

Sections 4.1, 4.2, 4.3, 4.4

1.   Ask the user to input an integer. Print "Even" if the number is even. Print "Odd" if the number is odd. Use the *rem* function to test for an even or odd number. The *rem(X, Y)* function returns the remainder of dividing *X* by *Y*. If *rem(X, 2) = 0*, *X* is even. Use an *if-else* statement in your solution. The following is a sample of an output from two separate executions of the program:

```
Type an integer: 2
Even

Type an integer: 3
Odd
```

2.   Modify your solution to the previous problem by checking whether the number entered by the user is an integer. One way to do this is to test if the rounded input is equal to the input. If it is, then the input is an integer. The *round* function returns the rounded value of the input argument. If the number is not an integer, print "Not an integer". Use an *if-elseif* statement in your solution. The following is a sample of the output from two separate executions of the program:

```
Type an integer: 2.5
Not an integer

Type an integer: 2
Even
```

3.   Ask the user to input a letter. Print "Vowel" if the character is a vowel. Print "Consonant" if the input is a consonant. Use a *switch* statement in your solution. You can use the *lower* function to convert characters to lowercase. Treat *Y* as a consonant. *Hint*: Use the string version of the *input* statement, which returns the argument as a string, rather than as a variable name or number—for example,

```
MyChar = input ('Type a letter: ', 's');
```

An example of the output for two separate executions of the program is

```
Type a letter: 'A'
Vowel
```

```
Type a letter: 'd'
Consonant
```

4. Modify your solution in the previous problem to test also if the input is a non-letter character (e.g., '<' or '3.5'). If not a letter, print "Not a letter". The example of an output for three separate executions of the program is

```
Type a letter: 5.3
Not a letter

Type a letter: *
Not a letter

Type a letter: d
Consonant
```

Sections 4.1, 4.2, 4.3, 4.5

5. Ask the user to input a character string. Count and display the number of vowels in the string. Do not count *Y* as a vowel. Recall that a string is a vector of characters. The *length* function returns the length of a vector. The *lower* function converts a character to lowercase. Use a *for* loop in your solution. The sample of the output is

```
Type a string: 'I am an American'
The number of vowels = 7
```

Recall that the *disp* function takes an array of strings as an argument. To convert a number to a string, use the *num2str* function.

6. Ask the user to input a number. Loop and ask the user to input another number. Keep looping until zero (0) is entered. Return the average of the numbers (not including the final zero). Use a *while* loop in your solution. The following is the sample of the output from a single execution of the program:

```
Input a number (zero to quit): 2
Input a number (zero to quit): 3
Input a number (zero to quit): 4
Input a number (zero to quit): 0
Average = 3
```

7. Modify your solution to Problem 4 so that the user continues to be prompted for input until the number zero is entered. When finished, print a good-bye statement. Use a *while* loop in your solution. The sample of the output for a single execution of the program is

```
Type a letter: q
Consonant
Type a letter: I
Vowel
Type a letter: 0
All done, thank you!
```

Challenge Problems

8. Expressions connected with a logical AND are evaluated left to right. If the first expression is false, the second expression never gets evaluated. Look at

the conditional expression on line 4 of Figure 4.14. Exchange the first and second parts of the conditional expression, placing the test for the letter X before the test for the string length. This will change the order of evaluation. Does the algorithm still work? Why or why not?

Write a pseudocode, draw a flowchart, and write the MATLAB code for Problems 9–13.

9. The factorial of a nonnegative integer N is defined to be

```
Fac(N) = 1 if N = 0 or 1,
Fac(N) = N (N-1) (N-2),...,(3)(2)(1), otherwise.
```

The mathematical factorial operator is the exclamation point (!). The factorial of 3 is computed as follows:

```
3! = (3)(2)(1) = 6.
```

Write a script that returns the factorial of a nonnegative integer. Use an *if* statement and a *for* loop in your solution. Do not use the MATLAB *factorial* function in your solution! Do use the MATLAB *factorial* function to check your answer. Here are several examples of the output sessions:

```
Type a nonnegative integer: 0
The factorial of 0 is 1.

Type a nonnegative integer: 1
The factorial of 1 is 1.

Type a nonnegative integer: 3
The factorial of 3 is 6.

Type a nonnegative integer: 4
The factorial of 4 is 24.
```

10. Does your solution for Problem 9 test for invalid inputs? Try typing a negative number or a fixed-point number such as 5.4. What happens? Modify your solution to test for invalid numerical inputs. The example of the output is

```
Type a nonnegative integer: -1
Sorry, that is a negative number.

Type a nonnegative integer: 5.4
Sorry, that is not an integer.

Type a nonnegative integer: 4
The factorial of 4 is 24.
```

11. The constant e can be approximated by using the following Taylor series:

$$e = 1 + \frac{1}{1!} + \frac{1}{2!} + \frac{1}{3!} + \frac{1}{4!} + \ldots$$

Write a script that approximates the value of e to five elements of the series. (The denominator will be 4!) You may use the MATLAB *factorial* function in your solution. Check your answer by using the MATLAB function $exp(1)$, which returns e^1.

12. Write a script that prompts the user with a menu for one of four trigonometric functions sine, cosine, tangent, and secant. The user selects a number

from the menu, and the script then plots the selected function from $-\pi$ to π in increments of 0.1. Use help to find the MATLAB functions for the trigonometric functions. To see the effect, undock your Command window and place it side by side with the Plot window. Use *disp* statements to create your menu. The menu should look like this:

```
1) sine
2) cosine
3) tangent
4) secant
Make a selection:
```

13. Modify your solution to the previous problem so that the plot is drawn and then the program loops to accept another input. Also, add a menu item that accepts upper- or lowercase "q" to quit. The program should loop until the user types "q" or "Q". Test the input to make sure that only the numbers 1, 2, 3, and 4, and the letter "q" or "Q" are accepted. If the user types anything else, the menu is redrawn with an error message, and the user is asked to try again.

14. Modify your solution to the previous problem to use the *menu* function to create the menu. The *menu* function displays a graphical menu for the user. For example, the following menu command results in the menu shown in Figure 4.15:

```
>> Choice = menu('Make a choice', 'Steak', ...
'Chicken', 'Tofu')
```

Figure 4.15. Example of the result of the *menu* function.

The first argument to the *menu* function is the menu title. The succeeding arguments are the menu items. If the user selects the first menu item, the *menu* function returns the number 1. If the user selects the second menu item, the *menu* function returns the number 2, etc.

5

Arrays and Matrix Operations

5.1 THE PRIMARY MATLAB DATA STRUCTURE

As we have previously stated, the basic data element in the MATLAB system is the array. A scalar is represented as a 1×1 array—that is, an array with one row and one column. Vectors are one-dimensional arrays. An $m \times 1$ array is called a *column vector*, where m is the number of rows in the single-column array. A $1 \times n$ array is called a *row vector*, where n is the number of columns in the single-row array. Array elements may be numbers, characters, strings, other arrays, or structures. Recall that the elements in an array must be uniform. A special type of array, called a cell array, allows nonuniform elements.

MATLAB supports multidimensional arrays. A *matrix* is a special case of an array. A matrix is a rectangular array containing elements of any specified algebraic system, usually real or complex numbers. The English mathematician Arthur Cayley first introduced the concept of a matrix in the mid-19th century. Matrices are employed to help solve systems of linear equations and to perform linear transformations. This chapter describes several applications of matrix algebra to scientific and engineering problems.

MATLAB arrays are, by default, self-dimensioning. That is, if we initialize an array with a set of values, MATLAB automatically allocates the correct amount of space for the array. If you append an element to an array, MATLAB automatically resizes the array to handle the new element. This is different from many programming languages, where memory allocation and array sizing takes a considerable amount of programming effort.

OBJECTIVES

After reading this chapter, you should be able to

- Create arrays and matrices.
- Access elements in arrays and matrices.
- Add, modify, and delete elements from arrays.
- Perform element-by-element arithmetic operations on arrays.
- Perform vector and matrix multiplication.
- Perform matrix exponentiation.
- Compute the transpose, determinant, and inverse of a matrix.

Matrix A consisting of m rows and n columns is said to be of *order* $m \times n$. If $m = n$, then matrix A is called a *square matrix*. The following matrix A is a square matrix of order three:

$$A = \begin{bmatrix} 2 & 4 & 6 \\ 3 & 5 & 7 \\ 1 & 2 & 3 \end{bmatrix}$$

Recall that you can reference the cells in a matrix by subscripts, representing the row number and column number, respectively. Thus, $A(2,3) = 7$. We call the collection of cells in a matrix for which the row numbers equal the column numbers the *main diagonal*. The main diagonal of A is [2, 5, 3].

5.2   ENTERING ARRAYS AND MATRICES

You can create arrays and matrices several ways in MATLAB. You have already been shown how to enter arrays in the Command window by typing text commands. There are several other ways to enter arrays in MATLAB. You can enter arrays by loading a script file that creates the arrays. You can view and edit arrays and matrices by using a graphical user interface called the Array Editor. Finally, you can quickly enter several types of special matrices by using some of MATLAB's built-in matrix generators.

5.2.1   Command Line Entry

Let us review how to enter arrays in the Command window. The syntax includes brackets for the whole array and delimiters for rows and columns. Elements in the same row are separated by commas or spaces. A new row is created by using a semicolon or a new line. The whole array is bracketed by square braces. The array

$$\begin{bmatrix} 1 & 3 & 5 \\ 2 & 4 & 6 \\ 7 & 7 & 7 \end{bmatrix}$$

is entered as

```
>> [1, 3, 5; 2, 4, 6; 7, 7, 7]
ans =
        1       3       5
        2       4       6
        7       7       7
```

You can also create the same array by using spaces to separate the elements in the same row instead of commas:

```
>> [1 3 5; 2 4 6; 7 7 7];
```

You can also create the same array by moving to a new line every time you designate a new row:

```
>> [1 3 5
    2 4 6
    7 7 7]
```

Note that the continuation symbol (...) is not required.

Moreover, you can enter array elements in series more concisely by using the *colon operator*.

5.2.2 The Array Editor

The Array Editor is a graphical interface that displays the contents of workspace objects and allows you to edit them. If the Workspace window is not visible, select **View → Workspace** from the Menu bar. Enter the following command in the Command window:

```
>> A = 5 : 0.5 : 7
A =
     5.0000    5.5000    6.0000    6.5000    7.0000
```

The workspace contents will now include a 1×5 array named A as depicted in Figure 5.1.

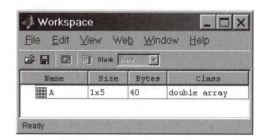

Figure 5.1. The Workspace window.

To see the Array Editor window, you should double-click anywhere on the line of the variable that you want to edit. In our example, click the mouse on the variable A in the Workspace window. The Array Editor will appear as depicted in Figure 5.2.

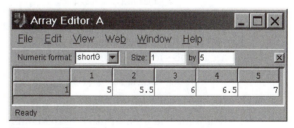

Figure 5.2. The Array Editor.

From the Array Editor, you can click on any cell in the array and edit the cell contents. You, can also change the array dimensions by changing the sizes in the window titled "Size". You can modify the display format by choosing a format from the drop-down menu titled "Numeric format".

5.2.3 Formatting Output

Numbers may be formatted several ways for display on the screen. The formatting does not affect the way the numbers are stored internally. Table 5.1 describes the MATLAB numeric formats. The numeric formats that you choose in the Array Editor window will return to the default of type "short" when you exit MATLAB. If you want to save your favorite format, then choose **File → Preferences → Array Editor** from the Menu bar. Preferences saved in this manner will persist when you exit and restart MATLAB.

TABLE 5.1. Numeric Formats.

Type	Format	Precision
short	fixed point, scaled	5 digits
short e	floating point	5 digits
short g	fixed or floating point (most accurate)	as many significant figures as possible with 5 digits
long	fixed point, scaled	15 digits
long e	floating point	15 digits
long g	fixed or floating point (most accurate)	as many significant figures as possible with 15 digits
rat	rational expression	approximates a rational fraction
hex	hexadecimal	base 16

You can also modify the display format by using the *format* command in the Command window. In addition, you can change the display format by choosing **File** → **Preferences** → **Command Window** from the Menu bar. The syntax of the *format* command is

```
format format-type
format ('format-type')
format
```

where *format-type* is one of the types listed in Table 5.1. Note that every MATLAB command may be represented in command form or functional form. The *command form* uses the command name followed by one or more spaces and then uses the command arguments—for example,

```
>> format long
```

The *functional form* uses the command named, followed by the arguments (if any) in parentheses. When using the functional form, you must place quotes around a string argument—for example,

```
>> format ('long')
```

We will not repeat the functional form in every example in the text, but it is understood that it may be used in place of the command form. The functional form is useful when programming because it allows you to manipulate the argument as a variable.

The *format* command without arguments resets the format to the default type. The default format is "short".

In addition to numeric formats, the *compact* and *loose formats* may be used to add or to delete extra line feeds in the display. Here are some examples:

```
>> format loose
>> log(2)

ans =

    0.6931

>> format compact
>> log(2)
ans =
    0.6931
```

If you forget what format you are utilizing, you can display the current format by using the *get* function. The *get* function gets an object attribute—in this case, the *format* attribute. The first argument is the number of the graphics object that contains the attribute. A graphics object in MATLAB is simply a named graphical structure (e.g., the Command window). The object number for the Command window screen is 0, as shown here:

```
>> get(0, 'format')
ans =
long
```

As an aside, you can see all of the attributes for an object by using the *get* function with the object number alone as an argument. The following command returns all of the attributes of the Command window:

```
>> get(0)
    CallbackObject = []
    Language = english
    CurrentFigure = []
    Diary = off
    DiaryFile = diary
    Echo = off
    ErrorMessage = Error: Expected a variable,
                    function, or constant, found ")".
    FixedWidthFontName = Courier
    Format = long
    ...
    (many more lines of output)
```

5.2.4   Built-In Matrix Generators

We use several types of arrays so frequently that MATLAB has provided special functions to support the generation of these arrays. We call a matrix in which all of the elements are zero a *zero matrix*. You can create a zero array or matrix by using the *zeros* function. The syntax of the *zeros* function is

```
zeros(dim1, dim2, dim3, ...)
```

If you specify a single, scalar parameter *dim1*, MATLAB returns a square zero matrix of order *dim1*. For example, the following command creates a 2×2 matrix of zeros:

```
>>A = zeros(2)
A =
      0      0
      0      0
```

If you specify multiple parameters, a multidimensional zero array of order *dim1* $\times$ *dim2* $\times$ *dim3*... is returned. The following command creates a 2×4 matrix of zeros:

```
>> A = zeros(2, 4)
A =
      0      0      0      0
      0      0      0      0
```

We call a matrix in which all of the elements are the number one a *ones matrix*. You can create a ones matrix by using the *ones* function. The syntax of the *ones* function is identical to the syntax of the *zeros* function. The following command creates a 3 × 2 matrix of ones:

```
>> A = ones(3, 2)
A =
       1      1
       1      1
       1      1
```

Similarly, you can generate an array of pseudorandom numbers by using one of MAT-LAB's several random array generator functions. One of these, the *rand* function, generates an array of random numbers whose elements are uniformly distributed in the range (0, 1). A uniform distribution is one in which there is an equal probability of occurrence for any value within the given range (0, 1)—for example,

```
>> A = rand(2,5)
A =
     0.9501     0.6068     0.8913     0.4565     0.8214
     0.2311     0.4860     0.7621     0.0185     0.4447
```

Another commonly used matrix form is the identity matrix. An *identity matrix* is a matrix in which every element of the main diagonal is one and every other element is zero. You can generate an $n \times n$ identity matrix by using the *eye* function with the syntax, as shown here:

```
eye(n)
```

Here is an example:

```
>> eye(3)
ans =
       1      0      0
       0      1      0
       0      0      1
```

You can use two arguments to specify both dimensions. An $m \times n$ identity matrix with ones on the diagonal and zeros elsewhere can be generated by using the syntax

```
eye(m,n)
```

For example, we might have

```
>> eye(4,3)
ans =
       1      0      0
       0      1      0
       0      0      1
       0      0      0
```

The *eye* function does not support more than two dimensions. Specifying more than two dimensions will result in a syntax error—for example,

```
>> A = eye(3,4,5)
??? Error using ==> eye
Too many input arguments.
```

5.3   ACCESSING AND MANIPULATING ARRAY ELEMENTS

5.3.1   Accessing Elements of an Array

You have already accessed array elements by using subscripts. Let us review what you have learned and cover a few more tricks for accessing array elements. We will use the following two-dimensional array A for the next few examples:

```
>> A = [1 3 5; 2 4 6; 3 5 7]
A =
        1       3       5
        2       4       6
        3       5       7
```

An element in a two-dimensional array can be accessed by using two subscripts, the first for the row and the second for the column; for example,

```
>> A(2,3)
ans =
        6
```

You can also access elements in a two-dimensional array by using a single subscript. In this case, imagine the columns lay end to end as follows:

```
A = [ 1
        2
        3
        3
        4
        5
        5
        6
        7 ]
```

This makes more sense if we look at how MATLAB stores arrays internally. Data are stored internally in a linear sequence of memory locations. MATLAB stretches out an array into a single sequence for storage.

We think of array A as a two-dimensional array. If A were stored one row at a time in memory, it might look like this:

```
1 3 5 2 4 6 3 5 7
```

This is called *row-major order*. However, if A were stored one column at a time in memory, it would look like the following:

```
1 2 3 3 4 5 5 6 7
```

This is called *column-major order*. MATLAB stores arrays in column-major order. MATLAB functions are written to take advantage of the underlying storage mechanism to speed up array operations.

The following examples demonstrate how to access an array element by using a single subscript:

```
>> A(1)
ans =
        1
>> A(4)
```

```
          ans =
                3
          >> A(8)
          ans =
                6
```

We have already used the colon operator to generate arrays. You can also use the colon operator to access multiple array elements simultaneously. You do this by using the colon operator to define a subscript range. For example, the use of 1:2:9 as a subscript returns the first, third, fifth, seventh, and ninth elements of *A*:

```
          >> A(1:2:9)
          ans =
                1       3       4       5       7
```

When used alone, the colon denotes all rows or columns. The following command returns all columns of row two from array *A*:

```
          >> A(2,:)
          ans =
                2       4       6
```

The following command returns the second and third rows of the first and second columns from array *A*:

```
          >> A(2:3, 1:2)
          ans =
                2       4
                3       5
```

5.3.2   Expanding the Size of an Array

You can dynamically expand an array simply by adding more elements—for example,

```
          >> A = [3 5 7]
          A =
                3       5       7
          >> A = [A 9]
          A =
                3       5       7       9
```

When appending arrays to multidimensional arrays, the newly appended parts must conform to the dimensions of the original array. For example, if adding a new row to a two-dimensional array, the row must have the same number of columns as the original array:

```
          >> A = [3 5 7];
          >> B = [1 3 5];
          >> C = [A; B]
          C =
                3       5       7
                1       3       5
```

If you try to append to an array and the appended part does not conform dimensionally, an error will result. Here's an example:

```
          >> A = [3 5 7];
          >> B = [2 4];
```

```
>> C = [A; B]
??? Error using ==> vertcat
All rows in the bracketed expression must have the same
number of columns.
```

PROGRAMMING TIP 5.1!

MATLAB supports preallocation of arrays by allowing the creation of an array that is filled with all zeros or ones. If you are using very large arrays in your programs, preallocation is more efficient than slowly growing an array.

If you know the size of your array ahead of time (e.g., 20,000), create a zero-filled array by using

```
zero(20000);
```

which is much faster than extending the size of the array one element at a time.

5.3.3   Deleting Array Elements

You can delete array elements by replacing them with the empty array, which we designate as []. In the following example, the second element of vector *A* is removed:

```
>> A = [3 5 7];
>> A(2) = []
A =
     3     7
```

You cannot remove a single element from a multidimensional array, since the array would no longer be conformant. This results in an error, as shown in this example:

```
>> A = [1 3 5; 2 4 6]
A =
     1     3     5
     2     4     6
>> A(2,3) = []
???  Indexed empty matrix assignment is not allowed.
```

You can use the colon operator in deletion operations. The colon operator allows deletion of whole rows or columns. In the next example, the second row of the 2 × 3 array *A* is removed:

```
>> A = [1 3 5; 2 4 6]
A =
     1     3     5
     2     4     6
>> A(2,:) = []
A =
     1     3     5
```

The following example removes the first, third, and fifth columns from array *A*:

```
>> A = [1 2 3 4 5 6; 7 8 9 10 11 12]
A =
     1     2     3     4     5     6
     7     8     9    10    11    12
```

```
>> A(:, 1:2:5) = []
A =
        2     4     6
        8    10    12
```

PRACTICE 5.1!

Let array

```
>> A = [ 1  0  1  0
         0  2  0  2
         3  1  3  1 ]
```

Write commands that will perform each of the following operations on array A:

1. Return the second column of A.
2. Return the first and third rows of A.
3. Delete the first and second columns of A.
4. Append the column vector [7; 8; 9] to A.

Re-create array A again before each problem. Check your answers by using **MATLAB**.

5.4 ELEMENT-BY-ELEMENT ARRAY OPERATIONS

5.4.1 Array Addition

MATLAB performs addition or subtraction of two arrays of the same order by adding or subtracting each pair of respective elements. The result is an array of the same order. For example, given that

$$A = [1\ 3\ 5] \text{ and } B = [10\ 12\ 14]$$

$A + B$ is calculated as follows:

$$[A(1) + B(1)\ \ A(2) + B(2)\ \ A(3) + B(3)] = [11\ 15\ 19].$$

Here is another example, this time we are using two-dimensional arrays. Given that

$$A = \begin{bmatrix} 1 & 3 & 5 \\ 2 & 4 & 6 \\ 7 & 7 & 7 \end{bmatrix}$$

and

$$B = \begin{bmatrix} -5 & 6 & 14 \\ 0 & -2 & 4 \\ 2 & 8 & 3 \end{bmatrix}$$

the sum of A and B is

$$A + B = \begin{bmatrix} -4 & 9 & 19 \\ 2 & 2 & 10 \\ 9 & 15 & 10 \end{bmatrix}$$

If two arrays are not of the same order, we say they are not *conformable* for addition or subtraction. For example, the following matrices C and D are not conformable for addition or subtraction because C's dimensions are 1×3 and D's dimensions are 2×3:

```
>> C = [1,3,5]
C =
      1       3       5

>> D = [2,4,6;3,5,7]
D =
      2       4       6
      3       5       7

>> C + D
??? Error using ==> +
Matrix dimensions must agree.
```

As you see, attempting to add them will result in an error.

The addition of arrays is commutative—that is,

$$A + B = B + A.$$

The addition and subtraction of arrays is associative—that is,

$$A + (B + C) = (A + B) + C.$$

5.4.2   Array Multiplication

MATLAB performs array multiplication by multiplying each pair of respective elements in two arrays of the same order. The symbol for array multiplication is a period followed by an asterisk (.*). The following example demonstrates array multiplication:

```
>> A = [1, 3, 5; 2, 4, 6]
A =
      1       3       5
      2       4       6

>> B = [2, 3, 4; -1, -2, -3]
B =
      2       3       4
     -1      -2      -3

>> A .* B
ans =
      2       9      20
     -2      -8     -18
```

To be conformable for array multiplication, the two arrays must be of the same order, unless one array is a scalar, in which case, each element of the other array is multiplied by the scalar—for example,

```
>> A = [5]
A =
      5

>> B = [2, 4, 6]
B =
      2       4       6

>> A .* B
ans =
     10      20      30
```

In this case (where at least one operand is a scalar), the period before the multiplication symbol is not required. The "*" alone will produce the same result. (See Section 5.5.2, titled "Matrix Multiplication" for details.) Here's an example:

```
>> A*B
ans =
      10     20     30
```

5.4.3   Array Right Division

MATLAB performs array right division of arrays A and B by dividing each element in array A by the respective element in array B. The symbol for array right division is a period followed by a forward slash (./). To be conformable for array right division, the two arrays must be of the same order, unless one array is a scalar. The following example demonstrates array right division:

```
>> A = [2, 4, 6]
A =
     2     4     6

>> B = [2, 2, 2]
B =
     2     2     2

>> A./B
ans =
     1     2     3
```

5.4.4   Array Left Division

MATLAB performs array left division of arrays A and B by dividing each element in array B by the respective element in array A. The symbol for array left division is a period followed by a back slash (.\). To be conformable for array left division, the two arrays must be of the same order, unless one array is a scalar. The following example demonstrates array left division, using the arrays A and B from the previous example:

```
>> A.\B
ans =
    1.0000    0.5000    0.3333
```

5.4.5   Array Exponentiation

MATLAB performs array exponentiation of arrays A and B by raising each element in array A to the power of its respective element in array B. The symbol for array exponentiation is a period followed by the caret symbol (.^). To be conformable for array exponentiation, the two arrays must be of the same order, unless one array is a scalar. The following example demonstrates array exponentiation:

```
>> A = [2, 3, 4]
A =
     2     3     4

>> B = [3, 2, 0.5]
B =
    3.0000    2.0000    0.5000
```

```
>> A.^B
ans =
        8      9      2
```

PRACTICE 5.2!

Given

$$A = [2\ 0\ 2;\ 1\ 0\ 1]$$

and

$$B = [4\ 4\ 4;\ 9\ 9\ 9]$$

calculate the following by hand:

1. A + B
2. A * 3
3. A .* 3
4. A .^ 3
5. (A + B) ./ B
6. (A + B) ./ A

Use MATLAB to check your answers.

5.5 BINARY MATRIX OPERATIONS

A binary operation is a mathematical computation performed by using two matrices as inputs. Binary matrix operations are not as straightforward to compute as element-by-element operations. Binary matrix operations have many applications, such as the solution of systems of linear equations.

5.5.1 Vector Multiplication

We will first describe vector multiplication mathematically and then show you how to perform the operation by using MATLAB. Two vectors α and β are multiplied by computing their dot product. The *dot product*, sometimes called the *inner product*, is calculated by adding the products of each pair of respective elements in vectors α and β. To be conformable for vector multiplication α must be a row vector and β must be a column vector. In addition, the vectors must contain the same number of elements, unless one is a scalar. If row vector

$$\alpha = [a_1 \quad a_2 \quad \ldots \quad a_n],$$

and column vector

$$\beta = \begin{bmatrix} b_1 \\ b_2 \\ \ldots \\ b_n \end{bmatrix}$$

the dot product

$$\alpha \cdot \beta = a_1 b_1 + a_2 b_2 + \ldots + a_n b_n.$$

The MATLAB symbol for vector multiplication is the asterisk (*)—for example,

```
A = [1, 5, -6]
A =
      1   5   -6
B = [-2; -4; 0]
B =
      -2
      -4
       0
C = A * B
C = -22
```

The result was calculated as follows:

```
A*B = (1*-2) + (5*-4) + (-6*0) = -22
```

Note how this differs from array multiplication, which would fail, since A and B are not conformable for array multiplication.

If you attempt to use nonconformable vectors, MATLAB returns an error. Here's an example:

```
>> A = [1, 2, 3]
A =
      1      2      3

>> B = [2, 3, 4]
B =
      2      3      4

>> A * B
??? Error using ==> *
Inner matrix dimensions must agree.
```

5.5.2   Matrix Multiplication

MATLAB performs the multiplication of matrix A by a scalar by multiplying each element of A by the scalar. Any array or matrix can be multiplied by a scalar. The following is an example:

```
A = [1, 3; -2, 0]
A =
      1   3
     -2   0
B = A * 5
B =
      5   15
    -10    0
```

MATLAB performs multiplication of nonscalar A and B by computing the dot products of each row in A with each column in B. Each result becomes a row in the resulting matrix. We will try to make this clearer by walking through an example:

```
>> A = [1 3 5; 2 4 6]
A =
      1      3      5
      2      4      6
```

```
>> B = [-2 4; 3 8; 12 -2]
B =
      -2      4
       3      8
      12     -2
```

Note that the number of rows in $A(m_A = 2)$ equals the number of columns in $B(n_B = 2)$. To be conformable for matrix multiplication, the number of rows in A must equal the number of columns in B. The result will be an $m_A \times n_B$ matrix. In the example, the result will be a 2×2 matrix.

The first step is to compute the dot product of row one of A and column one of B:

```
(1 * -2) + (3 * 3) + (5 * 12)= 67
```

Place the result in cell $(1, 1)$ of the result matrix. Next, compute the dot product of row one of A and column two of B:

```
(1 * 4) + (3 * 8) + (5 * -2)= 18
```

Place the result in cell $(1, 2)$ of the result matrix. Next, compute the dot product of row two of A and column one of B:

```
(2 * -2) + (4 * 3) + (6 * 12)= 80
```

Place the result in cell $(2, 1)$ of the result matrix. Finally, compute the dot product of row two of A and column two of B:

```
(2 * 4) + (4 * 8) + (6 * -2)= 28
```

Place the result in cell $(2, 2)$ of the result matrix. The resulting product is

```
>> A*B
ans =
      67     18
      80     28
```

For most cases of A and B, matrix multiplication is not commutative; that is,

$$AB \neq BA.$$

5.5.3   Matrix Division

The operations for left and right matrix division are not straightforward. We will not walk through the underlying algorithm for their computation in this text. However, we will show you an application of the left matrix division operator.

A common and useful application of matrices is the representation of systems of linear equations. The linear system

$$3x_1 + 2x_2 + x_3 = 5$$
$$x_1 + 2x_2 + 3x_3 = 13$$
$$-5x_1 - 10x_2 - 5x_3 = 0$$

can be represented compactly as the matrix product $AX = B$:

$$\begin{bmatrix} 3 & 2 & 1 \\ 1 & 2 & 3 \\ -5 & -10 & -5 \end{bmatrix} \begin{bmatrix} x_1 \\ x_2 \\ x_3 \end{bmatrix} = \begin{bmatrix} 5 \\ 13 \\ 0 \end{bmatrix}$$

MATLAB uses a complex algorithm to compute the solution to a linear system of the form $AX = B$. The operation is denoted by the matrix left division operator (the backslash) $X = A \backslash B$.

The solution to the preceding linear system can be determined as follows:

```
>> A = [3 2 1; 1 2 3; -5 -10 -5];
>> B = [5; 13; 0];
>> X = A\B
X =
      2.5000
     -4.5000
      6.5000
```

Verify that MATLAB produced a correct answer by substituting the results into the original three equations. You will learn more about solutions to linear systems when you take a course in linear algebra.

PRACTICE 5.3!

Given vectors

```
A = [ 2 -3 4 0]
B = [ 4; -12; 4; -12]
C = [ 2 12 0 0]
```

compute the following operations by hand and then check your answers by using MATLAB:

```
1. A * B
2. A * C
3. B * C
4. C * B
```

Given the matrices

```
A = [ 12 4; 3 -5]
B = [ 2 12; 0 0]
```

compute the following operations by hand and then check your answers by using MATLAB:

```
5. A * B
6. B * A
```

5.6 UNARY MATRIX OPERATIONS

Unary matrix operations are mathematical computations that are performed by using a single matrix as an input.

5.6.1 Transpose

We call the matrix that is created by exchanging the rows and columns of matrix A the *transpose* of A. For example, given

$$A = \begin{bmatrix} 1 & 2 & 3 \\ 4 & 5 & 6 \\ 7 & 8 & 9 \end{bmatrix}$$

the transpose of A, denoted in mathematics as A^T, is

$$A^T = \begin{bmatrix} 1 & 4 & 7 \\ 2 & 5 & 8 \\ 3 & 6 & 9 \end{bmatrix}$$

The MATLAB prime operator ($'$) returns the transpose of its argument—for example,

```
>> A = [1, 2, 3; 4, 5, 6; 7, 8, 9]
A =
        1       2       3
        4       5       6
        7       8       9
>> A'
ans =
        1       4       7
        2       5       8
        3       6       9
```

5.6.2   Determinant

The *determinant* of a matrix is a transformation of a square matrix that results in a scalar. We denote the determinant of a matrix A mathematically as $|A|$ or det A. In this text, we will use the second notation, since it resembles the MATLAB function for computing a determinant.

If a matrix has a single entry, then the determinant of the matrix is the value of the entry. For example, if $A = [3]$, the determinant of $A = 3$. We write this as

$$\det A = 3.$$

If a square matrix A has order 2, then the determinant of A is calculated as follows:

$$\det \begin{bmatrix} a_{11} & a_{12} \\ a_{21} & a_{22} \end{bmatrix} = a_{11} \cdot a_{22} - a_{21} \cdot a_{12}$$

MATLAB has a function that computes the determinant named *det*. The syntax for the *det* function is

$$\det \ (A)$$

where A must be a square matrix—for example,

```
A =
        2       3
        6       4
>> det(A)
ans =
      -10
```

First, we will show you how to calculate mathematically the determinant of a matrix with order $n > 2$. Then we will show you how to use MATLAB to perform the same computation.

The strategy for calculating the determinant of a matrix with order $n > 2$ involves subdividing the matrix into smaller sections called *minors* and *cofactors*. If row i and column j of a square matrix A are deleted, the determinant of the resulting matrix is called the minor of a_{ij}. We denote the minor as M_{ij}. For example, given

$$A = \begin{bmatrix} 1 & 2 & 3 \\ 4 & 5 & 6 \\ 7 & 8 & 9 \end{bmatrix}$$

then the minor of a_{12} (deleting row 1 and column 2) is

$$M_{12} = \det \begin{bmatrix} 4 & 6 \\ 7 & 9 \end{bmatrix}.$$

The cofactor of a_{ij} is denoted as A_{ij} and is calculated as follows:

$$A_{ij} = (-1)^{i+j} M_{ij}.$$

In our example, the cofactor of a_{12} is

$$A_{12} = (-1)^{1+2} \left((4 \cdot 9) - (6 \cdot 7) \right) = 6.$$

The general form for the calculation of a determinant is

$$\det A = a_{i1} A_{i1} + a_{i2} A_{i2} + \cdots + a_{in} A_{in}$$

where i is any row in square matrix A of order n. The answer is the same no matter which row is chosen. A similar formula works by choosing any column in A. Let us follow the example and expand A around row 2:

$$\det A = 4 \cdot (-1)^{2+1} \cdot \det \begin{bmatrix} 2 & 3 \\ 8 & 9 \end{bmatrix} + 5 \cdot (-1)^{2+2} \cdot \det \begin{bmatrix} 1 & 3 \\ 7 & 9 \end{bmatrix}$$

$$+ 6 \cdot (-1)^{2+3} \cdot \det \begin{bmatrix} 1 & 2 \\ 7 & 8 \end{bmatrix}$$

$$= (-4 \cdot -6) + (5 \cdot -12) + (-6 \cdot -6)$$

$$= 0.$$

We find that by using MATLAB to compute the determinant of A results in

```
A =
        1        2        3
        4        5        6
        7        8        9

>> det(A)
ans =
        0
```

As you can see, the determinant of a high order matrix is tedious to calculate by hand. Moreover, because the calculation of a higher order determinant is computationally intensive and involves a series of recursive steps, the rounding error can be significant.

5.6.3   Inverse

The *inverse* of a square matrix A, if it exists, is defined to be a square matrix such that

$$AA^{-1} = I,$$

where I is the identity matrix of the same order as A. The matrix inverse operation is denoted mathematically by using a negative one exponent, A^{-1}.

There is a method for determining if and when the inverse of a matrix exists. It depends on understanding the concept of matrix *singularity*. A square matrix is singular if and only if its determinant is equal to zero. Otherwise, a matrix is nonsingular. Furthermore, a square matrix has an inverse if and only if it is nonsingular. So, a square matrix A has an inverse if and only if $det(A) \neq 0$.

However, on a computer, zero is not always zero. Computer representations of real numbers are usually approximations. Thus, calculations can result in highly accurate, but approximate results. If the determinant of a matrix is close to zero, MATLAB will give a warning that the inverse of A may not be correct.

The syntax for MATLAB's inverse function *inv* is

```
inv(square-matrix)
```

Recall from the previous example that the determinant of the matrix

```
A =
     1     2     3
     4     5     6
     7     8     9
```

is singular (i.e., $det(A) = 0$) and should not have an inverse. MATLAB returns a warning noting this:

```
>> inv(A)
Warning: Matrix is close to singular or badly scaled.
         Results may be inaccurate. RCOND = 1.541976e-
         018.
ans =
  1.0e+016 *
    -0.4504      0.9007     -0.4504
     0.9007     -1.8014      0.9007
    -0.4504      0.9007     -0.4504
```

5.6.4   Matrix Exponentiation

MATLAB computes the positive integer power of a square matrix A by multiplying A times itself the requisite number of times. The multiplication operation that is performed is matrix multiplication, not element-by-element multiplication—for example,

```
>> A = [1, 2; 3, 4]
A =
     1     2
     3     4
>> A^2
ans =
     7    10
    15    22
>> A^3
ans =
    37    54
    81   118
```

The negative integer power of a square matrix A is computed by performing matrix multiplication of the inverse of A the requisite number of times. For example, to compute the second negative root of A, we type

```
>> A^-2
ans =
     5.5000    -2.5000
    -3.7500     1.7500
```

This only works if the matrix is nonsingular. MATLAB issues a warning if the computed determinant of A is equal or very close to zero. Here's an example:

```
>> A = [1,1; 0,0]
A =
     1     1
     0     0

>> det(A)
ans =
     0

>> A^-2
Warning: Matrix is singular to working precision.
ans =
   Inf   Inf
   Inf   Inf
```

PRACTICE 5.4!

Given the square matrices

```
A = [ 2 0; 1 -5]
B = [ 3 -2 0; 4 1 5; 0 -3 4]
```

compute the following operations by hand and then check your answers by using MATLAB:

1. A'
2. det(A)
3. B'
4. det(B)

Compute the following with MATLAB:

5. A^2
6. inv(A)
7. inv(B)
8. A^-2

5.7 MULTIDIMENSIONAL ARRAYS

We have previously used examples of two-dimensional arrays. Many of MATLAB's array operations can be extended to more than two dimensions.

The following command creates a three-dimensional array of order $2 \times 3 \times 2$. Since MATLAB cannot display the whole array at once, it displays the array a page at a time. There are two pages in the following example, as the third dimension takes two levels:

```
>> A = ones(2,3,2)
A(:,:,1) =
     1     1     1
     1     1     1
```

```
A(:,:,2) =
      1      1      1
      1      1      1
```

5.8   USEFUL ARRAY FUNCTIONS

MATLAB contains scores of useful functions for manipulating and extracting information from arrays. This section presents a few of the most commonly used array functions.

ndims

The *ndims* function returns the number of dimensions of its argument—for example,

```
>> A = ones(2,3,2);
>> ndims(A)
ans =
      3
```

size

The *size* function returns the length of each dimension, or the order of the array. The result is a vector that contains the size of dimension 1, dimension 2, dimension 3, etc. Here's an example,

```
>> A = zeros(2,3,2,4);
>> size(A)
ans =
      2      3      2      4
```

You can also use the size function to return the size of each dimension to a separate variable—for example,

```
>> [m, n, s, t] = size(A)
m =
      2
n =
      3
s =
      2
t =
      4
```

diag

The *diag* function returns the elements of the main diagonal. For a matrix, *diag* returns the elements with equal row and column indices (i.e., elements (1,1), (2,2), (3,3), etc.):

```
>> A = [1 3 5; 2 4 6; 0 2 4]
A =
      1      3      5
      2      4      6
      0      2      4
```

```
>> diag(A)
ans =
     1
     4
     4
```

The main diagonal is also called the *zero diagonal*. A second argument may be passed to *diag* that specifies the nth diagonal above or below zero. If the second argument is positive, the nth diagonal above the zero diagonal is returned, as in this example:

```
>> diag(A,1)
ans =
     3
     6
```

If the second argument is negative, the nth diagonal below the zero diagonal is returned. Here's an example:

```
>> diag(A,-1)
ans =
     2
     2
```

length

The *length* function returns the length of the largest dimension of an array. For a one-dimensional array (vector), this equals the number of elements in the vector. The length of A in the following example is three, which is the size of the largest dimension:

```
>> A = [1 3; 2 4; 0 2];
>> length(A)
ans =
     3
```

reshape

The *reshape* function reshapes an array. It has the syntax

```
reshape(A, m, n, p, ...)
```

where A is the array to be reshaped, and $m, n, p, \ldots$ are the new dimensions. The number of elements in the old array must equal the number of elements in the new array. Consider the array

```
>> A = ones(2,6,2);
```

Since the number of elements in $A = 2 \times 6 \times 2 = 24$, we should be able to reshape A into any order in which the product of the dimensions equals 24—for example,

```
>> reshape(A,2,12)
ans =
     1  1  1  1  1  1  1  1  1  1  1  1
     1  1  1  1  1  1  1  1  1  1  1  1
```

An attempt to reshape an array into a nonconforming array results in an error. Here's an example:

```
>> reshape(A,3,5)
??? Error using ==> reshape
To RESHAPE the number of elements must not change.
```

We shall consider another example. The following transformation makes sense, since you know that MATLAB stores arrays in column-major order:

```
>> A = [ 1 2 3; 4 5 6; 7 8 9; 10 11 12]
A =
     1     2     3
     4     5     6
     7     8     9
    10    11    12
>> reshape(A, 2, 6)
ans =
     1     7     2     8     3     9
     4    10     5    11     6    12
```

sort

The *sort* function sorts arrays. When used on a vector, the sort is in ascending order:

```
>> A = [4 2 3 9 1 2];
>> sort(A)
ans =
     1     2     2     3     4     9
```

When used on a two-dimensional array, MATLAB performs the sort on each column:

```
>> A = [5 0 4; 2 2 1]
A =
     5     0     4
     2     2     1
>> sort(A)
ans =
     2     0     1
     5     2     4
```

For more than two dimensions, MATLAB performs the sort on the first dimension with the size greater than one. We call a dimension of size one a *singleton dimension*. Another way of stating this rule is that the sort is performed on the first nonsingleton dimension.

You can specify the dimension on which to sort as a second argument. For example, if we want to sort the two-dimensional array *A* across rows instead of down columns, we could use the following command:

```
>> A = [5 0 4; 2 2 1]
A =
     5     0     4
     2     2     1
>> sort(A,2)
ans =
     0     4     5
     1     2     2
```

You can perform descending sorts by using the colon operator. We describe descending sorts and other array manipulation tricks in Chapter 10.

max, min, mean, median

The *max*, *min*, *mean*, and *median* functions each work in a similar fashion to the *sort* function. Given a vector argument, the functions return the maximum, minimum, mean, or median value, respectively. If given a two-dimensional array, each function returns a vector that contains the result of the operation on each column.

Because these functions each work in a similar fashion, we will demonstrate their use with the *min* function. First, we will use a vector as an example:

```
>> A = [ 3 2 -6 1 10];
>> min(A)
ans =
    -6
```

Next, we will show an example that uses a two-dimensional array:

```
>> A = [ 2 1 3; 4 2 2; 5 0 -2]
A =
      2    1    3
      4    2    2
      5    0   -2
>> min(A)
ans =
      2    0   -2
```

Note that *min* returns the minimum for each column.

PRACTICE 5.5!

Each of the five columns in matrix A represents the four exam grades for a student in a MATLAB programming class:

```
A = [ 89  97  55  72  95
     100  92  63  85  91
      82  96  71  91  82
      90  98  48  83  70 ]
```

1. Give a command that sorts each student's grades and returns a matrix with the sorted grades.
2. Give a command that computes the mean of each student's grades and returns a vector with the results.
3. Give a command that computes the median of each student's grades and returns a vector with the results.
4. Give a single command that returns the overall mean grade for all five students in the course.

   Now, change your view of matrix A. Assume that each of the four rows in matrix A represents the five exam grades of a student. *Note:* Each row represents a student.

5. Give a command that sorts each student's grades and returns a matrix with the sorted grades.
6. Give a command that computes the mean of each student's grades and returns a vector with the results.
7. Give a command that computes the median of each student's grades and returns a vector with the results.
8. Give a single command that returns the overall mean grade for all five students in the course.

APPLICATION! COMMUNICATION ROUTES

The calculation of the number of communication paths is important in a variety of fields, for example, the control of network router traffic. Scientists use the same theory to model behavior in fields such as human communication, political influence, and the flow of money through organizations.

A common example, used to demonstrate principles of communication routes, is the number of roads connecting cities. In this diagram we depict four cities along with the roads connecting them:

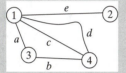

Table 5.2 shows the number of direct routes between each pair of cities. A direct route does not go through any intermediate city. For example, there are two direct routes between City 1 and City 4. The table expresses this information redundantly. You can see the routes between City 1 and City 4 by looking at either (row 1, column 4) or (row 4, column 1). We have presented the data in such a manner, so that it can be stored in a square matrix.

The square matrix A summarizes the connectivity between the cities. For example, $A(1,4) = 2$ indicates that there are two direct routes from City 1 to City 4:

$$A =$$

$$\begin{matrix} 0 & 1 & 1 & 2 \\ 1 & 0 & 0 & 0 \\ 1 & 0 & 0 & 1 \\ 2 & 0 & 1 & 0 \end{matrix}$$

Note that A is symmetric. This means that the cells above the main diagonal are a mirror image of the cells below the diagonal when reflected along the diagonal. Symmetry is also defined as $A(n, m) = A(m, n)$ for any m and n.

It is known that the matrix $A\char`^2$ represents the number of ways to travel between any two cities by passing through only one intermediate city.

```
>> B = A^2
B =
```

$$\begin{matrix} 6 & 0 & 2 & 1 \\ 0 & 1 & 1 & 2 \\ 2 & 1 & 2 & 2 \\ 1 & 2 & 2 & 5 \end{matrix}$$

Matrix B summarizes the number routes between pairs of cities if the route contains one intermediate city: Note the six ways to travel from City 1 back to City 1 by passing through exactly one other city: a–a, c–c, c–d, d–c, d–d, and e–e. The two ways to travel from City 2 to City 4 by passing through exactly one other city are e–c and e–d.

We count traveling in one direction differently than traveling the same route in the opposite direction. Thus, there are two routes from City 1 to City 4, c–d and d–c.

TABLE 5.2. Number of routes among four cities.

	City 1	City 2	City 3	City 4
CITY 1	0	1	1	2
CITY 2	1	0	0	0
CITY 3	1	0	0	1
CITY 4	2	0	1	0

KEY TERMS

cofactor	determinant	main diagonal
colon operator	dot product	matrix
column-major order	functional form	minor
column vector	identity matrix	ones matrix
command form	inner product	order
compact format	inverse	row-major order
conformable	loose format	row vector

short format   square matrix   zero matrix
singleton dimension   transpose
singularity   zero diagonal

NEW MATLAB FUNCTIONS, COMMANDS, AND RESERVED WORDS

clock—returns current date and time
det—returns the determinant of a square matrix
diag—returns the diagonal of a matrix
etime—returns time elapsed between 2 times
eye—returns identity matrix
format—formats numeric output
get—returns the named properties of an object
inv—returns the inverse of a square matrix
length—returns the number of elements in a vector
max—returns the maximum element(s) along the first non-singleton dimension
mean—returns the mean element(s) along the first non-singleton dimension
median—returns the median element(s) along the first non-singleton dimension
min—returns the minimum element(s) along the first non-singleton dimension
ndims—returns the number of dimensions of an array
ones—returns an array of ones
rand—returns uniformly distributes pseudo-random numbers in [0,1]
reshape—reshapes an array
size—returns the order (size) of an array
sort—sorts an array in ascending order
zeros—creates an array of zeros

SOLUTIONS TO PRACTICE PROBLEMS

5.1. 1. `A(:,2)`
      2. `A(1:2:3,:)`
      3. `A(:,1:2) = []`
      4. `A = [A [7; 8; 9]]`

5.2. 1. `A+B = [6 4 6; 10 9 10]`
      2. `A*3 = [6 0 6; 3 0 3]`
      3. `A.*3 = [6 0 6; 3 0 3]`
      4. `A.^3 = [8 0 8; 1 0 1]`
      5. `(A + B)./B = [1.500 1.000 1.500;`
                      `1.1111 1.0000 1.1111]`
      6. `(A + B)./A = Warning: Divide by zero.`
                    `[ 3 Inf  3`
                    `  10 Inf 10]`

5.3. 1. `A*B = 60`
      2. `A*C = ??? Error using ==> *`
              `Inner matrix dimensions must agree.`
      3. `B*C =  [ 8     48     0     0`
              `  -24   -144     0     0`
              `    8     48     0     0`
              `  -24   -144     0     0]`
      4. `C*B = -136`

```
5. A*B = [ 24   144;   6 36 ]
6. B*A = [ 60   -52;   0  0 ]
```

5.4.
```
1. A'     = [ 2   1; 0 -5 ]
2. det(A) = -10
3. B'     = [ 3      4      0
             -2      1     -3
              0      5      4 ]
4. det(B) = 89
5. A^2 = [ 4   0; -3   25 ]
6. inv(A) = [ 0.5000 0; 0.1000 -0.2000 ]
7. inv(B) = [ 0.2135      0.0899    -0.1124
             -0.1798      0.1348    -0.1685
             -0.1348      0.1011     0.1236]
8. A^-2 = [ 0.2500    0; 0.0300    0.0400 ]
```

5.5.
```
1. sort(A)
2. mean(A)
3. median(A)
4. mean(mean(A))
5. sort(A,2)
6. mean(A,2)
7. median(A,2)
8. mean(mean(A,2))
```

Problems

Section 5.1.

What is the order and main diagonal of the following matrices?

1. `[3, 4; 5, 6; 7, 8]`
2. `[2 3 4 5; 6 7 8 9]`
3. `[2 1 0; 2 −3 1; 4 0 0; 3 2 1]`

Verify your answers by using appropriate MATLAB functions.

Section 5.2.

4. Create a vector A that contains the following fractions:

    ```
    >> A
    A =
        1/2 2/3 3/4 4/5 5/6
    ```

    What command changes your format so the vector displays rational fractions instead of decimals?

5. What command creates a 4×5 matrix that contains all zeros?

Section 5.3.

6. The loads in kilograms on the center points of five beams are

    400.3

    521.1

212.1

349.5

322.2

Create a row vector named "Loads" that contains the five values. What is a single command that replaces the second and fourth values of "Loads" with zero? What is a single command that deletes the third and fifth elements of "Loads"?

7. Re-create the original row vector "Loads" from the previous problem. The lengths in meters of the five beams are, respectively,

14.3

6.2

22.6

2.4

10.2

Create a row vector named "Lengths" that contains the five beam lengths in meters. In a single command, create a matrix named "Beams" by concatenating "Loads" and "Lengths". "Beams" should have two rows with the load values on the first row and the respective lengths on the second row. Your answer should look like the following:

```
>> Beams =
   400.3000   521.1000   212.1000   349.5000   322.2000
    14.3000     6.2000    22.6000     2.4000    10.2000
```

Section 5.4.

8. Assume that the loads for the five beams in Problem 6 are distributed evenly across the length of each beam. Using array arithmetic, and the original vectors "Loads" and "Lengths", create a vector that represents the average load in kg/m for each beam.

9. The command $rand(1,n)$ produces a row vector of n uniformly distributed, pseudorandom numbers between 0.0 and 1.0. Use array arithmetic and the $rand$ function to create 100 uniformly distributed pseudorandom numbers between 8.0 and 10.0.

Section 5.5.

10. Express the following linear system in matrix form as matrices A and B:

$$3x_1 + 2x_2 = 4$$
$$-5x_1 + 10x_2 = 0$$

11. Use the MATLAB left matrix division operator to find the solution of the linear system in the previous problem.

Section 5.6.

12. The transpose of the transpose of a matrix equals the original matrix. This can be stated as $(A^T)^T = A$. Using MATLAB, demonstrate that the theorem is true for the following matrix:

```
A = [1 2 4 6; 4 3 2 1].
```

13.   Experiment with the transpose operator on a few example matrices. What conclusion do you reach about the main diagonal of a matrix and the main diagonal of its transpose?

14.   Given a matrix representation of a system of linear equations $AX = B$, if the determinant of A equals zero, the system does not have a unique solution. Two possibilities are that the system has no solutions and that the system has an infinite number of solutions. Determine if the following system has a unique solution:

$$2x_1 + 3x_2 + 4x_3 = 10$$
$$-x_1 + 3x_2 - x_3 = 12$$
$$x_1 + \frac{3}{2}x_2 + 2x_3 = 0$$

15.   The inverse of an array A multiplied by itself should equal the identity matrix of the same order as A. Show how you would test this assumption. Use matrix multiplication and the *inv*, *eye*, and *size* functions.

16.   The following matrix represents the numbers of direct paths between four network routers:

	R1	R2	R3	R4
R1	0	2	1	3
R2	2	0	0	2
R3	1	0	0	2
R4	3	2	2	0

How many paths are there from router two to router four if each path passes through exactly one other router?

Section 5.7.

17.   Create a 2 × 4 × 3 array of random numbers. Replace the cell contents in the third page of the array with zeros.

18.   Create a three-dimensional array of order 6 × 2 × 3. Fill page one with 1's, page two with 2's, and page 3 with 3's. Can you solve the problem in a single command?

Section 5.8.

19.   Create the following array:

$$A = [1{:}10; 11{:}20; 21{:}30].$$

Reshape A into a two-column array. What is the bottom number in each column?

Challenge Problem

20.   Reread Programming Tip 5.1. Test the assertion in the tip by writing a program that creates a 1 × 20000 row vector of ones in a single command. Write another program that creates a 1 × 1 row vector and then builds a 1 × 20000 vector of ones a single cell at a time using a loop.

Time both programs and compare the efficiency of the two methods. *Hints*: The function *clock* returns a six-element vector containing the current date and time. The meaning of each element in the vector is [year, month, day, hour, minute, seconds].

The elapsed time function, *etime(t2, t1)*, returns the elapsed time in seconds between time *t2* and time *t1*. The following code segment computes the time taken to execute the code between *t1* and *t2*:

```
t1 = clock
...
...
t2 = clock
ElapsedTime = etime(t2,t1)
```

6

Plotting and Graphing

6.1 INTRODUCTION

Creating plots of data sets and functions is very useful for engineers and scientists. You can use plots to present results for papers and presentations or to visually search for approximate solutions to problems. MATLAB has a rich set of plotting commands. In this chapter, we describe MATLAB's basic plotting operations.

6.2 THE *PLOT* COMMAND

The basic plotting command in MATLAB is *plot*. If you give the *plot* function a vector argument, MATLAB plots the contents of the vector against the indices of the vector.

The following command creates a vector Y, with 10 elements indexed from 1 to 10, that crudely approximates the sine function from zero to 4π:

```
>> Y = sin(0: 1.3: pi*4);
```

The command *plot*(Y) automatically opens the Plot Editor window and creates the plot depicted in Figure 6.1.

If you pass two vectors, X and Y, to the plot command, MATLAB plots the corresponding X_i, Y_i pairs and draws a single line connecting the points. The following example is a plot of two vectors—indeed, the same plot as that in the previous example (Figure 6.1):

```
>> X = 0 : 1.3 : pi*4;
>> Y = sin(X);
>> plot(X,Y)
```

Figure 6.2 shows another example, resulting from the following commands:

```
>> X = sin(0:0.1:10);
>> Y = cos(0:0.1:10);
>> plot(X,Y)
```

OBJECTIVES

After reading this chapter, you should be able to

- Create plots at the command line.
- Use MATLAB's graphical Plot Editor.
- Use line and marker styles.
- Label a plot.
- Create multiple plots in the same figure.
- Create log–log and semilog scaled plots.

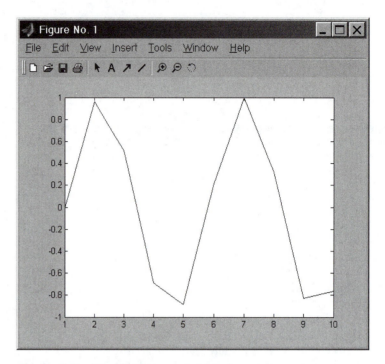

Figure 6.1. The Plot Editor and a plot of vector *Y*.

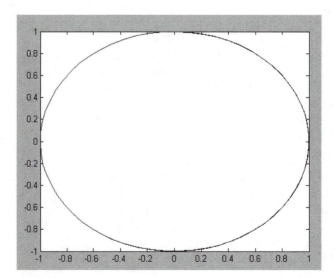

Figure 6.2. A plot of two vectors *Y* and *X*.

If one or both of the arguments to *plot* are matrices, then MATLAB plots the corresponding elements as before, but draws multiple connecting lines, for each column or row, depending on which is conformant. The following example plots matrix *Y* against vector *X*:

```
>> X = [9 8 7 6 5 4];
>> Y = [1 3 2 4 3 5; 12 13 14 15 16 17];
```

Since the columns of X and Y are of the same order, but the rows are not, the plot function creates two lines, one for each row. The first line is a plot of row one of Y against X. The second line is a plot of row two of Y against X. Figure 6.3 shows the resulting plot.

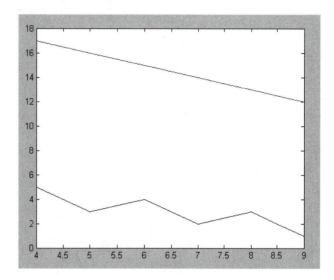

Figure 6.3.   A plot of matrix Y versus vector X.

6.3   USING THE PLOT EDITOR

Choose **Insert** from the Menu bar of Plot Editor, and a drop-down menu will appear. Figure 6.4 shows the Insert drop-down menu of the Plot Editor. From this menu, you can insert and modify many plot elements.

Figure 6.4.   The Insert drop-down menu.

Click on the arrow in the Figure toolbar of the Plot Editor. (See Figure 6.5 for the location of the depressed arrow.) After you have clicked on the arrow, click on the plot line. The data points should appear as shown in Figure 6.5. Now, right click the mouse, and a drop-down menu will appear, as indicated in the figure. From this drop-down

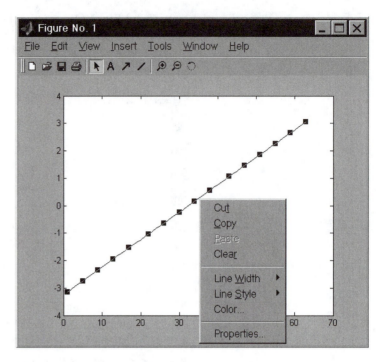

Figure 6.5. Changing attributes with the Plot Editor.

menu, you can change attributes of the plot line, such as the line width, line style, color, and other properties.

Oddly enough, now that we have shown you this technique, we are going to abandon it. The reason for doing so is that you can create and manipulate the same elements from the command line by using MATLAB function calls. Since this is a text on MATLAB programming, we will focus on the function calls. You should be able to figure out how to perform the same functions by using the Plot Editor on your own.

6.4 LINE AND MARKER STYLES

In this section, we will show you the command line options for adding and modifying the color and texture of the plot lines, as well as the command line options for changing the marker styles.

6.4.1 LineSpec Argument

You can control the color and texture of plot lines by using an additional argument of the *plot* command, called the line specification or *LineSpec*. This argument is a cryptic collection of characters that specifies the line character, the marker symbol, and the colors of both.

Let us look at three of these attributes as an example: the line character, the marker symbol, and the color. The available line characters are as follows:

- solid line (-)
- dashed line (- -)
- dotted line (:)
- dotted-dashed line (-.)

The default is a solid line. The marker symbol is one of 13, and the marker codes are as follows:

- point (.)
- circle (o)
- x-mark ($\times$)
- plus ($+$)
- star (*)
- square (s)
- diamond (d)
- down triangle (v)
- up triangle ($^\wedge$)
- left triangle ($<$)
- right triangle ($>$)
- pentagram (p)
- hexagram (h)

The following are the color codes:

- r–red
- g–green
- b–blue
- c–cyan
- m–magenta
- y–yellow
- k–black
- w–white

Now we will create a plot of the sine function with a diamond-shaped marker, a dashed line, and the color red. The symbols for the dashed line, diamond marker shape, and red color are enclosed in quotes as an argument to the *plot* command. The arguments within the quotes can be placed in any order. Figure 6.6 displays the results, except that your results should be in color. The MATLAB code is

```
>> X = 0 : 0.4 : 4*pi;
>> Y = sin(X);
>> plot(X,Y, '- -dr')
```

6.4.2   Line Properties

You can control other line qualities by using property-value pairs as additional arguments to *plot*. Examples of line attributes are *LineWidth* and *MarkerSize*. You can find the complete list of line attributes by choosing **Help** → **Index**. Type *line* in the box labeled *Search index for*, and choose **Properties** from the resulting list. Do not forget that the Help Index feature is case sensitive: Typing *Line* will get different results than typing *line*.

Let us re-create the previous plot, but use a solid line with LineWidth = 2 and a circular marker with MarkerSize = 6. In the following command, the lowercase character *o* designates a circular marker:

```
>> plot(X,Y, '-o', 'LineWidth', 2, 'MarkerSize', 6)
```

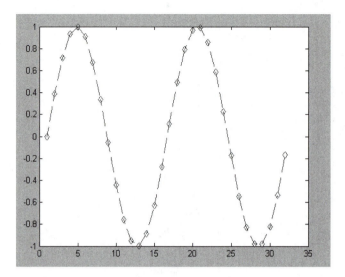

Figure 6.6. Sample use of the LineSpec argument.

Note that the property *names* are always placed in quotes, since they are always strings. If the property *values* are strings, place them in quotes, too. If the property *values* are numeric types, do not place them in quotes. Figure 6.7 shows the resulting plot.

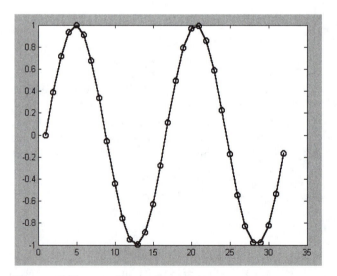

Figure 6.7. Sample use of line properties.

6.5 LABELING A PLOT

You should label a plot carefully. Plot labeling includes a title, axis labels, and if necessary, a legend. Labels, titles, legends, and other text can be created with the *xlabel, ylabel, legend, title*, and *text* commands.

6.5.1   Creating axis labels and titles

The *xlabel* command has several syntactic variants. The first variant takes a string argument and displays it as the X-axis label:

```
xlabel('string')
```

The second form takes a function as an argument:

```
xlabel(function)
```

The function must return a string.

You can use additional arguments to specify property-value pairs, in a manner similar to the way *Line* properties are specified in the *plot* statement. For *xlabel*, the properties are derived from the *Text* class, whereas the properties used in the *plot* statement are derived from the *Line* class. (We will explain more about classes and objects in Chapter 9, "Object-Oriented Programming." The term *class* refers to a group of characteristics shared by a group of objects.)

Some of the *Text* class properties are as follows:

- HorizontalAlignment
- FontName
- FontSize
- Color

You can see the full list of *Text* properties by choosing **Help** → **Index**. Type *text* in the box labeled *Search index for*, and choose **Properties** from the resulting list.

The *ylabel* command has the same syntactic variants and properties as *xlabel* and performs the same operations, but on the Y-axis instead of the X-axis.

The *title* command, too, has the same syntax and properties as *xlabel*, but creates a title for the graph. The *xlabel, ylabel*, and *title* commands share the same *Text* class properties.

6.5.2   Creating general text

The *text* command is the underlying function for the other labeling commands. By specifying its coordinates, text can be placed anywhere on the graph.

By default, text formatting for string objects uses a formatting language called *TeX*. MATLAB supports a subset of the TeX formatting commands. This subset is listed as properties of the *String* class. To see the available formatting commands, choose **Help** → **Index**. Type *string* in the box labeled *Search index for*, and choose **Text Property**. Table 6.1 displays a few of the most common TeX formatting codes.

The *text* command

```
>>text(0.5,0.5,'y \leq \pi * x^2')
```

will place the following in the Plot window, beginning at point (0.5, 0.5):

$$y \leq \pi * x^2$$

6.5.3   Creating a legend

The *legend* command creates a legend for the plot. You can pass the *legend* command either a list of strings that describe the legend's contents or a matrix of strings. In the

TABLE 6.1. A few of the TeX formatting codes.

Code	Character or Format
\bf	**bold font**
\it	*italics font*
\rm	normal font
\pi	π
\theta	θ
\rightarrow	$\rightarrow$
\leftarrow	$\leftarrow$
\leq	$\leq$
\geq	$\geq$
^	superscript
_	subscript

second case, each row of the string matrix becomes a line in the legend. The syntax for the legend command is

```
legend('str1','str2',...)
legend(string_matrix)
```

You can optionally supply an additional argument to *legend* that indicates the position of the legend in the graph:

```
legend('str1','str2',...,position)
```

Table 6.2 lists the codes for the position argument. The default position is the upper right corner of the plot. If position code is zero, **MATLAB** tries to obscure as few of the plotted points as possible.

TABLE 6.2. Position codes for the *legend* command.

Code	Placement
−1	outside the axes (on the right side of the chart)
0	inside the boundaries of the axes
1	at the upper right corner
2	at the upper left corner
3	at the lower left corner
4	at the lower right corner

The M-file in Figure 6.8 creates the labeled plot of the sine function displayed in Figure 6.9. Copy this file and execute it. Modify the plot formatting arguments until you feel comfortable using them.

6.6   MULTIPLE PLOTS

You can display multiple, simultaneous overlapping plots by using the *hold* command. The *hold* command is an example of a *toggle*. A toggle has two values: on or off.

The command

```
>>hold on
```

```
1   % Plots the sine function from 0 to 4 pi
2   % at intervals of 0.4 radians.
3
4   % create a vector containing the plot points
5   X = 0 : 0.4 : 4*pi;
6   Y = sin(X);
7
8   % create the plot with a solid line; use a circle as
9   % the marker, line width of 2, and marker size of 6
10  plot(X,Y, '-o', 'LineWidth', 2, 'MarkerSize', 6)
11
12  % create a title and axis labels
13  title('\bf Trigonometric Sine')
14  ylabel('\bf sin(x)')
15  xlabel('\bf 0 to 4\pi')
16
17  % create a legend
18  legend('sin(x)')
```

Figure 6.8. An M-file that demonstrates plot formatting commands.

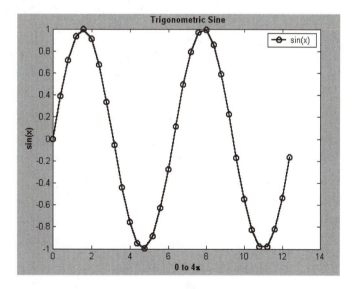

Figure 6.9. Example of labeled plot.

causes subsequent plot commands to superimpose new plots on the current plot. The command

    >>hold off

causes the next plot command to refresh the Plot window.

You can display multiple nonoverlapping plots by using the *subplot* command, which divides the Plot window into $m \times n$ subwindows called *panes*. The syntax is

```
subplot(m, n, pane_number)
```

For example, the command

```
>> subplot(2,1,2)
```

results in the Plot window being divided into 2 rows by 1 column of panes. The *pane_number* argument 2 indicates that the next plot command will place the subplot in pane number 2.

6.7   SCALING A PLOT

By default, the axes in MATLAB plots are linear. To plot a function with a logarithmic scale on the X-axis, use the *semilogx* command. Similarly, the *semilogy* command creates a logarithmic (or log) scale on the Y-axis. To create log scales on both axes, use the *loglog* command. These three commands have the same syntax and arguments as the *plot* command.

You may want to superimpose a grid over the graph when using semilog and log–log plots. Such a grid visually emphasizes the nonlinear scaling. Use the *grid* command to toggle a grid over the graph.

The M-file in Figure 6.10 uses the *semilogx* command to demonstrate that a log function plotted on a log scale is a straight line. This M-file also demonstrates how to

```
 1   % Plots a log function on linear and log scales.
 2
 3   % create a vector containing the plot points
 4   X = 1 : 100;
 5   Y = log(X);
 6
 7   % create a subplot using linear scale
 8   subplot(2,1,1)
 9   plot(X,Y)
10   title('\bf Log Plot on Linear Scale')
11   ylabel('\bf log(x)')
12   grid on
13
14   % create a subplot using log scale on X axis
15   subplot(2,1,2)
16   semilogx(X,Y)
17   title('\bf Log Plot on Semilog Scale')
18   ylabel('\bf log(x)')
19   grid on
```

Figure 6.10.   Example of *subplot* and *semilogx* commands.

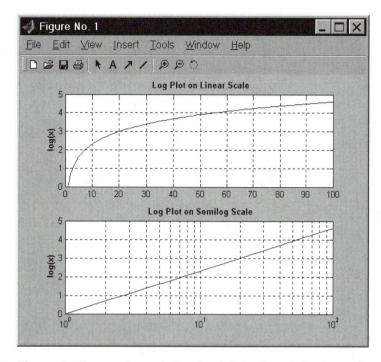

Figure 6.11. Log function plotted on linear and semilog scales.

use the *subplot* command to place two plots on the same graph. Figure 6.11 shows the results.

PRACTICE 6.1!

Write a script that performs the following tasks:

1. Create a vector X containing the values from -10 to 10 in increments of 0.5.
2. Create a vector Y that contains the square of each value in X.
3. Plot X and Y, using a dashed line and a pentagram marker.
4. Create a title in italics that reads $Y = X^2$.
5. Create appropriate labels for the X- and Y-axes.

KEY TERMS

panes   TeX   toggle

NEW MATLAB FUNCTIONS, COMMANDS, AND RESERVED WORDS

comet—plots an animated graph
grid—toggles plot grid on or off
hold—toggles multiplot on or off
legend—creates a plot legend
Line—the line graphics class, used in *plot* command
LineSpec—line type, property of the Line class
LineWidth—line width, property of the line class
loglog—creates a log–log scale plot
MarkerSize—marker size, property of the line class

plot—plots vectors and matrices
polar—plots polar coordinates
semilogx—creates a plot with log scale on the X-axis
semilogy—creates a plot with log scale on the Y-axis
String—the String graphics class, used in *text* command
subplot—creates a multiwindow plot
text—places text on named coordinates
Text—the text graphics class, used in *xlabel, ylabel, title* commands
title—creates a plot title
xlabel—creates a label on the X-axis of a plot
ylabel—creates a label on the Y-axis of a plot

SOLUTIONS TO PRACTICE PROBLEMS

6.1.

```
% Plot of x^2 in the range [-10, 10]
X = -10 : 0.5 : 10;
Y = X.^2;
plot(X,Y, '--p');
title('\it Y=X^2');
xlabel('-10 to 10'); ylabel('X ^2');
```

Problems

Section 6.1.

1. Create a plot of the function $Y = 3X^2 + 5X - 3$ for $X = [-5:0.1:5]$. Turn the grid on. Look at the graph. What is the approximate minimum of Y?

Section 6.2.

2. Create vector $X = [-5:0.1:5]$. Create a matrix Y that consists of rows $sin(X), sin(X + 1), sin(X + 2)$, and $sin(X + 3)$. Plot matrix Y against vector X.

Section 6.4.

3. Write an M-file that creates a plot of the function $Y = 5X^2 - 2X - 50$ for $X = [-10:1:10]$. Use a pentagon-shaped marker of size 10 and a dotted line of width 2.

Section 6.5.

4. Create an appropriate legend, labels for the axes, and a title for the plot in Problem 2.

5. Create appropriate labels for the axes and a title for the plot in Problem 3. Create the title in bold font.

Section 6.6.

6. Write an M-file that creates multiple superimposed plots of $Y = nX^2$ for $n = [1:10]$ and $X = [-10:0.01:10]$. Label the plot appropriately.

7. Write an M-file that creates subplots (not superimposed) of $Y = X^n$ for $n = [1:5]$ and $X = [-10:0.01:10]$. Each subplot's Y axis should have an appropriate

bold face title. Use a *for* loop to minimize the size of your code. Your results should resemble Figure 6.12.

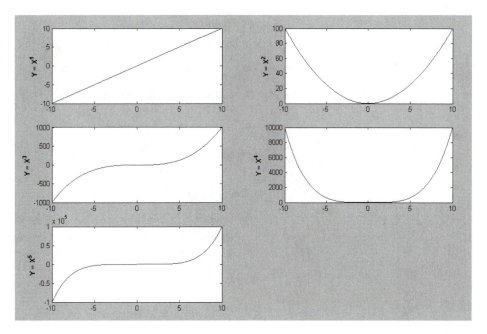

Figure 6.12. Subplots of $Y = X^n$ for $n = [1:5]$.

Section 6.7.

8. A graph that uses logarithmic scales on both axes is called a log–log graph. A log–log graph is useful for plotting power equations, which appear as straight lines on a log–log graph. A power equations has the form

$$y = bx^m$$

Plot the data in Table 6.3. Use a log–log plot. After viewing the plot, what can you infer about the relationship between the resistance and area of a conductor?

TABLE 6.3. Resistance vs. Area of a Conductor.

Area (mm²)	Resistance (milliohms/meter)
0.009	2000.0
0.021	1010.0
0.063	364.0
0.202	110.0
0.523	44.0
1.008	20.0
3.310	8.0
7.290	3.5
20.520	1.2

Challenge Problems.

9. The plots that have been shown so far use rectangular, or Cartesian, coordinates. Another method of plotting uses polar coordinates. In a polar coordinate system, the points are plotted as an angle and radius (theta, rho) instead of vertical (Y) and horizontal (X) components. The *polar* command creates a plot that uses polar coordinates. The syntax of the *polar* command is

    ```
    polar(theta, Rho, LineSpec)
    ```

    Plot the following function over the range 0 to π, using the polar command:

    $$\rho = \cos(3\theta).$$

    This function is known as the three-petal rose. Label the graph appropriately.

10. The *comet* command has the syntax

    ```
    comet(X,Y)
    ```

    and the effect is to trace a plot in slow motion with a tail. Use the *comet* command with $sin(X)$ for $X = [0:0.01:4\pi]$. Create a loop so that the sine function is plotted forwards and then backwards continuously.

7

Procedural Abstraction

7.1 THE PROCEDURAL PARADIGM

Computer programming is an art and a craft that is supported by mathematics and science. The craft of programming consists of many techniques. A group of related techniques that serves to focus the programmer on a particular view or way of programming is called a *programming paradigm*. One paradigm for programming is *procedural programming*.

In the procedural paradigm, you can think of the programmer's task as the design of a procedure or function that implements a certain *algorithm*. An algorithm is a set of steps or a recipe for solving a computational problem. Once the algorithm is coded and packaged in a procedure or function, the algorithm can be repeatedly used without rewriting it.

Functions in programming languages are modeled after mathematical functions. In mathematics, a function is a mapping that associates each element in a set X with one and only one element in a set Y. If the function f associates $y \in Y$ with $x \in X$, then we say that $y = f(x)$.

In a programming language, a *pure function* is a function that has no effect on the workspace other than to compute a value. A function in MATLAB is properly termed a *pseudofunction* or *procedure*, since the workspace might be changed as the result of the action of the function. In this text, we will use the terms *function* and *procedure* interchangeably.

We call any change in the system other than returning a value a *side effect* of the function. A programmer purposefully creates some side effects. Since the user of a function does not always know the internals of its behavior, it is important to reduce unnecessary side effects. Side effects should also be described in the function's documentation.

OBJECTIVES

After reading this chapter, you should be able to

- Use the procedural paradigm to solve problems.
- Write MATLAB functions.
- Use global, local, and persistent variables in your programs.
- Pass a variable number of arguments into functions.
- Create subfunctions and private functions.
- Understand how MATLAB resolves a name.
- Pass functions as arguments to other functions.

We usually pass one or more arguments into a function. The function then returns either a set of results or an error. For example, the trigonometric sine function is passed a real-valued scalar or array and returns the sine of the argument. Similarly, the MATLAB *sin* function takes a real-valued argument and returns either the sine of the argument or an error. The following example computes the sine of 5.3 and then returns and stores the answer in the variable *A*:

```
>> A = sin(5.3)
A =
    -0.8323
```

In the case of the *sin* function, we are interested in the value that is returned. We want a pure function; we do not want any side effects. In the following example, we expect that the *sin* function will not change the value of its input argument, *A*:

```
>> A = [ pi, pi/2, pi/4 ]
A =
    3.1416    1.5708    0.7854
>> B = sin(A)
B =
    0.0000    1.0000    0.7071
>> A
A =
    3.1416    1.5708    0.7854
```

We see that after we call the sine function, the value of *A* is not changed.

In certain cases, a side effect is really the main effect that we want. For example, the *plot* function draws a plot based on its input arguments. It does return a value—a vector of handles to line graph objects—but we are not usually interested in this return value. We are just interested in the side effect of the function: the visual plot.

This chapter introduces you to the concept of structuring a program with the use of functions or procedures, a process called *procedural abstraction*. By using the techniques presented here, you will be able to create and organize code that implements computational algorithms. As long as these algorithms are not too long or complex, and as long as they do not need to interface with many other concurrently running algorithms, the procedural programming paradigm will suffice.

In a subsequent chapter, we will introduce you to another programming paradigm that allows you to encapsulate data and algorithms into abstractions called *objects*. This paradigm is called *object-oriented programming*. The techniques used in the current chapter also are relevant to object-oriented programming. Later, you will see that the object-oriented paradigm provides groups of programmers and software engineers a natural means for building large, reliable, and reusable bodies of code that model complex, real-world phenomenon.

PROGRAMMING TIP 7.1!

Except as a learning exercise, you should not try to write functions that already exist in the MATLAB library. These functions are highly optimized to run efficiently and to handle error conditions.

MATLAB has a large number of built-in functions and library functions. Familiarize yourself with them by choosing **Help → MATLAB Help → Contents** from the Menu bar. Open the Contents menu by clicking on the + signs. Choose **MATLAB → MATLAB Function Reference → Functions by Category**. Browse through the available functions.

7.2   DEFINING AND USING FUNCTIONS

7.2.1   Functions vs. Scripts

A MATLAB function definition is stored in an M-file. A MATLAB function differs from M-file scripts in that a function may have input and output arguments and may use local variables. In addition, a function has a more defined structure than a script.

Arguments

MATLAB strictly defines the mechanisms for passing information into and out of a function. We call the information passed to and from a function the function's *arguments*. The information passed into the function is called the function's *input arguments* or *input parameters*. The information returned from the function is called the function's *output arguments* or *output parameters*.

Local Variables

We call a variable defined within a function a *local variable*. A function has a local namespace. That is, variables defined within the function are local to the function and cannot be seen outside of the function. This means that you can create both a local variable and a variable in the workspace that have the same name!

7.2.2   Structure of a Function

Let us examine a simple function used to compute the positive square root of a nonnegative number by Newton's method. Before describing how Newton's method works, we look at the syntax of the function definition. The function has three basic parts:

- the definition line
- the H1 line and help section
- the function body

In addition, other local functions, called subfunctions may be defined after the function body. We describe subfunctions in Section 7.5.1. Figure 7.1 shows the code for the square-root function. For now, don't worry about how Newton's method works. Just try to understand the different parts of the function definition; we will explain Newton's method in the next section.

Definition Line

The first noncomment line of the function is called the *definition line* and consists of

- the *function* keyword,
- the output argument(s),
- the function name, and
- the input argument(s).

The name of the function when it is called is defined by the name of the M-file. If you name the M-file *foo.m*, the function will be called *foo*. Most programmers also give the function the same name in the definition. We recommend this practice, but it is not required.

The following is the definition line in the *my_sqrt* function:

```
function Out = my_sqrt(x)
```

```
 1   function Out = my_sqrt(X)
 2   %  my_sqrt(X) - returns the positive square root of X.
 3   %  This function uses Newton's method for
     %  approximating
 4   %  the positive square root of a nonnegative scalar or
 5   %  array.
 6
 7   % first approximation
 8   A = X/2;
 9
10   % initialize X1
11   X1 = X;
12
13   % loop until the answer is small enough
14   while abs(X1 - A) > (10*eps)
15     X1 = X/A;
16     A  = (X1 + A)/2;
17   end
18
19   % return results
20   Out = A;
```

Figure 7.1. Function definition of Newton's square-root method.

Note that we have named the input parameter *X*, although it could be any lexically correct variable name. The output of the function will be the last value stored in the output argument *Out* before the function exits.

If there is more than a single input or output argument, the order of the arguments is defined in the definition line. The following definition line is for a function that takes four input arguments and returns two output arguments:

```
function [Volume, SurfaceArea] = f(Shape, X, Y, Z)
```

A function might not return a value. If a function does not return a value, then the definition line may either leave the output argument blank or use empty square brackets. The following definition lines are for examples of functions that do not return a value:

```
function draw_rectangle(X, Y)
function [ ] = draw_rectangle(X, Y)
```

H1 Line and Help Section

The first comment line after the definition line is called the HELP 1, or H1, line. This line provides a one-line summary of the function.

All comments that include the H1 line up until the first noncomment line are called the *help section*. This section contains the text that is returned when the help command is invoked for a function. If you have typed and saved the function in Figure 7.1 as *my_sqrt.m*, typing *help my_sqrt* returns

```
>> help my_sqrt

  my_sqrt(X) - returns the positive square root of X.
     This function uses Newton's method for
     approximating the positive square root of a
     nonnegative scalar or array.
```

If the help command is invoked for a directory instead of a function name, only the H1 line of each help section is displayed. For example, on my computer, the *my_sqrt* function is stored in the *examples* directory. Thus, when the help command is invoked for that directory,

```
>> help D:\Dave\MATLAB2001\examples

  my_sqrt(X) - returns the positive square root of X.
```

is displayed.

Function Body

The function body is the section of the function that contains the code for computing the algorithm. Results are returned by assigning them to the output argument(s). You can assign results in more than one place in the function body. The last assignment before the function exits is the value that the function returns to the calling program. In Figure 7.1, the variable *Out* is assigned a value once, on line 20.

The function definition is stored in a file named *my_sqrt.m*, and the file must be located in your current search path in order for MATLAB to find it. If you have not done so, type and save the example in Figure 7.1. Call the function a few times, as in the following examples:

```
>> my_sqrt(25)
ans =
     5
>> my_sqrt(2)
ans =
    1.4142
```

7.2.3 Function Example: Newton's Method

Now let us discuss how Newton's method for finding an approximation of the square root works. The basic trick of Newton's method is to compute successive approximations.

The first approximation, A, is a guess at the square root of X. The method then averages A with X/A, and the result is used as the next approximation. The same three steps continue until the algorithm halts.

The test for halting is the conditional expression on line 14 in Figure 7.1. The *abs* function returns the absolute value of its argument. We will explain the *eps* function shortly.

Table 7.1 demonstrates the results of the algorithm for computing an approximation of the square root of $X = 25$. The starting approximation is $X/2$, or 12.5. The results are displayed to four decimal places of accuracy.

TABLE 7.1.   Newton's method for approximating a square root.

Iteration	X/A	A = (A + X/A)/2
0		12.5000
1	2.0000	7.2500
2	3.4483	5.3491
3	4.6737	5.0114
4	4.9886	5.0000

Stopping Rule

Two decisions must be made about the algorithm. The first is deciding when to stop. The second is choosing the initial guess for the answer.

First, consider the stopping rule. A simple solution is to choose a fixed number of iterations. We could simply run the algorithm for 10 iterations and then stop. However, finding a square root that is far from the initial guess might take more iterations than finding a square root that starts close to the answer. In addition, finding the accurate square root of a small number may take fewer iterations than finding the square root of a large number. Therefore, if we used a fixed number of iterations, our answers for different inputs would have a wide range of accuracy.

Another method for meeting the required accuracy is to keep iterating until the difference between the current approximation and the previous approximation is small enough. For example, if we care only about having answers that are accurate to three decimal places, we can stop when $X_n - X_{n-1} < 0.001$, where n is the current number of iterations.

Since a computer stores only an approximation of a floating-point number, another possibility is to stop when we have reached the computer's accuracy limit. What is MATLAB's limit of accuracy? It is returned by the epsilon, or *eps*, function:

```
>> eps
ans =
   2.2204e-016
```

We can stop when the absolute value of the difference between the current approximation and the previous approximation is less than or equal to *eps*. By doing this, we have computed the most accurate value of the square root that is possible for MATLAB's double type. That value, however, is a little too accurate: Because of rounding errors, we must choose a value slightly greater than *eps*. The example code uses *eps* * 10.

First Approximation

The second decision that we need to make is how to choose the starting approximation value. If we do not care about computation time, we can choose almost any starting value. The one exception is that we cannot use the input argument as the starting value. If we did, then the algorithm would stop before the first iteration, since $X - X = 0 < eps * 10$.

The sample code in Figure 7.1 uses $X/2$ as the first approximation. This is not an optimal choice, but it works. There are some problems with the code when taking square roots of very large or very small numbers. We will not deal with those issues here, since they are topics for a course in numerical methods.

PRACTICE 7.1!

Walk through the code in Figure 7.1 line by line. Start with $X = 25$, and write the values of A and $X1$ each time line 17 is reached. Can you duplicate the first four iterations of the algorithm listed in Table 7.1?

You may be impressed by how few iterations are needed to compute most square roots with Newton's method. Try placing a counter in the sample code, and display the number of iterations. How many iterations of the while loop are needed to find the square root of 25? 100?

7.2.4 Calling a Function

The use of a function on the command line or within program code is termed a *function call*. You must define a function before you can call it. A function is called by invoking the name of its M-file, along with a suitable set of arguments. For example, you call the *my_sqrt* function by invoking its name, along with the appropriate arguments:

```
>> my_sqrt(9)
ans =
      3
```

You can use a user-defined function in an expression. The following numerical expression includes several function calls, including a built-in function and our newly defined *my_sqrt* function:

```
>> tan(pi/4) + my_sqrt(9)
ans =
      4
```

You can use a function call in an argument to another function. In the following example, the *pi* function is used as part of an expression that is an argument to the *sin* function, and the results of the *sin* function are used as an argument to the *my_sqrt* function:

```
>> my_sqrt(sin(pi/2)* 4)
ans =
      2
```

A function call may not be used on the left-hand side of an assignment. Recall that MATLAB dynamically defines variables. The effect of the following statement is to create a new 1×4 array named *my_sqrt* and assign the value two to the last element of the array:

```
>> my_sqrt(4) = 2
my_sqrt =
      0    0    0    2
```

Note that the effect also is to hide *my_sqrt* function's name: The use of *my_sqrt* now refers to the variable *my_sqrt*, not the function of the same name.

A function that returns multiple arguments is called by returning the outputs to an array. For instance, the *size* function returns the size of each dimension of an array. In the following example, the array A has two dimensions, and the size of each dimension is output to variables **M** and **N**, which are elements of the output array:

```
>> A = ones(5,2);
>> [M, N] = size(A)
M =
      5
N =
      2
```

PROGRAMMING TIP 7.2!

It is good programming practice to separate the name space of functions from the name space of variables. One method of doing this is to begin all function names with lowercase letters and begin all variable names with capital letters. This will help you avoid accidentally hiding function names.

PRACTICE 7.2!

Write a function that returns the sum of its two input arguments. Assume that the inputs are conformant double arrays. The body of the function will be very simple. Focus on correct form and documentation. After you have saved the function as *my_sum*, try using the help command for your new function. A sample call for *my_sum* is

```
>> A = 5;
>> B = 6;
>> my_sum(A,B)
ans =
     11
```

7.2.5   Returning from a Function

A function normally returns when the code in the function body has finished executing. At times, you may want to end a function early. In that case, control is passed back to the caller before the function has finished its normal execution.

You can immediately return from a function by using the *return* statement. The *return* statement returns control to the caller. The most recently assigned output value is returned. If the function has not yet been assigned an output value, nothing is returned.

As an example, let us modify the *my_sqrt* function to handle characters. If the current version of *my_sqrt* in Figure 7.1 is called with a character value, the square root of the ASCII code is returned. This is not an intuitively correct result. For example, using *my_sqrt* to compute the square root of 'd' returns the square root of 100, which is the ASCII code for the letter 'd'.

```
>> my_sqrt('d')
ans =
     10
```

The code segment in Figure 7.2 tests whether the value passed into argument X is a character type. The *isa* function tests for the class or type of the first argument. The return statement causes the function to end prematurely so that the rest of the function body is not executed.

```
% test for character type
if isa(X, 'char')
   return
end
```

Figure 7.2.   Test for input argument type.

PRACTICE 7.3!

Add the code in Figure 7.2 to the body of the *my_sqrt* function definition immediately after the help section of the function (line 6). If the improved *my_sqrt* is used with a character argument, nothing is returned.

```
>> my_sqrt2('c')
>>
```

The code in Figure 7.2 is an improvement, but it still has problems. If we try to use the new, improved *my_sqrt* in a more complex expression or assign it to a variable, we get the following error:

```
>> A = my_sqrt2('c')
Warning: One or more output arguments not assigned
during call to 'my_sqrt2'.
```

The error occurs because we did not assign the function a value before exiting. The modification to the code in Figure 7.3 corrects this problem by assigning a string to *my_sqrt* before the function returns.

```
% test for character type
if isa(X, 'char')
  Out = 'Type char is not handled.';
  return
end
```

Figure 7.3.   Revised test for input argument type.

PRACTICE 7.4!

Replace the code that you added to *my_sqrt* in the previous **PRACTICE** session with the code in Figure 7.3. Now if you execute *my_sqrt* with a character or string argument, a nice error message such as the following one will appear!

```
>> my_sqrt('foo')
ans =
Type char is not handled.
```

7.3   TYPES OF VARIABLES

7.3.1   Local Variables

Variables that are defined within a function body are local to that function. A variable name that is used within a function body does not overwrite the same name in the global workspace. This is a major difference between MATLAB scripts and functions.

For example, if we have an array named *A* in the global workspace, and we reuse the name *A* in a function definition, the two names will not collide. Both versions of *A* can coexist at the same time. The function definition in Figure 7.4 defines *A* to be the array [3, 4, 5].

```
function Out = test
% test whether local variable collides with global
% workspace
A = [3, 4, 5]
```

Figure 7.4. Example of local variable.

The following interactive commands define *A* as a string in the global workspace and then call the function *test*:

```
>> A = 'I am a string.';
>> test
A =
     3   4   5
>> A
A =
I am a string.
```

Note that the value of the global variable *A* does not change after the function call.

The use of local variables helps to encapsulate the inner working of the function. Data may be manipulated within the function body without risking the modification of external data. This helps reduce unwanted side effects of functions.

7.3.2   Global Variables

If variables are to be shared among functions, it is usually better to pass them into and out of functions by using parameters. We discuss parameter passing in the next section.

Occasionally, it is useful to modify variables globally. For example, if a variable is used by almost every function in an application and in the global workspace, it becomes tedious to put the variable in every argument list.

In the example in Figure 7.5, the variable *Counter* is first declared and initialized outside of the function in the global workspace. A *global variable* is declared by using the keyword *global* in its definition, as in the following code:

```
>> global Counter
>> Counter = 5
Counter =
     5
```

```
function [ ] = increment
% increment the global variable 'counter'
global Counter;
Counter = Counter + 1
```

Figure 7.5. Example of a global variable.

Within the function, you must declare the variable global again, or the effect of the increment will disappear when the function returns. For example, the *increment* function in Figure 7.5 increments *Counter*. We want to be able to initialize a variable in the global workspace and then call the *increment* function to add one to the variable and display the results. Note that we declare *Counter* global again inside the function body.

The following interactive session demonstrates that the modification of the *Counter* variable within the *increment* function has a persistent effect on the global variable:

```
>> global Counter
>> Counter = 5
Counter =
      5
>> increment
Counter =
      6
>> increment
Counter =
      7
>> increment
Counter =
      8
>> disp(Counter)
      8
```

If *Counter* were a local variable, the increment would be lost each time the function returned, and the global value would not be incremented. However, as you can see from the example, the value of the *Counter* variable inside the function is the same as the value of the *Counter* variable outside the function.

One way to think of this uniformity is to note that both *Counter* names point to the same place in memory when the name is global. When a name is local, it points to a different place in memory than does the same name of another variable.

A problem with using global variables is that they may be inadvertently modified elsewhere in the code; they are not protected by being encapsulated inside the function. If you use global variables frequently, it is easy to create unwanted side effects.

7.3.3 Persistent Variables

A problem with local variables is that they exist only during the execution of the function; they disappear completely after the function is finished executing. At times, we want to have the value of a local variable persist over a number of function calls. Still, we may not want to expose the variable to accidental changes by making it global.

MATLAB calls this type of variable a *persistent variable*. Figure 7.6 shows a function called *count_down* that demonstrates the use of a persistent variable.

The definition of a persistent variable results in an empty array [] being initially assigned to the variable. We get the counter started by using the *isempty* function, which tests whether a variable is empty and returns true if it is empty and false otherwise.

Repeated calls to *count_down* return 10, 9, 8, . . . , 1 and then start again with 10:

```
>> count_down
ans =
     10
>> count_down
ans =
     9
```

```
>> count_down
ans =
        8
```

Note that the value of counter is not lost between function calls.

```
1   function Out = count_down
2   % count_down - Counts down from 10 to 1 then repeats.
3   %  Uses the persistent variable 'counter'.
4   persistent Counter
5   if isempty(Counter) | Counter == 1
6      Counter = 10;
7   else
8      Counter = Counter - 1;
9   end
10  Out = Counter;
```

Figure 7.6. Example of a persistent variable.

The persistent *Counter* variable is protected within the function: You cannot modify *Counter* from the global workspace or from another function. Another way of saying the same thing is that the persistent variable *counter* is not *visible* from the workspace or from another function. The only way to modify it is by calling the *count_down* function. A global variable is visible in the workspace and from other functions.

You can create a variable named *Counter* in the global workspace, but that name is bound to another memory location. For example, in the following interactive session, *count_down* is called several times, and then a *Counter* variable is defined in the global workspace:

```
>> count_down
ans =
        6
>> count_down
ans =
        5
>> Counter = 25;
>> count_down
ans =
        4
```

You can see that when *count_down* is called again, the persistent variable has been protected.

PRACTICE 7.5!

Create an M-file with the code in Figure 7.6 and save it as *count_down.m*. Change the variable *Counter* from a persistent variable to a local variable. Assign the local variable the empty array to initialize it. What is the effect on the output of the function?

7.4   PARAMETER PASSING

7.4.1   Introduction

The two basic methods for passing parameters are called *pass by value* and *pass by reference*.

Before defining the types of parameter passing, it is important to introduce a few other definitions. The terms *argument* and *parameter* are used interchangeably. A *formal parameter* is defined to be an argument within a function definition. For example, in the function definition in Figure 7.7, the formal parameter is named *X*.

An *actual parameter* is defined to be an argument that is used in the function call. For example, in the following function call of *add_one*, the actual parameter is *Y*:

```
>> Y = 14;
>> add_one(Y)
ans =
    15
```

```
function Out = add_one(X)
%   add_one(X) - returns the successor of X
Out = X + 1;
```

Figure 7.7.   Example of a formal parameter.

7.4.2   Pass by Value

If a programming language uses the *pass-by-value* method of parameter passing, then the formal parameter (X in our example) is a copy of the actual parameter (Y in the example). More accurately, at the time of the function call, the formal parameter is bound to the value of the actual parameter.

This method is easy to understand and leads to fewer coding errors than do other methods. The value of the actual parameter is not modified in the function. In the previous example, the value of *Y* does not change. (Y is still equal to 14.) If the programmer wants to change the value of Y, then an explicit assignment must be made to *Y*. For example, we might have

```
>> Y = 14;
>> Y = add_one(Y)
Y =
    15
```

7.4.3   Pass by Reference

In certain cases, the-pass-by-value mechanism becomes unwieldy. One such case is when one is dealing with very large data objects. The following statement causes MATLAB to allocate 32 megabytes (Mbytes) of memory:

```
>> Y = ones(2000);
```

If MATLAB passed all parameters by value, the following statement would create a copy of the array Y during the execution of the function:

```
>> add_one(Y);
```

MATLAB would now have allocated at least 64 Mbytes of memory. You can see that this type of action will quickly exhaust the available physical memory on your computer. Because of this problem, some programming languages do not make a copy of a variable's contents when passing parameters. Instead, the function is passed a pointer to the actual parameter. More accurately, at the time of the function call, the formal parameter is bound to the address of the actual parameter.

Many programming languages, including FORTRAN, Pascal, and Ada, provide the ability to pass parameters by reference. Passing parameters by reference is a very memory-efficient method, since a memory address requires only a few bytes of storage. The downside of passing by reference is that a programmer may inadvertently modify an actual parameter within a function. This is another example of an unwanted side effect.

Consider the function *max* that finds the maximum element of array Y. It is not necessary to modify the actual parameter Y in order to find the maximum element. It seems wasteful to make a copy of Y, but this is the case if the language uses the pass-by-value method.

Suppose, however, that the programmer who wrote the *max* function inadvertently modifies the formal parameter inside the function body. If Y is passed by reference, then the actual parameter Y may by modified by mistake. This is the case if the language uses the pass-by-reference method.

7.4.4 MATLAB's Parameter-Passing Mechanism

The MATLAB parameter-passing mechanism is a combination of pass by value and pass by reference. If a parameter is not modified in the function body, then it is automatically passed by reference. If the parameter is modified in the function body, then it is passed by value.

This mechanism is a compromise that combines the security of pass by value with the efficiency of pass by reference. It is secure because it keeps the programmer from modifying the value of the actual parameter inside the function. The programmer can only modify a copy of the actual parameter. The method is efficient because no copy is ever made of a parameter that is not modified inside the function.

Another optimization that MATLAB makes is to pass slices of arrays without passing the whole array. Consider the example in Figure 7.8, which increments the odd elements of a vector. The *length* function used in the figure returns the number of elements in the vector.

```
function Out = add_odd(X)
% add_odd(X) - Increments the odd elements of X.
X(1:2:length(X)) = X(1:2:length(X)) + 1;
Out = X;
```

Figure 7.8. The *add_odd* function.

If *add_odd* is called with Y as a $1 \times 2{,}000{,}000$ array, the computer will use 16 Mbytes of memory to store Y. Then the call to *add_odd*, as in the following code, will use another 16 Mbytes:

```
>> Y = ones(1,2000000);
>> Z = add_odd(Y);
```

If we want to increment a small section of the array, we can do so without having the *add_odd* function make a copy of the complete array. The following call to *add_odd* increments only the first 10 elements of *Y*:

```
>> Y(1:10) = add_odd(Y(1:10));
```

This operation uses only 80 bytes of memory to store the formal argument, instead of 16 Mbytes!

7.4.5   Variable Numbers of Arguments

You can define MATLAB functions to accept a variable number of arguments. This approach is useful if you do not know ahead of time how many arguments will be used. For example, you should be able to define a function that computes the average or mean of a list of numbers without knowing how many numbers are to be used in the calculation.

The function definition in Figure 7.9 uses the MATLAB function *varargin*. The *varargin* function stores a variable number of arguments in a cell array, which can hold elements of varying types. The elements of a cell array are accessed with curly braces, as shown in line 7 of Figure 7.9.

```
1 function Out = my_average(varargin)
2 %  my_average
3 %     Computes the arithmetic mean of a variable
4 %     number of input arguments.
5 Total = 0;
6 for Index = 1:nargin
7    Total = Total + varargin{Index};
8 end
9 Out = Total/nargin;
```

Figure 7.9. Demonstration of variable number of input arguments.

The *varargin* function may be combined with other arguments, as long as *varargin* occurs last in the argument list. Within the function definition, the number of arguments can be determined by using the *nargin* (number of arguments in) function.

The *my_average* function can be used to compute the arithmetic mean of an arbitrary number of inputs, as in the following code:

```
>> my_average(1,2,3,4,5)
ans =
     3
>> my_average(2,6,10)
ans =
     6
```

MATLAB has a built-in *mean* function. Note the difference between *mean* and *my_average*: The *mean* function takes a single array argument; the *my_average* function takes a variable number of arguments.

PRACTICE 7.6!

Create and save an M-file with the code in Figure 7.9. Modify your code to return the maximum and minimum of a variable number of input arguments. Example of output is:

```
>> [A,B] = minmax(3,2,5,10,1)
A =
     1
B =
    10
```

There are similar functions for defining a variable number of output arguments. The *varargout* term is used in a function definition to indicate that a variable number of values may be returned. The *nargout* function is used to determine how many output arguments the caller expects.

The function definition in Figure 7.10 returns a variable-length sequence of integers. The input argument consists of the first integer in the sequence.

```
1 function [varargout] = sequence(First)
2 % sequence(First)
3 %    Returns a variable-length sequence of integers
4 %    starting with 'First'.
5 for Index = 1:nargout
6   varargout{Index} = First + Index - 1;
7 end
```

Figure 7.10. Demonstration of variable number of output arguments.

The use of braces here is somewhat confusing. In the definition line, multiple arguments are defined as an array of arguments; thus, they are enclosed in square brackets. The variable *varargout* is a cell array; hence, within the function body, the output arguments are placed into a cell array. Note the use of curly braces in line 6 to place each output argument into the cell array.

The *sequence* function may be called with a variable number of outputs. Each respective output argument is given the value of the next number in the sequence, as in the following code:

```
>> [A,B,C,D] = sequence(2)
A =
     2
B =
     3
C =
     4
D =
     5
>> [X,Y] = sequence(17)
```

```
X =
     17
Y =
     18
```

7.5   FUNCTIONS WITH LIMITED SCOPE

The function definitions that have been described so far are globally available to the MATLAB user. The level of visibility of a function or variable name is called its *scope*. We say that general functions have global scope. The only restriction is that the M-files that define the function must be in the MATLAB search path.

The functions that we have used as examples are small and relatively simple. As you begin to write programs that solve larger problems, you will want to decompose your solutions into smaller parts. This method of dividing a large problem into smaller problems is called *functional decomposition*.

Some of the smaller parts need not be visible to the general user, but are merely helper functions for the main solution. We need a mechanism for defining functions with limited scope. MATLAB provides several ways of doing this. One such mechanism is called a *subfunction* and another is called a *private function*.

For example, consider a function that searches through a string of words and looks for a particular kind of word. We might want to search for all capitalized words in a document, for all words that are in a banned word list, or for words that are misspelled.

We can decompose this problem into several subproblems:

1.   The first task is to find each word within the string. Let us call this type of function a *search function* and label it Function 1.

2.   The second task is to evaluate the word for particular characteristics. Let us call this type of function an *evaluation function* and label it Function 2.

Since the evaluation function (Function 2) is separated from the word search function (Function 1), we can easily replace the evaluation function. Doing so allows us to reuse Function 1 with different evaluation functions. Creating software in the form of reusable components is an important part of software development. Figure 7.11 shows a description of a reusable main function (Function 1) with several possible secondary components (Functions 2a, 2b, and 2c).

We would like the evaluation functions to be implemented so that they are visible only to the main function and are not directly usable outside of the main function. That is, the main function, and only the main function, can see the evaluation functions; outside of the main function, they are not visible. We say that the scope of the evaluation function is limited.

7.5.1   Subfunctions

One mechanism for meeting the conditions of functional decomposition and limited scope is the *subfunction*. Subfunctions are defined in the same M-file as the main function. The main function in an M-file is the first function definition and is visible to the global workspace. All other function definitions in that same M-file are subfunctions and are visible only to the main function. Let us walk through a demonstration that uses subfunctions to solve the problem of finding all palindromes in a given string.

Function 1.
Locate each word in a string.

Function 2a.
Evaluate–return true if first letter of word is capitalized.

Function 2b.
Evaluate–return true if word is a palindrome (The term *palindrome* is explained shortly).

Function 2c.
Evaluate–return true if word is misspelled.

Figure 7.11.   Example of a reusable function.

A *palindrome* is a string of characters that reads the same forwards and backwards. All single characters are palindromes. Other common words that are palindromes are *dad, mom*, and *peep*.

One of the more famous palindromes was invented after the opening of the Panama Canal. The palindrome is the string of letters that make up the phrase "A man, a plan, a canal—Panama!' The string is *amanaplanacanalpanama*.

Our solution will have the following form: The main function is called *get_match*. It parses one word at a time from the input string and repeatedly calls the *is_palindrome* subfunction until the end of the string is reached. If *is_palindrome* returns true (1), then the word is added to the output string. The result is a string of all words in the input string that meets the palindrome condition.

In Figure 7.12, the definition of the *get_match* function and its subfunction *is_palindrome* are shown. The problem of finding all palindromes in a string is decomposed into two smaller problems.

Note that we have introduced a new MATLAB function called *strtok* in the figure. This very useful function breaks a string into a set of tokens and returns the first token and the remainder of the string. A *token* is a string that is delimited by white-space characters. The default white-space characters are the space, the tab, and the carriage return.

In the following example, *strtok* is used to read successive tokens in a string:

```
>> A = 'I am  going to the store';
>> [word, remainder] = strtok(A)
word = I
remainder = am  going to the store
>> [word, remainder] = strtok(remainder)
word = am
remainder = going to the store
>> [word, remainder] = strtok(remainder)
word = going
remainder = to the store
```

PRACTICE 7.7!

Create and save an M-file with the code in Figure 7.12. What is returned from the following call?

```
get_match('I am a genius, dad')
```

What is returned from the following call?

```
is_palindrome('dad')
```

Why is this returned?

```
1   function Out = get_match(Str)
2   %  get_match(Str)
3   %     Returns all palindromes from a string of words.
4
5   % Main function
6   Remainder = Str;
7   NewStr = ";
8   while ~isempty(remainder)
9     [Word, Remainder] = strtok(Remainder);
10    if is_palindrome(Word)
11      NewStr = [NewStr, ' ', Word];
12    end
13  end
14  Out = NewStr;
15
16  % Subfunction
17  function Out = is_palindrome(Word)
18  %  is_palindrome(Word)
19  %     Returns true(1) if word is a palindrome,
20  %     otherwise, returns false(0). Word is a string
21  %     that does not contain white space.
22  Out = 1;
23  for Index = 1:length(Word)
24    if Word(Index) ~= Word(length(Word)-Index+1)
25      Out = 0;
26      break;
27    end
28  end
```

Figure 7.12.   Definition of the *get_match* function.

7.5.2   Private Functions

The use of subfunctions allows us to decompose a problem into a main function and one or more helper or evaluation functions. The subfunction has very limited scope, namely, to the main function in the same M-file.

How reusable is the main function or subfunction? Since they both reside in the same M-file, they are not directly reusable. We could copy the code with a text editor, but it would be nice if we could store the main function and the subfunction in separate files, which would make it easier to reuse them. One way to do this is to write the helper function as a private function.

A *private function* is a function definition that is placed in a special location—a subdirectory within the directory of the calling function. The subdirectory is appropriately named *private*. Any function that is placed in the *private* directory is visible only to functions in the parent directory.

In Figure 7.13, the current directory contains two M-files: *get_match* and *test_scope*. The three functions in the private directory are private functions. They are visible only to the two functions in their parent directory.

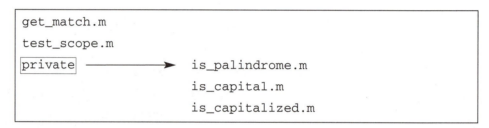

```
get_match.m
test_scope.m
private  ──────────►   is_palindrome.m
                       is_capital.m
                       is_capitalized.m
```

Figure 7.13.   Directory with private subdirectory.

Compare the scope of a subfunction with that of a private function: The subfunction's scope is limited to the same M-file; the private function's scope is limited to any M-file in its parent directory.

Figure 7.14 shows how easy it would be to change the *get_match* function to look for capitalized words instead of palindromes. Compare the code with the previous definition of *get_match* in Figure 7.12. Except for changing the documentation, the only change to the main function is replacing *is_palindrome* with *is_capitalized* in line 10.

PRACTICE 7.8!

Copy the code in Figure 7.14 into an M-file named *get_caps.m*. Note the location where you saved *get_caps*. Create a directory named *private* in that location. Copy the following code into an M-file and save it in the private directory under the name *is_capitalized.m*:

```
1   function Out = is_capitalized(Word)
2   % is_capitalized(Word)
3   %       Returns true (1) if the first letter of
    %       word is
4   %       capitalized. This is an example of a private
5   %       function.
6   if isequal(Word(1), upper(Word(1)))
7     Out = 1;
```

```
 8  else
 9    Out = 0;
10  end
```

Note the use of the *isequal* function: The function returns true if two arrays are the same size and contain the same elements. The upper function returns the uppercase version of a character. The two functions are used in combination in line 6 to determine whether the first character of the input string is the uppercase version of the same character.

Some sample output from *get_caps* is as follows:

```
>> A = 'Anne lives in Tallahassee';
>> get_caps(A)
ans =
  Anne Tallahassee
```

```
 1   function Out = get_match(Str)

 2   % get_match(Str)

 3   %    Returns all capitalized words from a string

 4   %    of words.

 5

 6   Remainder = Str;

 7   NewStr = ' ';

 8   while ~isempty(Remainder)

 9     [Word, Remainder] = strtok(Remainder);

10     if is_capitalized(Word)

11       NewWtr = [NewWtr, ' ', Word];

12     end

13   end

14   Out = NewStr;
```

Figure 7.14.   Modification of *get_match* to return all capitalized words.

7.6   NAME RESOLUTION

So far in this chapter, we have discussed user-defined functions, subfunctions, and private functions. In addition, MATLAB has a large number of predefined functions and built-in functions. What happens if two functions share the same name? The multiple use of a name is called *overloading* the name. MATLAB allows overloading of function names. The only restriction is that two functions with the same name may not reside in the same directory.

If a name may be overloaded, then how can we know which version of the name is being used at any time? MATLAB has a defined search order for resolving names. If we are executing a function from the command line, the location of the function may be determined by using the *which* function. Given a name as an argument, the *which* function returns the first location of the function in MATLAB's search order. The following example reveals that the first version of the *sin* function located by the *which* function is built into the MATLAB interpreter:

```
>> which sin
sin is a built-in function.
```

The *–all* flag to the *which* function tells it to return all of the versions of the sin function that are found by MATLAB. The following example shows that there are several other definitions of *sin* in the MATLAB search path:

```
>> which sin -all
sin is a built-in function.
C:\matlabR12\toolbox\symbolic\@sym\sin.m  % sym method
C:\matlabR12\toolbox\matlab\elfun\sin.m   % Shadowed
```

User-defined functions are also displayed. The next example shows the location on my computer of the *my_sqrt* function:

```
>> which my_sqrt
c:\dave\examples\my_sqrt.m
```

The order in which the functions are found is the same as the order of the search path. Built-in functions definitions are always first in the search path. MATLAB then searches for the name on the paths in the search path list and calls the first matching name that is found.

The search path can be viewed and modified by choosing **File → Set Path** from the Menu bar. The path can also be viewed by typing *path* from the command line. If you change the path order, then the search order for locating functions will be changed accordingly.

The resolution of names is complicated by the fact that names may also refer to variables or keywords. For example, if we assign the name *sin* to a variable and then use *which* to determine its meaning, we obtain the following results:

```
>> sin = 5
sin =
     5
>> which sin -all
sin is a variable.
sin is a built-in function.
C:\matlabR12\toolbox\symbolic\@sym\sin.m  % sym method
C:\matlabR12\toolbox\matlab\elfun\sin.m   % Shadowed
```

So far, we have been interested in resolving a name from the command line or global workspace. However, names also occur within function definitions, subfunction definitions, and private functions. The complete rules that MATLAB uses for resolving names are as follows: MATLAB starts with the first rule and proceeds through the list of rules until the name meets the rule's specification.

1. **Reserved word.** Reserved words are immutable and are always interpreted first. If a name is a reserved word, then MATLAB looks no further.
2. **Variable name.** If a name is not a reserved word, then the local workspace is checked to see whether the name is a local variable.
3. **Overloaded class method of the dispatching argument.** This rule and rule 7 probably won't make sense until you study the chapter on object-oriented

programming. A class method is a function that is associated with a particular object.

4. **Built-in function.** Built-in functions are compiled into the MATLAB interpreter. Built-in function names take precedence over all other function names except those defined in Rule 3.

5. **Subfunction of the calling function.** A subfunction that is defined within the same M-file as the calling function is used next to resolve a function name. A subfunction name is visible only from functions in the same M-file.

6. **Private function of the calling function.** Private functions reside in the *private* directory located in the same directory as the calling function. A private function is visible only to functions in the parent directory. Private directories do not have to be in your search path. MATLAB automatically searches the private subdirectory of any directory in your search path.

7. **Class constructor function.** A class constructor function is used to instantiate a new object. A constructor function or method has the same name as the object directory. This will be discussed further in the chapter on object-oriented programming.

8. **Current directory.** The current working directory is searched next.

9. **Search path.** Finally, all of the paths in the search path list are searched in order. The list of current search paths can be obtained by typing the *path* command or by choosing **File → Set Path** from the Menu bar.

If a name is not resolved by any of these rules, then an error message is returned. The following example shows that *foo* is not defined on my computer:

```
>> x = 3 * pi + foo
??? Undefined function or variable 'foo'.
```

PRACTICE 7.9!

Prove to yourself that subfunctions are resolved before private functions are (rules 5 and 6). If you have already created the *get_match* function in Figure 7.12, create a private function named *is_palindrome* that displays the string 'I am a fake' and then returns 1.

Execute *get_match* again. What happens?

```
1  function Out = is_palindrome(Word)
2  %  is_palindrome(Word)
3  %     Tests for private function resolution.
4  %     Always returns true(1).
5  %     Prints 'I am a fake'.
6  disp('I am a fake')
7  Out = 1;
```

Perform the following test of rules 2 and 5: On the command line create a variable named *is_palindrome*. Execute *get_match* again. What happens? Why?

7.7   FUNCTIONS AS ARGUMENTS

Many programs act on functions themselves. A simple example is a plot function that accepts a function as an argument along with minimum and maximum values for the function. The function returns a plot of the function for the given range of values. MATLAB has such a function, called *fplot*, in its library.

A function that uses a function as one of its arguments is called a *function function* by MATLAB. Functions can be passed as arguments in one of two ways. A function may be defined within a function for use only within that function's body. Such a function is called an *in-line function*. In-line function definitions are available in most modern programming languages.

The second way a function may be passed as an argument is by defining a reference to the function. In MATLAB, a reference to a function is called a *function handle*. Most other programming languages have a similar mechanism, usually called passing a pointer to a function.

7.7.1 Inline Functions

Inline functions are intended to be defined and used within the same scope. An inline function may be defined on the command line and used in the global workspace. Alternatively, an inline function may be defined within a function body, in which case it may be called elsewhere in the same function. However, an inline function cannot be called directly outside of the function in which it is defined. That is, its scope is local.

Two syntactic variations of an inline function are described here. The first variation assumes that a given argument is an isolated lowercase letter (usually x). For example, the following definition returns the value of the quadratic expression $x^2 - 2x + 3$:

```
>> g = inline('x^2 - 2*x + 3')
g =
     Inline function:
     g(x) = x^2 - 2*x + 3
```

Within the local scope, the function g may be called like any other function. Since it was typed on the command line, its definition will disappear when the current session is terminated. An example of a call to g is

```
>> g(3)
ans =
     6
```

A second syntactic variation of the *inline* function defines the input arguments explicitly. This is the preferred use, since the intended arguments are clearly stated. The syntax of the preferred variation is shown in Figure 7.15.

```
inline(expression, arg1, arg2, ...)
```

Figure 7.15. Syntax of the *inline* function.

The following code shows how to define the quadratic expression $x^2 - 2x + 3$ with the second syntactic variant:

```
>> h = inline('X^2 - 2*X + 3', 'X')
```

The reason for using the second variant is to make the names of the variables clear. This is helpful if multiple variables are used. The following example uses the second syntactic variant of the *inline* function to define a trigonometric expression:

```
>> h = inline('sin(Theta) - cos(Rho)', 'Theta', 'Rho')
h =
     Inline function:
     h(Theta, Rho) = sin(Theta) - cos(Rho)
```

Note that the arguments *Theta* and *Rho* are unambiguously defined.

An example of a call to the inline function *h* is

```
>> h(pi/2, pi/4)
ans =
     0.2929
```

PRACTICE 7.10!

Write an inline function with explicitly defined arguments that returns the result of the following algebraic expression:

$$3x^2 + 4y^2$$

7.7.2 Function Handles

A *function handle* is a reference to a defined function. The handle contains all of the information required to execute the function. You can pass a function handle as an argument to another function.

A function handle is created by placing the @ symbol before the function name. A function handle is evaluated (or "de-referenced") by using the *feval* function. The syntax of *feval* is shown in Figure 7.16.

```
[y1,y2,...] = feval(fhandle,x1,,x2,...)
```

Figure 7.16. Syntax of the *feval* function.

The following example creates a function handle for the *my_sqrt* function, after which the handle is evaluated using *feval*:

```
>> MySqrtHandle = @my_sqrt
MySqrtHandle =
    @my_sqrt
>> feval(MySqrtHandle,9)
ans =
     3
```

Why would we want to create a function handle and then evaluate the handle? The primary reason is that function handles can be passed as function arguments. For example, the MATLAB *fplot* function takes a function and minimum and maximum values as arguments and then plots the function for that range of values. The function argument to *fplot* may be given as a function handle, a string, or an inline function. The following example calls the MATLAB function *flpot* with the arguments MySqrtHandle and the range [0 3], whereupon MATLAB draws a plot of the square root function from zero to three:

```
>> fplot(MySqrtHandle,[0,3])
```

The next example uses a handle for the built-in cosine function to plot the cosine from pi to 6 * pi:

```
>> fplot(@cos,[pi, 6*pi])
```

The *fplot* function accepts inline functions as arguments. The following example creates an inline function for a polynomial and passes it to *fplot*, after which the polynomial is plotted for the range $[-2, 2]$:

```
>> fplot(inline('x^5 - tan(4*x)','x'),[-2,2])
```

A string containing a function name may also be passed into a function. The string can be converted into a function handle within the called function by using the MATLAB *str2func* function.

One example of how a string containing a function name might be used is the storage of function names in a database. The external database is not able to store a function handle, but the names of functions can easily be stored as strings. Within MATLAB, each string can be passed to a function that converts the string to a function handle by using *str2func*. The following example creates a phony database query result and then invokes the sample function *find_pi*, using the query result as the input argument:

```
>> database_query = {'cos', 'tan', 'my_sqrt'}
database_query =
    'cos'    'tan'    'my_sqrt'
>> find_pi(database_query)
cos(pi) = -1
tan(pi) = -1.2246e-016
my_sqrt(pi) = 1.7725
```

In this example, note that the database query is a cell array of strings.

The *find_pi* function evaluates each function in the list with the argument π and displays the results. The definition of *find_pi* is shown in Figure 7.17. The *str2func* function constructs and returns a function handle from a string consisting of the function name.

```
1   function [] = find_pi(FuncList)

2   %  find_pi(FuncList)

3   %      Evaluates each function in the list at pi.

4   for Index = 1:length(FuncList)

5     TempHandle = str2func(FuncList{Index});

6     TempResult = feval(TempHandle, pi);

7     disp([FuncList{Index},'(pi)
          = ',num2str(TempResult)])

8   end
```

Figure 7.17. Function that evaluates a function list at pi.

How do we decide whether to create a function handle and pass it into a function or pass a string into a function and create the handle within the function?

The function handle stores all information known about the function name at the time the handle is created. Recall that a function may have more than one definition (e.g., *which –all sin*). If new definitions have been created before the handle is evaluated, then the handle will not be up to date. The handle is then said to be *stale*. By contrast, if a string is passed into a function and converted to a handle at the time of execution, it will contain the latest definition.

Another issue involves understanding the scope of a function handle. At the time that a function handle is created, the function definition must be in scope. Thus, a handle for a private function must be created in the directory of the private function's main function. Outside of the main function's directory, the handle cannot be created. Recall that earlier in this chapter we created a private function named *is_capitalized*. If you created that function, you can see its type and location by using the *private* parameter to the *which* function as follows:

```
>> which private/is_capitalized
D:\Dave\Matlab2001\Examples\Private\is_capitalized.m
% Private to Examples
```

A valid function handle for *is_palindrome* cannot be created, except by functions in the *examples* directory. However, once a function handle has been created, it may be used outside of the scope of the function definition. This is an important distinction. When the string name of a function is passed as an argument and evaluated, the function definition must be in scope at the time of evaluation! However, a function handle need not have the function definition be in scope when the handle is evaluated.

The reason that a function handle may be used outside the scope of the function definition is that the handle carries the definition with it. Indeed, a function handle carries not only the primary function definition, but all other overloaded definitions. It is essentially a snapshot of all of the meanings of the function name.

To test the scope of a function handle, let us create a function in the examples directory that returns a function handle. Then we should be able to use the returned handle to access the *is_capitalized* function, even though *is_capitalized* is not in scope on the command line. We will use the function handle mechanism to bypass the normal scoping rules. The function definition used to bypass scope is called *bypass_scope* and is shown in Figure 7.18.

```
function Out = bypass_scope(FuncName)
%   bypass_scope(FuncName)
%       Returns a function handle for the named
%       function string. The function handle can be used
%       outside of the scope of the function definition.
Out = str2func(FuncName);
```

Figure 7.18. Demonstration of mechanism for bypassing scope of private function.

If we try to use *is_capitalized* directly, we get an error because the function is private and is not available from the command line:

```
>> is_capitalized('Foo')
??? Undefined function or variable 'is_capitalized'.
```

However, if we use our *bypass_scope* function to create a function handle, then we can use the handle to access the private function. The *bypass_scope* function works because *is_capitalized* is in the scope of the *bypass_scope* function. The relevant code is as follows:

```
>> cap_handle = bypass_scope('is_capitalized');
cap_handle =
    @is_capitalized
>> feval(cap_handle, 'Foo')
ans =
        1
```

Since a function handle is a snapshot of a function, you may wonder what happens to the handle if a function definition is modified or deleted after the handle is created. If the function definition is modified, the handle will note the update. A function handle stores references to each definition when it is created. Thus, *cap_handle* stores the locations of each definition of *is_capitalized* at the time it was called. Any modification in the function definition will still be contained in the handle. However, if the name or location of *is_capitalized* changes, the function handle will be out of date. For example, if we rename *is_capitalized* to *get_capitals*, then *cap_handle* will no longer evaluate properly, as the following code shows:

```
>> feval(cap_handle, 'Foo')
??? Error using ==> feval
Cannot reload file
   c:\dave\examples\private\is_capitalized for function
   handle.
```

7.7.3   Function Functions

A function that uses other functions as arguments is called a *function function* in MATLAB. A number of MATLAB library functions are *function functions*. The previously used *fplot* function is an example of a function function. Another example of a function function is *fzero*, which finds the zero of a function.

Most function functions allow the function argument to be a string, a function handle, or an inline function. If the function argument is a string, the string is converted to a function handle internally.

Another example of a function function in MATLAB's library is the *quad* function, which implements the adaptive Simpson quadrature method. This method is used to compute a definite integral. You may not have taken calculus yet, but you can think of a definite integral as the area under a function's graph from points x_1 to x_2 on the x-axis.

By using *fplot* with the periodic sine function from π to 3π, you can visually see that the area under the plot is zero. The *quad* function for this same range should return zero. As the following code shows, it returns a number very close to zero:

```
>> fplot(@sin, [pi, 3*pi])
>> quad(@sin, pi, 3*pi)
ans =
 -2.5666e-016
```

Numerical methods such as quadrature approximate the correct answers.

PROGRAMMING TIP 7.3!

Be careful when testing for equality. If possible, use another relational operator, such as > or <. In the following *while* loop, the variable *Index* will never equal zero, because the initial value is 15 and *Decrement Value* is 2.

```
Index = 15;
DecrementValue = 2;
Sum = 0;
while Index ~=0
   Sum = Sum + Index;
   Index = Index - DecrementValue;
end
```

A better solution for the loop is

```
while Index > 0
   Sum = Sum + Index
   Index = Index - DecrementValue;
end
```

Functions that use numerical methods can also present a problem. A numerical method results in an approximate solution, so a return value of zero may really be a number very close to zero. The following code will not perform as expected, because the *quad* function returns -2.5666e-016:

```
Area = quad(@sin, pi, 3*pi);
if Area == 0
   ...
   ...
end
```

The *eps* function returns the minimum difference between one floating-point number and its next closest number. This is called the epsilon or relative floating-point accuracy. A good rule of thumb is to assume that a numerical method will return a value of zero that is at least within $2 * eps$ of zero.

The foregoing code can be changed to test for the absolute value of the difference between zero and the return value. If it is less than $2 * eps$, it is presumed to be zero:

```
if abs(quad(@sin, pi, 3*pi)- 0) < 2*eps
   ...
   ...
end
```

APPLICATION! LOAN REPAYMENT

Suppose that, upon graduation, you decide to buy a new car that costs $21,000. You have the option of making a down payment. The rest of the amount owed will be paid off in equal monthly payments for 36 months. You also have the option of borrowing from various lenders who are offering different annual interest rates.

The monthly payment for the loan amount is given by

$$A = P\left(\frac{i(1 + i)^n}{(1 + i)^n - 1}\right),$$

where P is the principal or loan amount, i is the monthly interest rate, and n is the number of payments.

Let's write a program that accepts the following user inputs and displays the amount of the monthly payment

- price of car
- annual interest rate (simple interest)
- down payment

The program can be decomposed into four parts:

1. Get the inputs from the user.
2. Check for validity of the user's inputs.
3. Compute the monthly payments.
4. Display the monthly payment amount.

The main function in the program is very simple: It executes the four steps listed. If any step is more than a few lines long, it is placed into a subfunction. This makes the main program very readable.

A sample output for the program is

```
Car Payment Calculator.
   Please type the following information:
      Price of the car: 19000
      Annual interest rate (e.g., 6.5): 5.5
      Down payment: 2000
Your monthly car payment is $513
```

The code for the main function *newcar* is

```
function [] = newcar
% new_car - computes the monthly payments for buying a new car.
%           Accepts the following inputs:
%                  - car price
%                  - annual interest rate
%                  - down payment amount
%
% get user inputs
Inputs = get_user_inputs;

% check validity
if bad_inputs(Inputs)
  return
end

% compute monthly payment
Payment = get_payment(Inputs);

% display payment amount
disp(['Your monthly car payment is $', num2str(Payment)]);
```

There are three subfunctions. The code for the *get_user_inputs* subfunction is

```
function Out = get_user_inputs
% get_user_inputs - subfunction that prompts user for
%        interest rate, car price, and down payment
disp('Car Payment Calculator.');
disp('  Please type the following information:');
Out = input('    Price of the car: ');
Out = [Out input('    Annual interest rate (e.g. 6.5): ')];
Out = [Out input('    Down payment: ')];
```

The subfunction that checks for bad inputs only checks a couple of things—basically, the range of each input. There are many more validity checks that could be performed. This section could easily become the longest part of the code. The code for the subfunction *bad_inputs* is

```
function Out = bad_inputs(Inputs)
% bad_inputs - subfunction that checks for out of range inputs,
%              if bad, displays error message and returns false
Out = 0;
if Inputs(1) > 30000
  disp('Please look for a cheaper car!');
  Out = 1;
end
if Inputs(2) < 0 | Inputs(2) > 10
  disp('Interest rate should be between 0 and 10%)');
  Out = 1;
end
if Inputs(3) < 1000
  disp('You should save at least $1,000 for a down payment!');
  Out = 1;
end
```

The subfunction that performs the computation is called *get_payment*. The code is

```
function Out = get_payment(Inputs)
% get_payment - compute monthly payment for car
%               given int rate, down payment, and price
Price = Inputs(1);
% divide by 100 for percent then by 12 to get monthly rate
IntRate = Inputs(2)/1200;
DownPayment = Inputs(3);
% The loan term is 36 months
Temp = (1 + IntRate)^36;
Out = round((Price-DownPayment)*((IntRate*Temp)/(Temp-1)));
```

KEY TERMS

actual parameter	input argument	perfect number
algorithm	input parameter	persistent variable
argument	local variable	private function
definition line	object	procedural abstraction
formal parameter	object-oriented programming	procedural programming
function call	output argument	procedure
function function	output parameter	programming paradigm
function handle	overloading	pseudofunction
functional decomposition	palindrome	pure function
global variable	parameter	scope
help section	pass by reference	side effect
inline function	pass by value	subfunction

NEW MATLAB FUNCTIONS, COMMANDS, AND RESERVED WORDS

abs—returns absolute value of the argument's elements

cd—changes directory

eps—epsilon, the distance from 1.0 to next-closest floating-point number

feval—evaluates a function, given a function handle or name

fplot—plots a function within a given range

function—keyword in a function definition

fzero—finds the zero of a function nearest to given guess

global—keyword for definition of a global variable

inline—creates an inline function

isa—returns true if object is of given class (type)

isempty—returns true if argument is an empty matrix

isequal—tests whether arguments are same size and contain same elements

nargin—returns the number of arguments passed into a function

nargout—returns the number of arguments expected to be passed out of a function

path—displays the user's search path

pwd—prints working directory

quad—approximates an integral, using adaptive Simpson quadrature

return—causes function to return immediately to caller

str2func—converts a function name string to a function handle

strtok—finds next token in a string

upper—returns uppercase version of character argument

varargin—contains a cell array of variable number of input arguments

varargout—contains a cell array of variable number of output arguments

which—displays the path names of function definitions

SOLUTIONS TO PRACTICE PROBLEMS

7.1. Changes to function body:

```
% first approximation
A = X/2;
Index = 0;
% initialize X1
X1 = X;
% loop until the answer is small enough
while abs(X1 - A) > (2*eps)
  X1 = X/A;
  A  = (X1 + A)/2;
  Index = Index + 1;
end
% return results
Out = A;
disp(['Number of iterations = ', int2str(Index)])
```

Sample calls:

```
>> my_sqrt(25)
Number of iterations = 7
ans =
     5
>> my_sqrt(100)
Number of iterations = 8
ans =
    10
```

7.2.
```
function Out = my_sum(A, B)
% my_sum(A, B) - returns the sum of A and B.
%    It is assumed that A and B are conformant double
%    arrays.
Out = A + B;
```

7.5. Change line 4 to

```
Counter = [];
```

The new function always returns 10.

7.6.
```
function [min, max] = minmax(varargin)
% minmax(varargin)
%    Returns the maximum and minimum of a variable
%    number of input arguments.
Max = varargin{1};
Min = varargin{1};
for Index = 1:nargin
  if varargin{Index} > Max
    Max = varargin{Index};
  end
  if varargin{Index} < Min
    Min = varargin{Index};
  end
end
```

7.7.
```
>> get_match('I am a genius, dad')
ans =
 I a dad
>> is_palindrome('dad')
??? Undefined function or variable 'is_palindrome'.
```

The subfunction *is_palindrome* is not visible from the command line. It can be accessed only from its parent function.

7.9. The subfunction is seen before the private function. In the second test, the subfunction is seen before a global variable.

7.10.
```
g = inline('3*x^2 + 4*y^2', 'x', 'y')
```

Problems

Section 7.1.

1. Using the Index and Search features of the Help browser, find the names of the MATLAB functions that perform the following actions:

   a. Removes all items from the workspace
   b. Shows the MATLAB version number
   c. Produces a beeping sound
   d. Checks whether a file or variable exists
   e. Returns the largest floating-point number in the system
   f. Returns the current date and time as a date vector
   g. Transforms Cartesian coordinates to polar coordinates
   h. Returns the greatest common divisor of two integer arrays
   i. Converts a string to lowercase
   j. Plots a histogram

Section 7.2.

2. Look at the function definition in Figure 7.1. What are
   a. the name(s) of the output argument(s)?
   b. the function name?
   c. the name(s) of the input argument(s)?

3. In Figure 7.1, what are the line number(s) of
   a. the definition line?
   b. the H1 line?
   c. the help section?
   d. the function body?

4. Find the location of the MATLAB function *realmax*, using the *which* command. Open the M-file *realmax.m* in the editor. Identify the definition line, the H1 line, the help section, and the function body. Is the function well documented? What is the ratio of comment lines to lines of code?

5. The Taylor series approximation of e^x is

$$e^x = 1 + \frac{x}{1!} + \frac{x^2}{2!} + \frac{x^3}{3!} + \dots.$$

Write a function modeled after Figure 7.1 that iteratively approximates e^x until the answer converges to within $10 * eps$. Name the function *my_epowerx*. Some sample answers using long format are as follows:

```
>> my_epowerx(1) =   2.71828182845905
>> my_epowerx(-5) =   0.00673794699909
>> my_epowerx(0) =   1
```

Section 7.3.

6.   Write a function that accepts a single scalar argument and keeps a running average of the numbers that have been entered. You will need to use a persistent variable in your solution. When testing, use `clear all` between a series of executions to clear the persistent variable. A sample sequence of executions is

```
>> running_average(3)
ans =
     3
>> running_average(8)
ans =
     5.5000
>> running_average(14)
ans =
     8.3333
```

7.   What is the difference in visibility between a global variable and a persistent variable?

Section 7.4.

8.   Write a function that takes a variable number of string arguments and returns the longest string. If a tie occurs, return the first string in the argument list. Sample output is

```
>> longest_string('foo', 'gopher', 'howdy', 'Quincy')
ans =
gopher
```

9.   Write a function that takes a variable number of array arguments and returns the number of scalar arguments. (*Hint*: A scalar is a noncharacter array of size 1×1.) Sample output is

```
>> A = [3 4 5];
>> B = 3;
>> C = 'c';
>> D = 14.5;
>> count_scalars(A,B,C,D)
ans =
     2
```

10.   Write a function that returns a variable number of words from a string, starting with the first word and proceeding through the string. (*Hint*: Use the *strtok* function to parse the words out of the string.) Sample output is

```
>> Str = 'A little older and a little wiser';
>> [a, b] = get_words(Str)
```

```
a =
A
b =
little
>> [c,d,e,f] = get_words(Str)
c =
A
d =
little
e =
older
f =
and
```

Section 7.5.

11.   Modify the code in Figure 7.14 to return all words in a string shorter than five characters in length. Name the function *get_shortwords*. Create a subfunction named *is_shorter5* that checks the length. Sample output is

```
>> Str = 'A fool and his money are soon parted';
>> get_shortwords(Str)
ans =
 A fool and his are soon
```

12.   A *perfect number* is a number whose factors sum to itself. One (1) is included as a factor, but the number itself is not. An example of a perfect number is 6, since its summed factors $1 + 2 + 3 = 6$. Another perfect number is 28 $(1 + 2 + 4 + 7 + 14 = 28)$. Create a main program called *perfect_number* that prompts the user and accepts an integer as input. The main function should loop and continue to ask for input until a zero is typed. Create a private function named *is_perfect* that determines whether the user input is a perfect number. Display appropriate output. Sample output is

```
>> perfect_number
Type a perfect number (0 to quit): 4
   Sorry, Charlie!
Type a perfect number (0 to quit): 28
   28 is a perfect number!
   Its factors are 1   2   4   7   14
Type a perfect number (0 to quit): 0
>>
```

Section 7.6.

13.   MATLAB's rules for name resolution state that the current working directory is searched before the search path is traversed. Devise a simple test which demonstrates that the current working directory is searched before the search path is traversed. (*Hint*: Look up the *pwd* and *cd* commands in the Help Browser.)

Section 7.7.

14.   Which of the following has the broadest scope—an inline function, a normal function, or a function handle? Which has the narrowest scope? Explain.

15.   In some languages, programmers use an inline function because it executes more efficiently than a separately called function. Test this assertion by writing a function that implements the algebraic expression $5x^2 - 10x + 50$. Write a program that calls the function 1,000 times. Then call an inline definition of the same expression 1,000 times. Which one is faster? (*Hint*: Use the *clock* and *etime* functions to do the timing.)

16.   Write a program that stores the function handles of the functions $\sin(x)$, $\cos(x)$, $\exp(x)$, and $\log(x)$ in an array. Write a user interface that allows the user to select one of the functions. Use *feval, plot,* and the array index to plot the chosen function for $x = [1 : 0.1 : 10]$. A sample interface is

```
The following functions may be plotted.
  1. sin
  2. cos
  3. exp
  4. log
Choose a number (0 to exit):
```

8

Recursion

8.1 INTRODUCTION

Earlier in the text, we described a solution for finding an approximation of a square root by using Newton's method. The method described previously uses a loop and iterates until a satisfactory solution is reached. We call this type of solution method an *iterative solution*. In this section, we will describe another type of solution method called *recursion*.

In short, a *recursive function* is one that calls itself. Each time it calls itself, the function may use different inputs and return different outputs. Eventually, if we have programmed correctly, the function reaches a termination condition.

Some students find the notion of recursion difficult to grasp at first. An example of a natural recursion is the viewing of two mirrors that face each other. It appears that a smaller mirror is inside of the first mirror, and a yet smaller mirror is inside of the second mirror, ad infinitum.

Another example is a magazine that has a picture of the same magazine on its cover, and so on. Hence, there appear to be a series of successively smaller magazines inside each magazine that eventually disappear into a point.

The primary difference between natural recursion and a recursive function is that we do not want our function to continue indefinitely. We will start by showing you an iterative and a recursive solution for finding the factorial of a positive integer. Then, we will use this example to explain how recursion works.

OBJECTIVES

After reading this chapter, you should be able to

- Understand how recursion works.
- Describe how recursion is implemented by using a stack.
- Write recursive functions.
- Understand different types of recursion.
- Describe when to use recursion in a program.

8.2   A SIMPLE RECURSION EXAMPLE

Recall that the factorial of a nonnegative integer N is defined to be

$$Fac(N) = 1 \text{ if } N = 0 \text{ or } 1 ,$$
$$Fac(N) = N(N - 1)(N - 2), \ldots, (3)(2)(1), \text{ otherwise.}$$

The mathematical factorial operator is the exclamation point (!). The factorial of three is written as

$$3! = (3)(2)(1) = 6.$$

MATLAB has a factorial function named *factorial* as part of its function library. MATLAB's factorial function is accurate up to $N = 21$, since double precision numbers only have about 15 digits of accuracy. Above $N = 21$, the factorial of N requires more than 15 digits.

Figure 8.1 defines a simple iterative solution for finding the factorial of a number. Figure 8.2 defines a recursive solution for the same problem. In the recursive solution, a function handle is used to call the function recursively. Both solutions ignore perverse cases such as negative numbers and noninteger inputs. Do not worry about the perverse cases for now. We will cover them later.

```
1   function Out = my_iterative_factorial(N)
2   % my_iterative_factorial(N)
3   %    Iteratively computes the factorial of a
4   %    nonnegative integer.
5   Fac = 1;
6   for Index = N:-1:2
7     Fac = Fac * Index;
8   end
9   Out = Fac;
```

Figure 8.1.   A simple iterative solution for factorial.

```
1   function Out = my_factorial(N)
2   % my_factorial(N)
3   %     Computes the factorial of a nonnegative integer.
4   if N == 0          % base case for 0
5     Out = 1;
6   elseif N == 1      % base case for 1
7     Out = N;
8   else               % all other cases are recursive
9     Out = N * feval(@my_factorial, N-1);
10  end
```

Figure 8.2.   A simple recursive solution for factorial.

Let us walk through the definition in Figure 8.2. The algorithm uses a selection statement to break the problem into two parts, called the *base case* and the *recursive case*.

8.2.1   Base Case

The first part (lines 4–7) are two cases for which we know the answer, $N = 0$ and $N = 1$. We call these the base cases of the algorithm. The base cases provide a way to stop the algorithm.

8.2.2   Recursive Case

The second part (line 9) is the recursive case. If we do not know the answer (such as for $N = 2$), we call the function with the argument $N - 1$ and then multiply the return value by N. This only works because we know that if we keep subtracting one from N, eventually we will reach a base case ($N = 1$).

Figure 8.3 shows each function call to *my_factorial*. Three calls are made to *my_factorial* before the base case is reached. The base case is reached in call three. Then the return values begin to be passed back to the waiting function calls. Finally, the first call is reached and the answer of six is returned.

```
Call 1: my_factorial = 3 * feval(@my_factorial, 2)

Call 2: my_factorial = 2 * feval(@my_factorial, 1)

Call 3: my_factorial = 1

Call 2: my_factorial = 2 * 1

Call 1: my_factorial = 3 * 2

ans = 6
```

Figure 8.3.   A walk through of *my_factorial*(3).

8.3   STACK-BASED EXPLANATION

During execution, the values of local variables within a function call are stored in a stack structure. A *stack* structure is similar to a stack of plates. The last plate placed on the stack is the first one retrieved, assuming that you only grab plates from the top of the stack. This is called a last-in, first-out or *LIFO* mechanism. We call placing a new plate onto the stack a *push* operation. We call grabbing a plate off the top of the stack a *pop* operation.

The run-time organization of function calls is usually implemented internally by using a stack. When the first function call is made, its local variables are pushed onto the run-time stack in a structure called an *activation record*. When that function completes, the activation record is popped from the stack.

		N=1, mf=1		
	N=2, mf=?	N=2, mf=?	N=2, mf=2	
N=3, mf=?	N=3, mf=?	N=3, mf=?	N=3, mf=?	N=3, mf=6
t = 1	t = 2	t = 3	t = 4	t = 5

Figure 8.4.   Activation stack history for *my_factorial*(3).

In Figure 8.4, the history of activation records is shown for the function call *my_factorial(3)*. The columns represent time periods $t = 1 \ldots 5$, and each cell represents the local state of the function call at time t. The return value for *my_factorial* is abbreviated as *mf*.

At time $t = 1$, the activation record for *my_factorial(3)* is pushed onto the stack. The contents of the activation record are $N = 3$ and $mf = ?$, since the return value is not known yet.

At time $t = 2$, the call *my_factorial(2)* is made and the activation record is pushed onto the stack. Its activation record contains the local variable $N = 2$ and $mf = ?$, since the return value is not yet known.

At time $t = 3$, the call *my_factorial(1)* is made, and the activation record for this call is pushed onto the stack. The local state is $N = 1$, and the function computes the return value of $mf = 1$. Since the function has now completed, the return value is passed back to its caller, and its activation record is popped off the stack.

At time $t = 4$, the waiting function gets the return value of one and multiplies it by its version of N that equals 2. Now this call can complete and return the value 2. Its activation record is popped.

Finally, at time $t = 5$, the waiting function receives the value of two and multiplies it by $N = 3$. This final activation record is popped, and the final answer of six is returned.

The calls leading up to time $t = 3$ are all incomplete. Each function instance is waiting for a recursive call to return. We say that the recursive call is *pending*. The creation of all of the pending calls ($t = 1, 2, 3$) is called *winding the stack*. Between time $t = 3$ and time $t = 4$, the last (or most recent) activation record is popped. We call the sequence of popping recursive activation records *unwinding the stack*.

8.4 DESIGNING A RECURSIVE SOLUTION

The guidelines that follow may be helpful when designing a recursive solution to a problem. Remember, not all problems have recursive solutions, and we do not recommend recursion for all problems even if a recursive solution exists.

8.4.1 Designing Guidelines

The first design consideration is to determine whether you can decompose the problem into subproblems that resemble the main problem. In the factorial example, the main problem can be decomposed into a number of subproblems of multiplying N by $N - 1$.

The second consideration is to find a *base case* that you can solve without using recursion. In the factorial example, the base case is one factorial (1!).

If the answer to both of these questions is yes, you should write the recursive expression. Once you have written the recursive expression design a base case which guarantees that the function will terminate.

Let us try this method to solve the problem of generating a *Fibonacci sequence* of length N, where N is a natural number. The Fibonacci sequence is defined as

$$Fib(N) = 1, \text{ if } N = 1 \text{ or } 2,$$
$$Fib(N) = Fib(N - 1) + Fib(N - 2), \text{ otherwise}$$

In other words, the first two elements of a Fibonacci sequence are each unity, and we compute the other elements of the sequence by adding the two preceding elements.

The first eight elements of the Fibonacci sequence are

$$Fib(8) = 1, 1, 2, 3, 5, 8, 13, 21$$

The first step in designing a recursive solution is to find subproblems that resemble the main problem. The part of the algorithm that adds the two previous numbers in the sequence is such a subproblem. We can express the recursive case in the following MATLAB expression:

```
feval(@Fib, N-1) + feval(@Fib, N-2)
```

This code will work for all cases, except when $N = 1$ or $N = 2$. We have to handle these cases separately. They are considered the base cases, since we can determine the results of $Fib(1)$ and $Fib(2)$ without using recursion. Figure 8.5 shows a recursive solution for generating the Nth number in a Fibonacci sequence.

```
1   function Out = Fib(N)
2   % Fib(N)
3   %      Returns the Nth Fibonacci number.
4   switch N
5     case {1, 2}
6        Out = 1;
7     otherwise
8        Out = feval(@Fib, N-1) + feval(@Fib, N-2);
9   end
```

Figure 8.5.   Recursive solution for generating a Fibonacci number.

Sometimes, a recursive solution requires the use of a helper function. Toward that end, consider Newton's method for finding an approximate square root. Figure 8.6 shows an iterative solution to the problem. The solution requires that we remember the original number for which we are finding the square root. This is because we must divide the original number by the new approximation (line 15), which occurs inside the main loop of the function. To implement the solution recursively, we would either have to make X a global variable or pass it as a separate parameter. We would like to create a recursive solution that requires a single parameter and does not expose any variable by making it global.

In Figure 8.7, we define a recursive solution for Newton's square root method. This solution uses a subfunction called *helper* to handle the recursion and extra parameters.

PRACTICE 8.1!

Type the code from Figure 8.7 into an M-file and save it as *recursive_sqrt.m*. Verify to yourself that the solution produces the same results as the iterative *my_sqrt* function. To help you understand how the function works, add a line to the recursive solution that displays partial results. Insert a line before line 21 that reads as follows:

```
disp(A)
```

```
1   function Out = my_sqrt(X)
2   %  my_sqrt(X) - returns the positive square root of X.
3   %   This function uses Newton's method for
4   %   approximating the positive square root of a
5   %   nonnegative scalar or array.
6
7   % first approximation
8   A = X/2;
9
10  % initialize X1
11  X1 = X;
12
13  % loop until the answer is small enough
14  while abs(X1 - A) > (10*eps)
15     X1 = X/A;
16     A  = (X1 + A)/2;
17  end
18
19  % return results
20  Out = A;
```

Figure 8.6.   Function definition of Newton's square-root method.

8.5   TYPES OF RECURSION

8.5.1   Tail Recursion

Recursive solutions can be categorized in several ways, depending on how the recursive call is structured. If there are no pending operations waiting to be performed when a recursive call returns, the type of recursion is called *tail recursion*.

The *helper* function in Figure 8.7 is an example of tail recursion. When the call to helper returns, it is immediately assigned to the return value. No other operations are performed on the returned value. Line 21 from Figure 8.7 is an example of tail recursion:

```
Out = feval(@helper, X, X/A, (X/A + A)/2);
```

Now, revisit the factorial solution in Figure 8.2, line 9:

```
Out = N * feval(@my_factorial, N-1);
```

This is the recursive step in the solution. Note that after the recursive call returns, the result is multiplied by N. This example is not a tail recursion because an operation is performed on the recursive solution after it returns.

The advantage of tail recursion is that memory storage requirements are lessened. If the call is not tail recursive (i.e., a pending operation exists), the results must

```
 1   function Out = recursive_sqrt(X)
 2   % recursive_sqrt(X)
 3   %       This function uses Newton's method for
 4   %       approximating the positive square root of a
 5   %       nonnegative scalar or array.
 6
 7   % first approximation
 8   A = X/2;
 9   % call recursive helper function
10   Out = helper(X, X, A);
11
12
13   function Out = helper(X, X1, A)
14   % helper(X, X1, A)
15   %      Auxiliary subfunction for finding sqrt.
16   if abs(X1 - A) <= (10*eps)
17     % we're done
18     Out = A;
19   else
20     % recursively call function until small enough
21     Out = feval(@helper, X, X/A, (X/A + A)/2);
22   end
```

Figure 8.7. A recursive solution for Newton's square root method.

be temporarily stored. Another advantage of tail-recursive solutions is that you can convert them to iterative solutions.

Another way of classifying recursive solutions is by the shape of the recursive calls. The two types are linear and tree shapes.

8.5.2   Linear Recursion

If there are no pending operations that require a **recursive** call to the function then the recursion is called *linear recursion*. Both the *helper* and *my_factorial* functions are examples of linear recursion. The *my_factorial* function has a pending operation: multiplication by N. The pending operation does not require a second call to *my_factorial*.

8.5.3   Tree Recursion

If there are pending operations that require a recursive call to the same function, we call the recursion a *tree recursion*. The solution for returning a Fibonacci number is an example of tree recursion. The following code is line eight from Figure 8.5:

```
Out = feval(@Fib, N-1) + feval(@Fib, N-2);
```

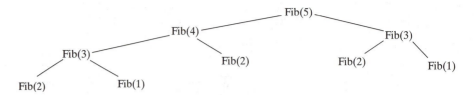

Figure 8.8. Example of tree recursion for Fibonacci sequence.

Note that the return call from *Fib* is added to another call to *Fib* before the function returns. Figure 8.8 demonstrates how the calls to *Fib*(5) form a tree structure.

8.6 WHEN TO USE RECURSION

The primary reason to use recursion is that a recursive solution often simplifies the code structure. A complex function may be easier to understand when presented in a recursive form. There are elegant recursive solutions to problems such as solving a maze, sorting, and searching through complex data structures.

However, recursion has a cost. An iterative solution involves a single function call for the primary iteration. A recursive solution involves many function calls. Each pending function call requires a new activation record, which takes up space in memory. This is especially true in a language such as MATLAB that uses the pass-by-value method of parameter passing. Recursive solutions may also be slower, since it takes time to push and pop activation records.

Fortunately, a problem that has a recursive solution also has a corresponding iterative solution. In fact, functions that use tail recursion can be converted automatically to an iterative solution. This is accomplished by replacing the recursive call with an assignment statement and a loop structure.

Figure 8.9 shows a conversion of the *helper* function from the recursive square root function in Figure 8.7. We have modified the *helper* function by assigning the input parameters new values and then looping.

One strategy used by programmers is initially to use a recursive solution if it makes the code easier to understand. After the programmer has validated the solution, the programmer converts the code to an iterative solution to conserve resources. The iterative solution will usually be faster and may require less memory (stack space) during execution.

```
13   function Out = helper(X, X1, A)
14   % helper(X, X1, A)
15   %    Auxiliary subfunction for finding sqrt.
16   while abs(X1 - A) > (10*eps)
17      X1 = X/A;
18      A = (X/A + A)/2;
19   end
20   % we're done
21   Out = A;
```

Figure 8.9. Example of converting tail recursion to iteration.

MATLAB gives us a clue that recursion uses memory by including a variable that sets the recursion limit. MATLAB limits the number of recursive calls for a function to 500. You may change this limit, but MATLAB gives a warning that raising the limit may crash your computer. We can see the warning by calling *my_factorial(520)*:

```
>> my_factorial(520)
??? Maximum recursion limit of 500 reached. Use
set(0,'RecursionLimit',N) to change the limit. Be
aware that exceeding your available stack space can
crash MATLAB and/or your computer.
```

KEY TERMS

activation record	pending call	stack
base case	pop	tail recursion
Fibonacci sequence	push	tree recursion
iterative solution	recursion	unwinding the stack
LIFO	recursive case	winding the stack
linear recursion	recursive function	

NEW MATLAB FUNCTIONS, COMMANDS, AND RESERVED WORDS

clf—clear current figure window (clears the plot editor)
gcd—returns the greatest common divisor of two nonnegative integers
mod—performs the modulus operation

Problems

Section 8.1.

1. What is the main difference between a correctly written recursive computer program and the example of two mirrors facing each other?

Section 8.3.

2. Write a script that calls *my_iterative_factorial* 5,000 times and then calls *my_factorial* 5,000 times, and computes the elapsed time for each. Which is faster, the iterative or recursive function? Why?

Section 8.4.

3. A chain letter is a form of recursion. Someone initiates an e-mail letter, sending it to 10 friends. Each recipient then sends it to 10 friends. Think of a base case that guarantees the chain letter will not repeat forever (i.e., that the recursion will stop).

Section 8.5

4. Write a recursive function named *my_circle* that plots a circle with an initial radius r and then calls itself with smaller and smaller values of r in intervals of 1 until $r \leq 1$. Turn *hold* on, so that the circles are all generated on the same plot. Write a subfunction to plot a single circle. The title for the plot

should display the number of concentric circles. Recall that the formula for a circle is

$$x^2 + y^2 = r^2.$$

(*Hint*: The *clf* command clears the graphics window.) Figure 8.10 displays the result of calling *my_circle* with the argument 8:

```
>> my_circle(8)
```

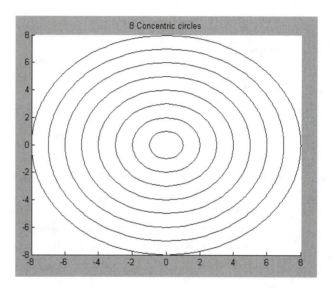

Figure 8.10. Example for Problem 4.

5. If a and b are nonnegative integers, then the greatest common divisor (GCD) of a and b is defined as the largest positive integer that divides both a and b. If $a > b \geq 0$, then a recursive definition for the GCD is

- Base case: $\gcd(a, b) = a$, if $b = 0$.
- Recursive case: $\gcd(a, b) = \gcd(b, a \bmod b)$ if $b \neq 0$.

Using these rules, the GCD of 26 and 8 can be found as follows:

$$\gcd(26, 8) = \gcd(8, 2) = \gcd(2, 0) = 2.$$

Write a recursive function that finds the GCD of two nonnegative integers using the modulus or mod operation. Use the MATLAB *mod* function to compute the modulus operation. The modulus operation returns the remainder of a/b. Here's an example:

```
>> mod(8,5)
ans =
      3
```

MATLAB has a *gcd* function that you can use to validate your program. *Hint*: Do not forget to test if $a > b$ and switch a and b, if necessary.

6. The Taylor series approximation of cosine is

$$\cos(x) = 1 - \frac{x^2}{2!} + \frac{x^4}{4!} - \frac{x^6}{6!} + \cdots$$

Write a recursive function that computes an approximation of cosine. Validate your solution by using the MATLAB *cos* function. Note the alternating plus and minus signs. You may use the MATLAB *factorial* function in your solution.

9

Introduction to Object-Oriented Programming

9.1 THE OBJECT-ORIENTED PARADIGM

Object-oriented programming is a programming paradigm—a way of viewing programming. Object-oriented programming languages arose because of the inflexibility of previous generations of programming languages.

The roots of object-oriented programming are derived from the Simula language in the 1960s and from Smalltalk in the 1970s. C++, Smalltalk, Delphi, Python, and Java are examples of modern object-oriented programming languages.

The first commercial computing systems with integrated object-oriented architectures and development environments were the Apple Macintosh (1984) and the NeXT machine (1988). The NeXT development environment included the first object-oriented visual interface development kit, something that is taken for granted in object-oriented software development systems today.

In the *modular programming* paradigm, the principles of data abstraction allow a programmer to *encapsulate* functions and data structures into modules. Thus, all functions related to a particular algorithm or computation are located in the same place and are protected.

In MATLAB, you have learned to protect functions by writing subfunctions and private functions, which are accessible only through the parent function. In addition, access to internal data structures is protected: Local variables can be accessed solely by using the function call. The separation of the interface of a module from the details of its implementation is called the *principle of encapsulation*.

One advantage of encapsulation is that it allows a programmer the flexibility to change the details of how a module is implemented without affecting code that uses the module. For example, the way a statistics module is implemented can be altered, but as long as the statistical functions

OBJECTIVES

After reading this chapter, you should be able to

- Describe the basic elements of the object-oriented programming paradigm.
- Overload an operator for a class.
- Write a polymorphic method for a class.
- Define and create a new MATLAB class.
- Write class methods.
- Instantiate and use objects from a class.
- Give an example of encapsulation.

require the same input parameters and return the same values, the user of the module does not have to change any code.

We have changed the implementation of the *my_sqrt* function several times in the text. For example, we have written both iterative and recursive version of the function. In both of those implementations, the interface remained the same. The user of *my_sqrt* does not even have to know that the underlying implementation changed.

Still, there are limitations to the modular programming paradigm. They are best illustrated with an example. Suppose we had a module that implemented a list of strings. Then a list implementation might include functions for creating a list, appending to a list, and sorting a list. This list implementation is called an *abstract data type*.

Can we use the same code for lists of integers? Not directly. One option is to create a second module for lists of integers, borrowing ideas and code from the list of strings. Another option is to create a module for lists in general that includes a list type. This would allow us to reuse code that is the same no matter what type of list is created. However, we would have to reexamine all the code to see what needs to be changed and what stays the same. If we add a third type, say lists of structures, then all of the code not only would need to be reexamined, but might have to be changed to handle the new type of list.

You can see that our current method's code is not very reusable. That is the basic problem with the modular programming paradigm.

The object-oriented programming paradigm handles this issue by allowing the common elements of different list types to be abstracted into what is called a *class*. A *class* is a group of characteristics that may be shared by a group of objects.

Some of the characteristics of a class may be specialized or refined into a *subclass*, or what is sometimes called a *derived class*. Common characteristics can be inherited by a subclass, but each subclass can contain its own specialized characteristics. This notion of being able to automatically share common characteristics among classes and subclasses is called *inheritance*. Inheritance is one of the essential aspects of object-oriented languages that are not found in procedural languages. Before demonstrating the mechanism for creating classes and objects in MATLAB, let us cover some of the basic terminology and concepts of object-oriented programming.

9.2   OBJECT-ORIENTED ELEMENTS AND MECHANISMS

9.2.1   Classes

The basic elements of an object-oriented language are *classes* and their instantiations, called *objects*. You can think of a class as an abstraction of a group of potential objects that share the characteristics of the class.

The characteristics typically include definitions of abstract data types and the procedures that operate on those data types. For example, the Bird class is an abstraction of many kinds of birds, which share certain attributes in common, such as feathers, wings, and beaks.

A class may contain *subclasses* or *derived classes*. For example, the Bird class contains the subclasses Finch and Owl. Instances of the Finch subclass and the Owl subclass share common characteristics of the Bird class (e.g., they have wings and beaks). However, members of the Owl subclass have some characteristics of their own that are not shared by the Finch subclass (e.g., owls are nocturnal and are carnivores). The idea of a subclass automatically sharing characteristics from a parent class is called *inheritance*. A subclass typically adds more features to its parent class, but may subtract features.

9.2.2 Objects

Objects are the things that are made from a class mold. Objects are dynamically created as needed. The act of creating an object from a class is called *instantiation*, and a created object is called an *instance* of a class.

In computer programming, an *object* is a program module that contains both data and the procedures for operating on the data. We do not invoke an object with a function or procedure call; instead, we think of sending a *message* to an object. The object then acts on that message.

The set of messages that an object may receive is well defined and is called the object's *protocol*. How the object acts on the message internally is hidden from the user of the object, which may be another object, a programmer, or the human user of the program.

In programming, the characteristics or attributes of an object are stored in variables. Variables that are shared among the members of a class are called *class variables*. Variables that are unique to each individual instance of a class are called *instance variables*.

The choice of the Bird class as an example is meant to demonstrate that an object-oriented programming class hierarchy resembles a biological taxonomy. (See Figure 9.1.)

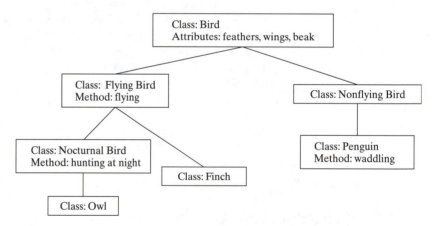

Figure 9.1. The (not biologically serious) Bird class hierarchy.

9.2.3 Methods

Functions that exist within objects and that operate on objects are called *methods*. Methods may perform computation on instance variables within an object and may send messages to other objects. A method for a Flying Bird object is *flying*.

A method derived from a class may be removed in a subclass. For example, the Owl subclass inherits the *flying* method from the Flying Bird class. However, a subclass called Injured Owls that removes the *flying* method could exist.

In classes developed for programming, methods tend to fall into certain categories. Some of these categories and their definitions are described next.

Constructor

A *constructor* method is a method used to create and initialize an object (an instance of a class). In some languages, including MATLAB and C++, the constructor method is given the same name as the class. Objects are created (or instantiated) by their class constructor. The constructor method is required because it is the only way to instantiate a new object.

Destructor

A *destructor* method is called when an object is about to be destroyed. In many cases, the destruction of an object is automatic when the object is no longer referenced by any other object. Some programming languages have explicit destructor methods. MATLAB does not use destructor methods; instead, objects are cleared from the workspace by using the *clear* command.

Iterator

An *iterator* is a group of methods that support moving through a sequence. For example, given a current state of 15, a positive iterator for integers would return 16. Similarly, given a current state of 'g', an iterator of characters would return 'h'. Iterators can produce complex sequences, such as walking through a graph in a certain order. Iterators usually handle the cases of pointing to the first element of a sequence and reporting when the end of the sequence has been reached.

Display

Most object-oriented languages include a kind of method that is used to create a string representation of an object in order to display the object on the screen. The MATLAB method for this purpose is called *display* or *disp*. You will want to create a display method for most classes that you design.

9.2.4 Polymorphism

A message may be treated entirely differently when received by different objects. The capability for the same message to be treated differently when received by different objects is called *polymorphism.*

A classic example is the *draw* method. When a message is sent to an object asking the object to execute the *draw* method, each object interprets the message according its own shape. Thus, the Square object draws a square on the basis of the method inherited from the Square class and using its own (internally stored) measurements. The Circle object has a different *draw* method inherited from the Circle class.

The beauty of polymorphism is that each object is responsible for its own methods. We can send a message to an object that says, "Draw yourself." We do not need to know how to draw every object. We just need to know how to communicate with every object.

9.2.5 Operator Overloading

A particular case of polymorphism is the ability of a class to redefine operators to act differently for its own purposes. For example, the + operator is typically used to mean addition for integers. In some languages, however, when used on strings, the + operator means concatenation, not addition. The following code is an example:

```
4 + 5 = 9
'Hello' + ', World.' = 'Hello, World.'
```

This type of polymorphism is called *operator overloading*. We will redefine the + operator in the example of a List class later in the chapter.

9.2.6 Multiple Inheritance

A subclass may inherit characteristics from several parents. The ability of a subclass to inherit methods and data structures from more than one parent class is called *multiple inheritance*. For example, a Bat subclass is derived primarily from the Mammal class, but may inherit certain methods, such as *flying*, from the Bird class.

9.2.7 Container Classes

A *container class* defines objects that hold something. Typically, a container class defines a common set of operations that manipulate the objects that are contained by the class.

For example, a *stack* class can be considered a container class. You can think of a stack data structure as being similar to a stack of plates. Normally, you add a plate to the stack by placing it on top of the stack. This is called *pushing* the plate onto the stack. When you remove a plate from the stack, you take it off the top of the stack. This is called *popping* a plate off the stack. Since the first plate popped is the last plate pushed, a stack is often called a last-in, first-out, or LIFO, structure.

A stack class will usually have a *push* method, a *pop* method, and a method that tests for an empty stack. A stack is a way of containing things. However, the definition doesn't constrain what types of objects are contained in the stack. You can have a stack of anything—poker chips, jet airplanes, or golf balls. Stacks are used extensively in computer programming. In Chapter 8, we discussed a stack of activation records used to store recursive function calls.

Other typical containers are queues and lists. A *queue* is an example of a first-in, first-out, or FIFO, data structure. A new item is placed on the end of the queue. As new items are added to the queue, items are removed from the front of the queue. You can think of a queue as being similar to a single ticket line at the movies, assuming that nobody breaks in line.

A simple *list* structure is a sequence of objects. Unlike an array, a list is not accessed by using subscripts. Instead, *append* and *remove* methods are respectively used to add and remove items from the list. We will define a simple list structure using MATLAB later in the chapter.

One type of list that is commonly used in computer programming is a *linked list*. A linked list has a logical ordering, which may or may not be totally different from the way the objects are actually stored in memory. The ordering is enforced by associating a link with each item. In Figure 9.2, a singly linked list is displayed. Each item in the list has contents and a link to another node. The FirstNode and the LastNode are two special nodes.

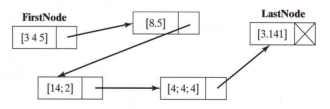

Figure 9.2. Example of a singly linked list.

9.3 DEFINING CLASSES IN MATLAB

A class is created in MATLAB by creating a special directory for the class and, at a minimum, creating a constructor method for the class. The convention is to create a directory named after the class name, but with the @ symbol appended in front of it. The constructor method is an M-file that resides in the class directory and has the same name as the class.

For example, to create a stack class, we would first create a directory named *@stack* in our search path. Then we would create a constructor method named *stack.m* and save it in the *@stack* directory. Of course, to make a useful Stack class, we would add other methods, such as *push* and *pop*.

The function that actually creates a new class is called *class*. The *class* function is used inside the constructor method to define the new class. Usually, this is the last line of code in the constructor method. For example, the last line of code in the Stack class constructor might be

```
S = class(S, 'stack');
```

The effect of this class function inside the constructor method is to create a *stack* object, using S as a template. The new object S will be returned by the constructor. This concept will become clearer as we walk through the example later in the chapter.

9.4 INSTANTIATING OBJECTS IN MATLAB

An object is instantiated by calling its class name. For example, to create an empty stack object, you would type

```
>> MyStack = stack
```

The effect of calling *stack* is to invoke the constructor method of the Stack class.

The *class* function has a different use outside of the constructor method. Here, it is used to find out the class of an object. To find out the class of MyStack, you would type

```
>> class(MyStack)
ans =
stack
```

9.5 A SAMPLE CLASS

The easiest way to learn how to build a class is to walk through an example. In this section, we will build a class and its associated methods. You should type, save, and execute the sample methods as you proceed through the section.

9.5.1 Class Design

One data structure that is frequently used in programming is a *list*. Our list class is defined to be a sequence of arbitrary objects. For example, the following list L contains a character, a fixed-point number, a string, and an array:

```
'c', 14.5, 'foo', [3,4,5]
```

Typical operations on lists include adding members to the list, removing members from the list, and sorting the list. In this and the next couple of sections, we will create a List class with the methods shown in Table 9.1.

TABLE 9.1. The methods for the List class.

Method Name	Description
list(…)	the list constructor method, used to create an instance of the List class
append(L, X1, X2, X3, …)	appends a variable number of variable types of objects to list L
size(L)	returns the number of elements in list L
remove(L, X)	removes the first occurrence of object X from list L
reverse(L)	reverses the order of elements in list L
display(L)	displays list L

A *constructor* method must be created for every class. A constructor is used to create an object of the class. Most classes will benefit from a *display* method, which is used to produce a viewable rendition of an object.

9.5.2 Class Definition

The first step in defining a new class is to create a folder with the class name preceded by the @ character. Place the new folder in your search path, or add the location of the folder to your search path. To modify your search path, choose **File → Set Path** from the menu bar.

I have chosen the name @*list* for the new List class. The path leading up to the @*list* folder is in my MATLAB search path:

```
D:\Dave\Matlab2001\Examples\@list
```

The M-files that are stored in the @*list* folder become the methods of the List class. For example, we will create an *append* method that will be defined in the file *append.m* and stored in the @*list* folder.

The Constructor Method

The first method that we will define for the List class is the constructor method, which defines how a new object of the class is instantiated. The MATLAB convention is to name the constructor M-file with the name of the class. In our case, the constructor M-file is named *list.m*.

The constructor method for a list should handle several cases. It should be able to create a new empty list. It should be able to create a new list and initialize the list with a variable number of objects. The following examples are illustrative:

```
% creates an empty list L
>>L = list

% creates a list L with 4 elements
>>L = list(5, 'foo', 3.14, [2,3;4,5])
```

Note that the objects in the list may be of various types, including scalars, arrays, strings, and even other lists. At least, that is how it appears from outside the class when you are using the list constructor.

How is the list constructed and stored inside the class? MATLAB's data types can be viewed as classes in a class hierarchy. All user-defined classes are descendants of the structure array class. Before, proceeding, review the section on structure arrays in Appendix C.

MATLAB requires that an object's data type be defined using *a structure array.*

The code in Figure 9.3 implements the List *constructor* method. The structure array that holds the List object is named *L* and has a single field, named *elements*. That single field holds the elements of the list. The field is accessed using the dot operator as *L.elements*.

```
1   function L = list(varargin)
2   %  list - List constructor
3   %  L = list(x1, x2, x3, ...) creates a list object
4   %       and initializes the list with the input
    %       arguments.
5   %  If no input arguments are given, an empty list is
6   %  returned.
7   if nargin == 0
8      L.elements = {};
9   else
10     for Index = 1:nargin
11        L.elements(Index) = varargin(Index);
12     end
13  end
14  L = class(L, 'list');
```

Figure 9.3.   The constructor method for the List class.

The next design decision to make is to choose the data structure that will be used internally to store a list. That is, of what data type is the *elements* field? We have chosen a cell array as the data structure to hold the members of the list. The reason for choosing a cell array is that it can contain arbitrary types of objects. Therefore, *L* is a structure array with one field named *elements*, and the *elements* field is a cell array.

Within a method definition, the variable *nargin* holds the number of arguments passed into the method. In the constructor method, we use the value of *nargin* to test whether the new object should be empty. If the new object is empty, we allocate a cell array of size zero. (See lines 7–8 of Figure 9.3.)

If *nargin* is greater than zero, then each argument is added to the cell array by means of a *for* loop. (See lines 10–12 of Figure 9.3.)

If the input argument is named *varargin*, MATLAB accepts a variable number of arguments. (See line 1.) A combination of fixed and variable arguments may be used, but *varargin* must be passed last in the argument list.

The last line in the constructor method actually creates the class by associating the name *L* with List class. (See line 14.) The new instance of the List class is returned to the calling program. As stated earlier, this form of the *class* function can be used only within a constructor method.

Congratulations, you have created a class. Now that you have created the one essential method for a class, try instantiating an object of that class—for example, with the code

```
>> A = list(5, [5 2], 'foo');
```

Use the *class* function to determine what type of object A is:

```
>> class(A)
ans =
list
```

PROGRAMMING TIP 9.1!

There are three cases to consider in creating a constructor. The constructor may be called with

1. No arguments, resulting in the creation of an empty object.
2. Some arguments, resulting in the creation of an initialized argument.
3. An object of its own class as an argument.

Try the following commands, which test the three cases for the List constructor:

First, with no arguments, we have

```
>> A = list;
class(A)
ans =
list
```

Next, with several arguments, the commands are

```
>> B = list('foo', [3 4; 5 6], 6);
>> class(B)
ans =
list
```

Finally, with a list as one of the arguments, we write

```
>> C = list(A, 'foo');
>> class(C)
ans =
list
```

The Display Method

The *display* method is usually defined for a class. Otherwise, an object of that class will be displayed in accordance with its underlying type. Create the following list and see what is returned:

```
>> A = list(3, 'foo')
A =
     list object: 1-by-1
```

This code is technically accurate, but not very informative. At a minimum, we want to see the number of items and perhaps their sizes. We might also want to see the contents of each item in the list.

There are many ways that you might choose to display a list. The code in Figure 9.4 defines one idea for the *display* method of the List class. We have chosen to display each list element on a separate line or lines.

The first section of the *display* method (line 5) uses the *length* function to determine how many elements are in the list. The next section uses the *inputname* function (line 9) to obtain the actual name of the formal parameter *L*. The name is used to display the name of the object.

The main body of code for the *display* method (lines 13–24) is a *for* loop that is used to examine the size and class of each member of the list. The results for each member are then displayed with the use of the *display* method for that type of object.

The *num2str* function (number to string) is used to convert the element number to a string, since the *disp* function argument consists of an array of type *char*. The *class* function is used to determine the class of each element.

Note the use of the *length* and *size* functions in lines 15–18. The expression

```
size(L.elements{Index},1)
```

```
1   function display(L)
2   % Display - displays a list object L
3
4   % get the number of elements in the list
5   Len = length(L.elements);
6
7   % display the name of the list
8   disp(' ');
9   disp([inputname(1),' ='])
10
11  % loop through each element and display it
12  Str = '';
13  for Index = 1:Len
14    % get size of each element
15    if isequal(size(L.elements{Index},1), 1)
16      elSize = length(L.elements{Index});
17    else
18      elSize = size(L.elements{Index});
19    end
20    % display element
21    disp(['  ',num2str(Index),':',...
22          class(L.elements{Index}),...
23          '(',num2str(elSize),')'])
24    disp(L.elements{Index})
25  end
26  disp(' ');
```

Figure 9.4. The *display* method for the List class.

returns the size of the first dimension of the element, which lets us determine whether the element is a vector or a multidimensional array. If it is a vector, we use the *length* function to return the length of the vector. Otherwise, we use the *size* function to return the size of each dimension.

The following is an example of how to use the *constructor* and *display* methods:

```
>> A = list(5, 'foo', 3.14, [2,3;4,5])

A =
  1: double(1)
     5

  2: char(3)
foo
```

```
3: double(1)
  3.1400

4: double(2  2)
  2    3
  4    5
```

In this example, a new List object was instantiated and initialized with four elements: the scalar five, the string 'foo', the fixed-point number 3.14, and a two-dimensional array.

Lists can also be created by using other lists as elements. For example, the following command produces a list *B* that has a copy of list *A* as one of its elements:

```
>> B = list(15, A, 'armadillo')

B =
  1: double(1)
    15

  2: list(1)
    list object: 1-by-1

  3: char(9)
armadillo
```

Note the size of item 2 of list B. It indicates that the list contains one element, but we know that it has four! The problem arises because the inherited *size* method is not appropriate for our List class. We will fix the problem in the next section.

The Size Method

I hope that you have been typing in the methods for the List class. If you have, try invoking the *size* function on a list. You should get results similar to the following:

```
>> A = list(3,4,5)

A =
  1: double(1)
    3
  2: double(1)
    4
  3: double(1)
    5

>> size(A)
ans =
  1    1
```

This is not exactly what we want. The inherited *size* method returns 1×1, meaning that there is a single object of type *List* named *A*. We want the *size* method to return the number of elements in *A*. Therefore, we will redefine the *size* method for the List class. This is an example of polymorphism. Copy the code in Figure 9.5 into an M-file named *size.m*, and save it in the @*list* directory.

Now try using the *size* method for object *A*. The results should be more satisfactory. The *size* method now shows that there are three elements in list A:

```
>> size(A)
ans =
  3
```

```
1   function S = size(L,varargin)
2   % size(L) - returns the number of elements in list L
3   %          - varargin is used to catch other arguments
4   %               and ignore them.
5   S = length(L.elements);
```

Figure 9.5.   The *size* method for the List class.

The Append Method

The *append* method is used to append new objects to an existing list. The code in Figure 9.6 defines the *append* method for the List class.

The *append* method demonstrates both fixed- and variable-length arguments. The first argument, *L*, is a fixed-length argument. An object of the *List* class is expected. The remaining arguments (two through *nargin*-1) may be of any type and number.

```
1   function L = append(L, varargin)
2   % append - appends one or more new elements to list L
3   for Index = 1:nargin-1
4     numElements = length(L.elements);
5     L.elements(1,numElements+1) = varargin(Index);
6   end
```

Figure 9.6.   The *append* method for the List class.

The following example illustrates the use of the *append* method (note that the results of the method must be assigned back to *A* in order for *A* to change):

```
>> A = list(1,3)
A =
   1: double(1)
      1
   2: double(1)
      3
>> A = append(A,5)
A =
   1: double(1)
      1
   2: double(1)
      3
   3: double(1)
      5
```

The Remove Method

The *remove* method is used to remove the first occurrence of an element with the same value as the second argument. For example, the command

```
L = remove(L, 'foo')
```

returns a list with the first occurrence of the string 'foo' in the list L removed. To change L, the results must be assigned back to L.

If the element is not found in the list, the method has no effect. Figure 9.7 shows the definition of the *remove* method.

```
1   function L = remove(L, E)
2   % remove(L, element) - deletes the first occurrence
3   %                      of element E from List L
4   for Index = 1:length(L.elements)
5     if isequal(E, L.elements{Index})
6       L.elements(Index) = [];
7       return
8     end
9   end
```

Figure 9.7. The *remove* method for the List class.

The *for* loop successively checks each element in the list until a match is found or the end of the list is reached. Once a match is found and deleted, it is no longer necessary to continue the loop. The *return* statement (line 7) is used to exit the function immediately and return control to the calling code. This makes the method more efficient for very long lists.

To see what methods exist for a particular class, use the *methods* function. For example, to see the methods that have been defined so far for the List class, type

```
>> methods(list)
Methods for class list:
append   display   list   remove   size
```

PRACTICE 9.1!

The remove method can easily be modified to remove all occurrences of an element with a certain value. Write a method named *remove_all* that removes all occurrences of elements with the value E from list L. Use the following syntax:

```
L = remove_all(L, E)
```

The Reverse Method

The next method that we will define for the List class is a method that reverses the elements in the list. Note that we do not have to walk through all of the elements of the list to reverse the list; we only have to iterate halfway through the list to complete the reversal. Figure 9.8 shows the definition of the *reverse* method.

```
1   function L = reverse(L)
2   % reverse(L) - reverses the elements of list L
3   Len = length(L.elements);
4   for Index = 1:Len/2;
5     Temp = L.elements(Index);
6     L.elements(Index) = L.elements(Len - Index + 1);
7     L.elements(Len - Index + 1) = Temp;
8   end
```

Figure 9.8.   The *reverse* method for the List class.

Overloading an Operator

We now consider an example of overloading the + operator for the List class. In this case, we want the + sign to denote the concatenation of two lists. For example, assume the following lists A and B:

```
>> A = list(4, 'd');
>> B = list('e', [3 5]);
```

We want the following result:

```
>> A + B
ans =
  1: double(1)
     4
  2: char(1)
d
  3: char(1)
e
  4: double(2)
     3     5
```

To create a meaning for an operator, place an M-file in the class directory with the function name of the operator. The + sign is associated with the name *plus*. To see the function names that MATLAB associates with operators, type

```
>>help +
```

at the command line. Figure 9.9 shows the definition of our *plus* method for the List class.

```
1   function L1 = plus(L1, L2)
2   % plus - use the + operator to concatenate two lists
3   for Index = 1:length(L2.elements)
4     numElements = length(L1.elements);
5     L1.elements(numElements+1) = L2.elements(Index);
6   end
```

Figure 9.9.   The *plus* method for the List class.

PRACTICE 9.2!

The function name that is associated with the minus sign ($-$) is called *minus.m*. Overload the minus operator with a new meaning for List objects. The effect of the minus operator is to remove all objects in the second list from the first list. Given lists

```
A = list('foo', 4, 5, 6);
B = list(5, 6, 7);
```

it follows that *A-B* is

```
>> A-B
ans =
  1: char(1  3)
foo
  2: double(1)
    4
```

(*Hint*: Use the *remove_all* function that you created in Practice 9.1.)

9.6   ENCAPSULATION

Note that the data elements within a method are protected: They can be accessed only by using the object's methods. Try accessing the element field of a List object directly from the command line. The following error is returned, consistent with the principle of encapsulation:

```
>> A = list(5, [3 12]);
>> length(A.elements)
??? Access to an object's fields is only permitted
within its methods.
```

Next, try to use a List class method on an object that is not a List object.

```
>> A = [ 3 4 5];
>> append(A, 4)
??? No appropriate methods for function append.
```

MATLAB does not find an *append* method associated with A, since the only *append* method or function in my search path is part of the List class. Both the methods and the data of the List class are encapsulated.

APPLICATION! GRAPHICAL USER INTERFACE

A natural application of object-oriented programming is the design and implementation of a *graphical user interface* (also called a *GUI*). There is a natural mapping of software objects to objects on the screen, such as scrollbars, buttons, menus, and toolbars. It makes sense for screen objects to exist in a hierarchy of classes. For example, an OK button might belong to the OK Button class, which is a subclass of the Button class.

Most modern programming languages have a graphical toolkit that allows the user to build graphical user interfaces, or GUIs, visually. MATLAB's GUI builder is called GUIDE, which stands for Graphical User Interface Development Environment.

Let us build a very simple GUI consisting of a single push button that, when pushed, creates a plot. First, invoke GUIDE by typing *guide* at the command prompt:

```
>> guide
```

The Guide Layout editor will appear as shown in Figure 9.10. Using the Layout editor, you can drop

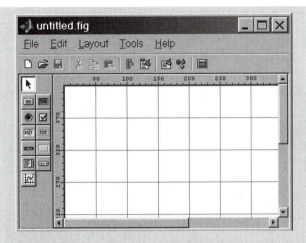

Figure 9.10. The GUIDE Layout editor.

GUI components onto the empty palette in the center of the editor window.

The toolbar along the left of the editor shows the available components. This toolbar is called the Component Palette. Click on the icon labeled *OK*, which is the top left icon on the Component Palette (just below the arrow). Now move your cursor over the layout area in the center of the screen, and click. A push button should appear as shown in Figure 9.11.

Figure 9.11. A sample push button.

Now choose **Tools → Activate Figure** from the Menu bar. The GUI will be saved into two files. The *fig* file contains the layout properties, and the M-file contains the actions that will occur when the button is pressed. An action associated with a graphical object is termed a *callback*. Give your new GUI the name *my_gui.fig*.

Once you have saved your file, a new box will appear that contains your push button. This box should be similar to Figure 9.12. You can actually push the button on your new GUI. The button responds by moving in

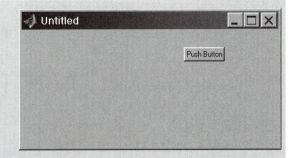

Figure 9.12. An activated push button GUI.

and out. However, the button does not do anything, because we have not told its callback to do anything.

In the Layout editor window, right click on the push button and choose **Edit Callback** from the drop-down menu. The file *my_gui.m* will automatically be opened in the M-file editor. The cursor will be taken to a section of code that looks like the following:

```
% ------------------------------------------------------------
function varargout = pushbutton1_Callback(h, eventdata, handles,
varargin)
% Stub for Callback of the uicontrol handles.pushbutton1.
disp('pushbutton1 Callback not implemented yet.')
```

This code is the callback for the push button. Let us change the *disp* statement to do something (e.g., plot the sine function). Remove the *disp* statement and replace it with the following two lines:

```
X = 0: 0.1 : 2 *pi;
plot(X, sin(X))
```

Save your M-file (*my_gui.m*) to a location that is in your MATLAB path, and again, choose **Tools → Activate Figure** from the Menu bar of the Layout editor. Your new GUI will appear, and now the push button actually does something: It creates a plot!

Spend some time reading the MATLAB on-line help for GUIDE. You should be able to pick up a lot on your own. For starters, try editing some of the push-button properties. From the Layout editor, choose **Tools → Property Inspector**. The Property Inspector window will appear. Play around by modifying some of the properties of your push button (e.g., color and font size). Choose **Tools → Activate Figure** to view the results. You can also invoke your new GUI by typing

```
>>my_gui
```

at the command line.

KEY TERMS

abstract data type	inheritance	object
class	instance	object-oriented programming
callback	instance variables	operator overloading
class variables	instantiation	polymorphism
constructor	iterator	pop
container class	linked list	principle of encapsulation
derived class	list	protocol
destructor	message	push
encapsulate	methods	queue
graphical user interface	modular programming	stack
GUI	multiple inheritance	subclass

NEW MATLAB FUNCTIONS, COMMANDS, AND RESERVED WORDS

class—creates an object (within a constructor)

class—returns the class of an object (outside of a constructor)

clear—destroys an object

guide—invokes MATLAB's GUIDE toolkit interface p. 9–19

inputname—returns the name of the input argument with the given number

methods—returns the methods for a given class p. 9–16

minus—the name of the method that is associated with the $(-)$ operator

plus—the name of the method that is associated with the $(+)$ operator p. 9–18

return—causes a function to immediately return to the caller

SOLUTIONS TO PRACTICE PROBLEMS

9.1.   Note in the following code that the *for* loop walks backwards through the list:

```
function L = remove_all(L, E)
% remove_all(L, E) - delete all occurrences
%                    of element E from List L
for Index = length(L.elements):-1:1
  if isequal(E, L.elements{Index})
    L.elements(Index) = [];
  end
end
```

Try walking forwards, and you will see that the algorithm doesn't work, since the list gets truncated inside the loop.

9.2.

```
function L1 = minus(L1, L2)
% plus - uses the '-' operator to remove items
%        in L2 from L1.
for Index = 1:length(L2.elements)
  L1 = remove_all(L1, L2.elements{Index});
end
```

Problems

1.   Write a Stack class that has the following methods: *stack* (the constructor), *push*, and *pop*. The syntax and definitions for *push* and *pop* are as follows:

- *push(S, E1, E2, ...)* pushes one or more elements *E* onto the top of stack *S* and returns a new *S*.
- *pop(S)* pops the top element from the top of stack *S* and returns the popped element and the new stack as [*E S*]. For example,

```
>> [E S] = pop(S)
```

will return the popped element into E and the new stack into S.

The Stack class need only handle scalars for this problem.

2. What happens if your stack is empty? Does the pop method create an error? Write a Boolean method *is_empty* for the Stack class. The method should take a Stack object as an argument and return True (1) if stack *S* is empty and False (0) otherwise. Use *is_empty* in your *pop* method to deal with an empty stack.

3. Write a *display* method for the Stack class. Here is one example of how a stack could be displayed:

```
>> A = stack
A =
        Top-------
    Bottom-------
>> A = push(A, 12)
A =
        Top-------
                12
    Bottom-------
>> A = push(A, 4.2)
A =
        Top-------
                4.2
                12
    Bottom-------
>> A = push(A, 5)
A =
        Top-------
                5
                4.2
                12
    Bottom-------
>> [E A] = pop(A)
E =
        5
A =
        Top-------
                4.2
                12
    Bottom-------
```

You may be able to design a better method.

4. Write a Circle class with the following methods:

- *constructor(R, Color)* creates a circle object with radius *R* and line color *Color*. The default radius is 1. The colors are the same symbols used in the

LineSpec argument of the *plot* command: 'r' = red, 'g' = green, 'b' = *blue*, etc. The constructor does not plot the circle; it only creates a Circle object.

- *display(C)* displays the name, radius, and color of a Circle object. The display method does not plot the Circle object; it only displays the object's characteristics. (Be patient, we will get to the *draw* method in Problem 6.)

You will need to define several numerical fields for the structure array that you use in your constructor method. These fields will hold the radius and color values. You no longer need the cell array *elements* as part of the structure.

Sample output is as follows:

```
>> A = circle(5,'r')
Circle object A =
   Radius: 5
    Color: r
```

5. Write the following two methods for the Circle class:

- *circumference(C)* returns the circumference of circle *C*.
- *area(C)* returns the area of circle *C*.

Sample output is

```
>> B = circle(56.3, 'b')
Circle object B =
   Radius: 56.3
    Color: b
>> circumference(B)
ans =
   353.7433
>> area(B)
ans =
   9.9579e+003
```

6. Write a *draw* method for the Circle class. The call *draw(C)* should plot circle *C* with the object's own radius and color. The results of the following commands are shown in Figure 9.13 (except that your plot should draw a red circle):

```
>> A = circle(5,'r')
Circle object A =
   Radius: 5
    Color: r
>> draw(A)
```

7. Write a method for the List class called *list2str*. The method takes a single List object as an argument and returns a string. The string should separate elements in the list with commas, enclose the list in parentheses, and bracket arrays with [ ]. For example, list *A* contains, respectively, a double scalar, a 1 × 2 vector, and the string 'chicken'. For this problem, your code should be able to handle scalars, vectors, and strings. Sample output is

```
>> A = list('foo', 5, [4 5]);
>> list2str(A)
ans =
('foo', 5, [4  5])
```

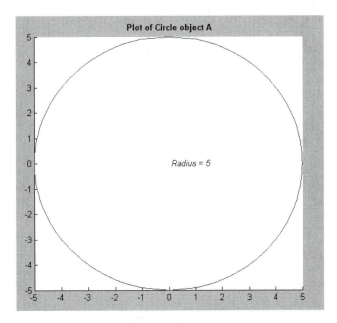

Figure 9.13. Results of the draw method on object *A*.

8. Extend the *list2str* method to include lists that contain two-dimensional arrays as elements. Display the array in one row, using a semicolon as a row delimiter. Sample output is

```
>> A = list([3 5; 14 2; 3 4], 'chicken');
>> list2str(A)
ans =
([3 5; 14 2; 3 4], 'chicken')
```

9. Extend the *list2str* method to include lists that contain other lists as elements. Use recursion to implement your solution. Sample output is as follows:

```
>> A = list(5, 'foo');
>> B = list(A, [3 4 5]);
>> list2str(B)
ans =
( (5, 'foo'), [3 4 5])
```

Here's another sample output session:

```
>> A = list(4, 5, 6);
>> B = list([9 9; 10,10]);
>> C = list('a', 'b', 'c');
>> D = list(A, B, C)
>> list2str(D)
ans =
((4, 5, 6), ([9  9; 10 10]), ('a', 'b', 'c'))
```

10

Software Development

10.1 INTRODUCTION

The art of software development involves writing reliable, efficient, error-resistant, and reusable code. One of my friends states that he likes to write code that is "lean, mean, and error free." There is a vast difference between writing short code segments such as the examples in this text and writing large real-world software applications. Software development merits a textbook of its own and is typically taught as part of a software-engineering course.

Writing a large real-world application usually requires the consideration of one or more of the following issues:

- Applications may require multiple graphical user interfaces that interact in complex ways.
- Considerations must be made for dealing with changes to the software, including upgrades, new versions, and bug fixes.
- Real-world applications often model complex dynamic systems that cannot be implemented with a simple single-threaded solution.
- Real-world applications are so complex that the design of the software application becomes the most time-consuming task.
- Large applications are usually written by a group of programmers. The issues of group dynamics, task sharing, and project management are formidable.
- Applications may need to be executed on several platforms under several operating systems and may need to interface with software modules written in other languages.

This is not a text on software engineering. However, every programmer should understand some of the issues related to writing reliable, reusable code. This chapter will cover

OBJECTIVES

After reading this chapter, you should be able to

- Describe the two main types of program errors.
- Write code that checks for valid inputs.
- Use the MATLAB debugger to locate and fix program bugs.
- Understand how algorithmic complexity affects a program's efficiency.
- Determine the complexity of a function or code segment.
- Vectorize your MATLAB code.
- Profile a MATLAB program.
- Understand how to compile and call C programs from MATLAB.

two of these issues in depth: reliability and efficiency. Topics that we will cover in less detail include source code control, compilation, and interfacing with other programming languages.

10.2   SOFTWARE RELIABILITY

One area that every programmer must face is the detection of errors. An error may arise from a number of sources. Methods for locating and tracking an error, called a *bug*, are part of a discipline in its own right. We call this discipline *quality assurance*. Even with extensive testing, errors occur when a program of significant complexity is executed in a real-world environment. A goal of a programmer is to catch errors before they occur. We call this activity *debugging* our code. If errors cannot be detected and removed, then the programmer's goal is to write code that handles the errors gracefully. This enterprise is called *error handling* and is concerned with the management of errors as they occur at run time.

10.2.1   Types of Errors

Syntax Errors

Software errors fall into several categories. The simplest type of error, because it is usually the easiest to detect, is an error in the syntax of a program. The syntax of a language is the set of linguistic rules that define the structure of programming code. The requirement that a function definition start with the keyword *function* is an example of MATLAB syntax. The MATLAB interpreter interprets syntax rigidly and will not execute code in which it detects a syntax error.

The function in Figure 10.1 is intended to compute the sum of the squares of a vector. Executing the function produces the following error:

```
>> sum_sqr([1 2 3])
??? Error: File: c:\examples\sum_sqr.m Line: 8
  Column: 3
"end" expected, "End of Input" found.
```

```
1   function out = sum_sqr(A)

2   % sum_sqr(A)

3   %    Computes the sum of the squares of the elements

4   %    in vector A.

5   out = 0;

6   for Index = 1:length(A)

7     out = A(Index)^2;
```

Figure 10.1.   Function definition with errors.

The MATLAB interpreter detected the fact that the *for* loop did not have a corresponding *end* statement. Because *end* is a required syntactic element of a *for* loop, the absence of an *end* statement is an example of a syntax error. The program immediately terminates and displays an error message.

Algorithm Errors

A program may be syntactically correct and still produce incorrect results. One reason for this is that the program does not correctly solve the problem. That could be because the programmer did not correctly understand the problem, or it could be because the programmer did not correctly implement the solution. Either way, we call this error an *algorithm error* or semantics error. The code in Figure 10.1 contains an algorithm error: If the programmer corrects the syntax error by adding an *end* statement at line 8, the code produces the output:

```
>> sum_sqr([1 2 3])
ans =
      9
```

The algorithm correctly computes the square of each element in the vector, but the programmer has forgotten to add the results obtained. The correct code for line 7 should be

```
out = out + A(i)^2;
```

PRACTICE 10.1!

Find four errors in the following function, and identify each as a syntactic error or an algorithmic error:

```
1   function B = is_digit(Character)
2   %    is_digit - Boolean function, returns True if
3   %            C is a character digit, '0' - '9'
4   if ischar(C) and C >= 48 and C < 57
5     B = 1;
6   elseif
7     B = 0;
8   end
```

Input Errors

A common type of error is caused by incorrect input. Most of the example functions in this book have not checked for input errors. For example, the recursive function *my_factorial* shown in Figure 10.2 fails miserably if it is given an argument that is not a

```
1   function Out = my_factorial(N)
2   % my_factorial(N)
3   %    Computes the factorial of a nonnegative integer.
4   If N == 0        % base case for 0
5     Out = 1;
6   elseif N == 1    % base case for 1
7     Out = N;
8   else             % all other cases are recursive
9     Out = N * feval(@my_factorial, N-1);
10  end
```

Figure 10.2. A simple recursive solution for factorial.

nonnegative integer. When an incorrect argument is used, the following foreboding message is displayed:

```
>> my_factorial(-4)
??? Maximum recursion limit of 500 reached. Use
set(0,'RecursionLimit', N) to change the limit. Be
aware that exceeding your available stack space can
crash MATLAB and/or your computer.

Error in ==> c:\dave\examples\my_factorial.m
On line 8  ==>   out = N * feval(@my_factorial, N-1);
```

You can use the MATLAB internal variable *RecursionLimit* to limit the number of nested function calls that may be made. Usually, the default limit of 500 is adequate to tell us that we have an error in our code. With a recursive function, this usually means that we have not adequately defined the stopping condition. In fact, a review of the code in Figure 10.2 reveals that many arguments to *my_factorial* will result in an infinite recursion. These include negative numbers and fixed-point numbers.

It is good programming practice to test for invalid inputs and display an appropriate error message to the user. The foregoing error message tells the programmer something, but not anything particularly helpful for the user of the *my_factorial* function. The user needs to know *why* the input was incorrect (i.e., the input needs to be a nonnegative integer).

Figure 10.3 shows a revised version of *my_factorial* that checks for incorrect inputs. The logical expression

```
round(N)  ~= N
```

```
1   function out = my_factorial2(N)
2   % my_factorial(N)
3   %     Computes the factorial of a nonnegative integer.
4   % First, check for incorrect input
5   if round(N) ~= N | N <= 0
6     error('Input must be a nonnegative integer.')
7   else
8     if N == 0      % base case
9       out = 1;
10    elseif N == 1 % base case
11      out = N;
12    else
13      % recursive case
14      out = N * feval(@my_factorial2, N-1);
15    end
16  end
```

Figure 10.3. A revised version of *my_factorial* with argument checking.

tests whether the argument is not an integer. The second logical expression

```
N < 0
```

tests whether the argument is negative. The results of these two expressions are combined with the logical *OR* operator (|).

Note the use of the *error* function. This MATLAB library function displays a text string and then immediately returns control to the command line. In this case, lines 7–16 are not executed. In addition, any pending function calls are popped off the activation stack. If we use the new, improved *my_factorial2* with invalid arguments, a more appropriate error message is displayed:

```
>> my_factorial2(-4)
??? Error using ==> my_factorial2
Input must be a nonnegative integer.
```

PRACTICE 10.2!

> Try calling *my_factorial2* with other arguments. Can you find an argument type that is not tested by *my_factorial2*? What about nonscalar values? Add another condition to the logical expression in line 5 of Figure 10.3 that tests for nonscalar values.

The last error message generated in a MATLAB session is stored. You can retrieve the last error message by using the *lasterr* function:

```
>> lasterr
ans =
Error using ==> my_factorial2
Input must be a nonnegative integer.
```

10.2.2 Finding Errors

Finding program errors or bugs can be a frustrating and time-consuming task. What makes debugging even more annoying is that the most obstinate bug seems simple once you locate it. Fortunately, there are time-honored rules of thumb for locating programming errors. This section lists some hints from expert programmers. The next section demonstrates the use of a tool designed especially for locating difficult bugs: the MATLAB debugger.

Divide and Conquer

The most-used debugging technique is to break a program into smaller parts and test each part separately. In a large application, you can execute each function as a stand-alone code segment. Within a function, you can test each selection statement or loop independently.

Display Partial Results

It is difficult to break up a single loop into much smaller code segments. If a bug is part of a loop, it is usually helpful to display partial results as the loop executes. The simplest way to display partial results is to remove the semicolons that serve to hide such results. Alternatively, you can temporarily add a *disp* statement to the code.

If the loop iterates many times, the results may scroll past the screen faster than you can read them. There are several commands that will temporarily halt program execution. The simplest is the *pause* statement, which halts execution until any key is pressed.

Another command that temporarily halts program execution is the *keyboard* command. If you add a keyboard statement to a code segment, execution will stop and control will pass to the keyboard. The letter *K* is added to the prompt to notify you that the keyboard command has been invoked. The user may modify any local variables or type any MATLAB commands. To continue execution, the user types *return* and then presses the **Return** key.

You can use the *echo* command to turn on the display of each line of code as it is interpreted. The command can be added inside a function or can be called outside the function by using the function name as an argument. The following example turns on echoing for the *my_sqrt* function:

```
>> echo my_sqrt on
```

Test Interactively

You can use the MATLAB interpreter interactively to verify the action of short code segments or expressions. This is useful for testing your understanding of a code segment. For example, you could use the following code segment to verify your understanding of a conditional expression.

```
>> x = 5
>> x < 3 | ~(x > 7)
ans =
     1
```

Read Error Messages

Become familiar with the MATLAB error messages. You will quickly learn to recognize the most common syntax and run-time errors. The MATLAB errors messages contain a lot of information.

MATLAB usually displays the line number of the offending line of code in the message. The following example shows an error message that points directly to line 14 and column 24 of the named file:

```
> my_sqrt(2)
??? Error: File: C:\Dave\Examples\my_sqrt.m Line: 14
  Column: 24
")" expected, "identifier" found.
```

The message indicates that a right parenthesis is missing.

Some syntax error messages will point to the offending place in a line of code. MATLAB uses the vertical bar as the pointer symbol. The following example points to the location of the missing parenthesis:

```
>> (a +b
??? (a +b
        |
Error: ")" expected, "end of line" found.
```

Write Test Procedures

One method that software engineers use to validate program code is to write a series of tests for a function. The tests can be run whenever the function needs to be validated. A validation test of this type is often used to detect whether changes to the code have broken it. In other words, the test is used to see whether the function has regressed, and, accordingly, we call this type of test a *regression test*.

The script in Figure 10.4 tests the *is_palindrome* subfunction defined within the *get_match* function in Figure 10.5. The execution of *test_palindrome* produces the following results:

```
>> test_palindrome
Passed test 1.
Passed test 2.
Passed test 3.
```

```
function test_palindrome
% script to test the is_palindrome function
if is_palindrome('ada')
  disp('Passed test 1.')
end
if ~is_palindrome('adA')
  disp('Passed test 2.')
end
if is_palindrome('12345678900987654321')
  disp('Passed test 3.')
end
```

Figure 10.4. A test procedure for *is_palindrome*.

PRACTICE 10.3!

The following function is supposed to sort the odd columns of a matrix in ascending order:

```
1 function Out = sort_oddcols(A)
2 % sort_oddcols - sorts the odd columns of
3 %                matrix A in ascending order.
4 for Index = 1:size(A,2)-1
5   if rem(Index,2) == 0
6     A(:,Index) = sort(A(:,Index));
7   end
8 end
9 Out = A;
```

Use some of the tricks just described to debug the errors in the code. Sample correct output is

```
>> A = [1 2 3 4; 4 3 2 1; 0 1 0 8; 2 2 2 2]
>> sort_oddcols(A)
ans =
     0     2     0     4
     1     3     2     1
     2     1     2     8
     4     2     3     2
```

```
1   function Out = get_match(Str)
2   %  get_match(Str)
3   %     Returns all palindromes from a string of words.
4
5   % Main function
6   Remainder = Str;
7   NewStr = ' ';
8   while ~isempty(remainder)
9     [Word, Remainder] = strtok(Remainder);
10    if is_palindrome(Word)
11      NewStr = [NewStr, ' ', Word];
12    end
13  end
14  Out = NewStr;
15
16  % Subfunction
17  function Out = is_palindrome(Word)
18  %  is_palindrome(Word)
19  %     Returns true(1) if word is a palindrome,
20  %     otherwise, returns false(0). Word is a string
21  %     that does not contain white space.
22  Out = 1;
23  for Index = 1:length(Word)
24    if Word(Index) ~= Word(length(Word)-Index+1)
25      Out = 0;
26      break;
27    end
28  end
```

Figure 10.5.   Definition of the *get_match* function.

10.2.3 The MATLAB Debugger

The MATLAB debugger is a tool that allows you to stop and restart a program during its execution. While the program is stopped, the states of variables and function calls may be explored and even modified on the fly. A *breakpoint* is a pre-set place in the code where you wish to stop during the debugging process.

The effective use of the debugging tool involves learning how to stop and start the program where you want it to stop and start. One way to stop execution is to set one or more breakpoints. Another is to tell the debugger to stop on a warning or an error. A third way is to step through the code one line at a time.

There are two versions of the debugging tool, and the choice of which one to use is a matter of preference. One version employs a graphical interface, and the other is a set of functions used at the command line.

Graphical Editor/Debugger

The graphical version of the MATLAB debugger is invoked after opening an M-file in the MATLAB editor. Two items on the menu bar pertain to debugging: the *Breakpoints* and *Debug* items.

Figure 10.6 depicts the Breakpoints drop-down menu. The items on this menu tell the debugger when to stop. Before using these commands, you must first save your M-file. The options are as follows:

- **Set/Clear Breakpoint.** Select this item or use the function key **F12** to set or clear a breakpoint. When you create a breakpoint, a red dot is placed in the left margin of the chosen line. A breakpoint can be set only on an executable line. A breakpoint cannot be set on the function definition line or on a comment line.

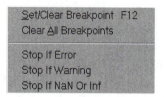

Figure 10.6. The BreakPoints drop-down menu.

- **Clear All Breakpoints.** Clear all breakpoints at once.
- **Stop if Error.** Stop execution if an error occurs.
- **Stop if Warning.** Stop execution if a warning occurs.
- **Stop if NaN or Inf.** Stop execution if an expression results in NaN (not a number) or Inf (infinity).

Figure 10.7 shows the Debug drop-down menu. You can use the items on this menu to stop and start program execution. The menu items, together with their respective shortcut keys, are explained as follows:

- **Step (F10).** Execute the current line.
- **Step In (F11).** Step into a function. This option is useful if the breakpoint contains a function call. For example, the Step In command makes a recursive

Figure 10.7. The Debug drop-down menu.

call to the function *my_factorial2* shown in Figure 10.8 because line 15 in Figure 10.9 is set as a breakpoint.

- **Step Out (Shift + F11).** Finish executing the current function, return to caller, and then pause.
- **Run (F5).** If the M-file contains unsaved changes, this item will appear as **Save and Run**. The command starts execution of the program. If the program requires one or more input arguments, don't use this command. Instead, start the program from the command window.
- **Continue (F5).** If the program is already executing, then Continue appears instead of Run. Use Continue to continue to the next stopping point.
- **Go Until Cursor.** Continue execution until the cursor is reached.
- **Exit Debug Mode.** Resume normal execution without debugging.

```
1    function out = my_factorial2(N)
2    % my_factorial(N)
3    %     Computes the factorial of a nonnegative integer.
4    %
5    %check correct arguments
6    if length(N) ~= 1 | round(N) ~= N | N <= 0
7        error('Input must be a nonnegative scalar
            integer.')
8    else
9       if N == 0     % base case
10         out = 1;
11      elseif N == 1 % base case
12         out = N;
13      else
14         % recursive case
15         out = N * feval(@my_factorial2, N-1);
16      end
17   end
```

Figure 10.8.   The *my_factorial2* function.

Sample Debugging Session

We will use the *my_factorial2* function shown in Figure 10.8 to demonstrate the debugger commands. First, however, load or type *my_factorial2* into your MATLAB editor.

During the debugging process, you can view the contents of the local workspace by using the Workspace window. The activation stack is made visible by clicking the item labeled Stack on the toolbar. Perform the following steps:

1.   Set breakpoints at lines 11 and 15. These lines are the base case of $N = 1$ and the recursive case of the *my_factorial2* function, respectively.

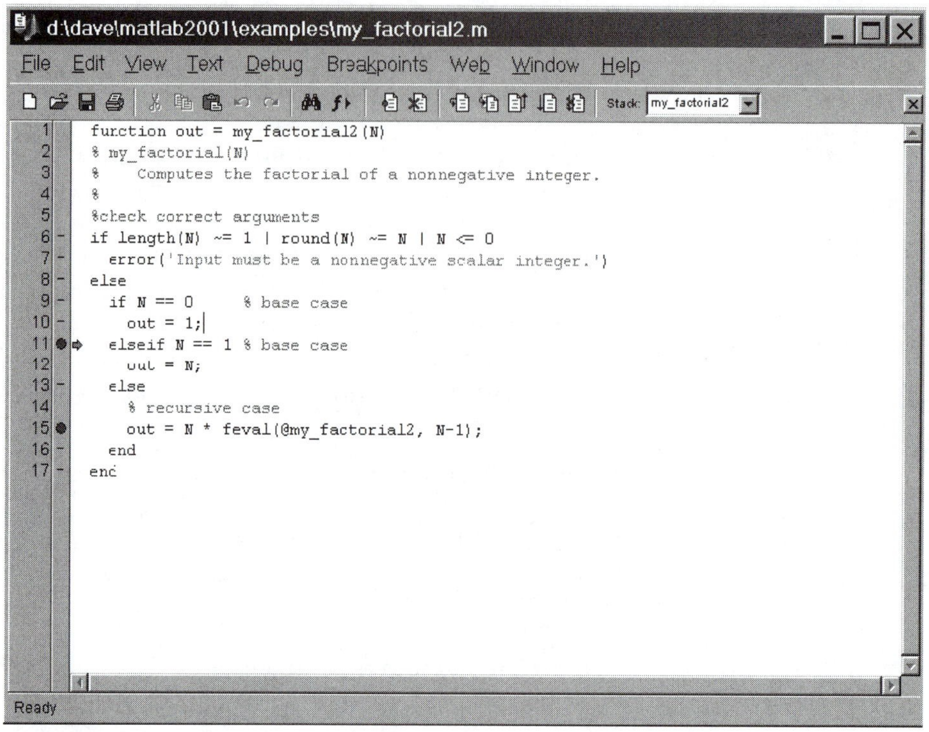

Figure 10.9. A sample debugging session.

2. In the Command window, type

```
>> my_factorial2(8)
```

3. The Editor window will now appear as depicted in Figure 10.9. Execution has stopped at line 11.

4. Use the F10 key to step through the program one line at a time. Each time line 15 is executed, click on the drop-down menu titled *Stack* in the Editor window. Notice the stack frames being added and subtracted to the stack.

5. Also, open the Array Editor and watch the value of *N* change as the program enters and exits each recursive call.

Command Line Debugging

The commands in the graphical editor have equivalent text commands that you can enter at the command line. For example, the command *dbstop* is used to set breakpoints, and the command *dbclear* is used to clear breakpoints. Most users prefer the graphical debugging interface. Table 10.1 lists the primary command line debugging commands.

10.2.4 Exception Handling

We call errors that occur during the execution of a program *run-time errors*. *Exceptions* are serious, often fatal, run-time errors. The process of dealing with serious run-time errors is called *exception handling*. Exceptions usually result from running out of some resource, such as memory; the inability to locate some resource, such as a file; or input that results in an impossible calculation, such as divide by zero. If you execute a program

TABLE 10.1. Command line debugging commands.

Name	Function
dbclear	clear breakpoints
dbcont	continue or resume execution
dbquit	quit debugging mode
dbstack	display the current function call stack
dbstatus	list all breakpoints
dbstep	step forward and execute one or more lines of code
dbstop	set breakpoints
dbtype	list an M-file with added line numbers (so that breakpoints can be set)

from the command line, an error in one of the functions of the program causes it to terminate. An error message is usually printed to the screen. Program termination and displaying an error message may be satisfactory for an interactive session. However, uncontrolled program termination is not always satisfactory.

Consider, for instance, a program that performs calculations on a supercomputer. The program may run for many hours or days, performing some complex computation. If the program happens to run across a bad data point on the fifth day, it would be nice if the program did not crash at that point. One possibility is for the program to skip that data point and continue processing, perhaps writing the bad data to a log.

Another example is an embedded program that runs on a satellite. The program that controls a rocket's flight to Mars cannot crash and wait for user input. The program must deal with errors as they occur and must continue to run.

Garbled or missing input data are common causes of exceptions. Computations that reach boundary conditions, such as an index that is out of range or an attempt to divide by zero, also cause exceptions.

One goal for the programmer is to detect errors before the program crashes. The programmer can then consciously decide how to handle the error. A number of alternatives exist:

1. If possible, the error may be bypassed, with the program continuing to run. You could skip the item that caused the error, or a default value could be used. Consider a program that uses repeated data from thousands of readings to predict the weather. A few missing data points are probably not going to change the overall result. In this case, skipping bad data and continuing the computation is a good solution.

2. The program may terminate, but you could shut the application down in a controlled manner. Before termination, you may wish to save some internal variables to a file or write a detailed error message to the screen or a log. One example that warrants this option is a network server that is about to crash due to an internal error. It would be convenient if the program logged the error to a file and saved any internal state, such as pending service requests. That way, once the server is restarted, it could continue where it left off and handle any pending requests. Service may have been delayed, but no requests were lost.

3. If the program is interactive, the user can be prompted for different input, and the program can continue instead of crashing.

4. Explicit error messages can be displayed or logged. MATLAB usually displays informative error messages, but you can make them more explicit, if necessary, by catching the errors.

MATLAB provides several facilities for detecting errors before they crash a program. One facility is the *try ... catch* statement. The syntax of this statement is shown in Figure 10.10. Normally, the block of code between the reserved words *try* and *catch* is executed. If an error occurs, control passes immediately to the block of code between the reserved words *catch* and *end*, and that block is executed.

```
try

   ...

   ...

catch

   ...

   ...

end
```

Figure 10.10. The syntax of the *try ... catch* statement.

One error that frequently appears during the use of MATLAB is an incorrect array size. If you try to add two arrays whose dimensions do not agree, MATLAB displays the following error:

```
>> A = [1, 2; 10, 11];
>> B = [4, 8];
>> A+B
??? Error using ==> +
Matrix dimensions must agree.
```

Figure 10.11 shows a new definition of addition that uses the standard MATLAB plus operator (+) to perform addition on arrays. However, we wrap up the addition operation with a *try ... catch* statement. This allows us to *trap* the error and display our own error messages. The following session shows the use of the new *add* function:

```
>> A = [1, 2; 10, 11];
>> B = [4, 8];
>> add(A,B)
Error: Argument dimensions do not agree.
   The size of the 1st argument is [2 2].
   The size of the 2nd argument is [1 2].
```

This modification of the error message is only one of the possibilities one might employ for dealing with a dimension mismatch. An alternative solution is to truncate the largest argument until the matrix dimensions agree and then to reperform the operation.

10.2.5 Handling Warnings

Less serious error conditions cause MATLAB to issue a warning message, but not to terminate a program. An example is the method by which MATLAB masks some floating-point exceptions.

```
1   function out = add(A, B)
2   %  add(A,B)
3   %       Adds two matrices, provides expanded error
4   %       message.
5   try
6      out = A + B;
7   catch
8      disp('Error: Argument dimensions do not agree.')
9      str = mat2str(size(A));
10     disp(['  The size of the 1st argument is ',str,'.'])
11     str = mat2str(size(B));
12     disp(['  The size of the 2nd argument is ',str,'.'])
13  end
```

Figure 10.11. Sample use of the *try . . . catch* statement.

In some programming languages, division by zero results in a floating-point exception. If the exception is not trapped and handled by the programmer, the program will "crash." If MATLAB detects a division by zero, it returns the special value *Inf*, which represents the IEEE value for positive infinity. If 0/0 is detected, MATLAB returns the special value *NaN*, which represents the IEEE value for *not a number*. In addition, MATLAB returns a warning message, as in the following examples:

```
>> 5/0
Warning: Divide by zero.
ans =
    Inf
>> 0/0
Warning: Divide by zero.
ans =
    NaN
```

Any further operations that contain the values *Inf* or *NaN* will result in *Inf* or *NaN*, respectively. The following is an example:

```
>> C = [ 3, 5/0, 14.3]
Warning: Divide by zero.
C =
    3.0000       Inf    14.3000
>> sum(C)
ans =
    Inf
```

Suppose now that we want to obtain the sum of the quotients of two vectors. MATLAB allows us to do this easily with the *sum* statement:

```
>> A = [4 6 8];
>> B = [2 3 4];
```

```
>> sum(A./B)
ans =
      6
```

However, if any of the quotients result in a floating-point warning, the operation fails. The following session demonstrates such a failure:

```
>> A = [4 6 8];
>> B = [2 0 4];
>> sum(A./B)
Warning: Divide by zero.
ans =
      Inf
```

We may want to perform a sum of quotients, but ignore any quotients that return a floating-point warning. Our first attempt might be to catch the exception by means of a *try . . . catch* statement. However, this will not work as expected, because division by zero returns only a warning, not an error.

Accordingly, we must deal with floating-point exceptions differently than we do other exceptions, because MATLAB masks these errors and returns a warning and a special value instead. The function in Figure 10.12 demonstrates how to turn off warning messages and trap floating-point exceptions. The function *sum_div* calculates the sum of the quotients of each respective element in two vectors, ignoring any quotients that return *Inf* or *NaN*.

```
1   function Out = sum_div(X, Y)
2   %  sum_div(X, Y)
3   %       Calculates the sum of the respective quotients
4   %       of the elements in vectors A and B. Quotients
5   %       that result in a floating-point exception are
6   %       ignored.
7   warning off;
8   Out = 0;
9   for Index = 1:length(X)
10    Element = X(Index)/Y(Index);
11    if isfinite(Element)
12      Out = Out + Element;
13    end
14  end
```

Figure 10.12. Function that demonstrates handling warnings.

The following example demonstrates the use of *sum_div*:

```
>> A = [0 2 4 6 8];
>> B = [0 2 1 0 2];
>> sum_div(A, B)
ans =
      9
```

Note that warnings generated during the execution of the function are not displayed. Therefore, it is not necessary to turn warnings back on after the *sum_div* function finishes executing. The lifetime of the command to turn warnings off is the same as the lifetime of the execution of the function. Once the function finishes executing, the warning flag returns to its previous status.

10.3 SOFTWARE EFFICIENCY

An important area of concern for programmers is the efficiency of an application. Programs must run in a reasonable amount of time and must use a reasonable amount of system resources, or they are worthless.

One of the most common tasks for programmers is to make their code more efficient. If the amount of memory or disk resources is a problem, we need to make the program more *space efficient*. If the program is too slow, we need to make it more *time efficient*.

In the scientific and engineering domain, many algorithms require large computational resources. Computer memory is a limited resource, and once it is used up by an application, the operating system must resort to saving partial results on computer disks. Disk access is an order of magnitude slower than memory access.

Although the amount of physical memory and disk space for personal computers and workstations is cheap and becoming cheaper by the year, the amount of space on embedded systems, such as cellular telephones and personal digital assistants, is more limited.

The time efficiency of a program may be critical in a real-time or embedded system. Some examples are code that is resident on satellites or code that is used in air traffic control systems. A gross example is the prediction of weather: A weather prediction program is not useful if it is so slow that it does not finish predicting Tuesday's weather until Wednesday.

More mundane software applications can still benefit from code optimization. We call the amount of time it takes a computer to respond to a keystroke or other user action the *interactive response time*. Programmers who create user interfaces typically spend a lot of time decreasing the interactive response time of their applications.

An area of special concern for efficiency is that of networking. Embedded applications that control network routers and Internet hosts must run efficiently, or all other network applications will slow down.

One type of Internet application that is especially concerned with time and space efficiency is the search engine. Often, time efficiency can be increased at the expense of space efficiency and vice versa. This is called the *space–time trade-off*. Search algorithms are victims of this kind of trade-off.

10.3.1 Algorithmic Complexity

Definition of Algorithmic Complexity

A number of factors contribute to the time efficiency of a program: the speed of the CPU, the quality of the program code, the amount of memory on the computer, the speed of the I/O devices such as the network and disk drives.

Another factor that contributes to time efficiency is the nature of the algorithm itself, called the algorithm's *complexity*. The *time complexity* of an algorithm is a measure of the time it takes the algorithm to complete execution as a function of the input size. If n is the size of the input, then we are interested in how fast the computational time increases as n increases. (Most of what follows concerning time complexity also applies to *space complexity*.)

We are interested in the worst-case, or *asymptotic complexity*, of an algorithm. The asymptotic complexity of an algorithm is also called the *order of complexity* and is denoted by the Greek letter omicron, or *big-O* notation.

An algorithm that has constant complexity is denoted as $O(1)$. An example of a piece of MATLAB code that has constant order of complexity is the statement

```
y = 4 * x - 3;
```

where x is a scalar. No matter what scalar value we assign to x, it will take MATLAB approximately the same amount of time to compute y. The speed of the processor is not important for the determination of complexity. What is important is that, on the *same* processor, the complexity of the algorithm is constant.

An example of a linear complexity is a typical *for* loop. For example, the time it takes to execute the following loop is linearly related to the loop variable n:

```
for i = 1:n
    y = 4 * x -3;
end
```

As the size of n is increased, the time it takes to iterate through the loop roughly increases as $c \times n$ for some constant c. For the sake of complexity, we ignore the constant term and say that the preceding example has complexity $O(n)$.

Algorithms that are more complex may have several terms in their growth equation. For example, the following code contains a nested loop, and the assignment statement is executed n^2 times:

```
for i = 1:n
    for j = 1:n
        y = 4 * x - j;
    end
end
```

The complexity of this algorithm is said to be $O(n^2)$.

The complexity of an algorithm is determined by evaluating the growth function of the algorithm. If the growth function is $f(n)$, then

$$f(n) = O(g(n))$$

if and only if there exist positive constants c and n_0 such that

$$f(n) \leq c \cdot g(n)$$

for all $n \geq n_0$.

In other words, $g(n)$ is an upper bound for $f(n)$. There are many functions that could satisfy $g(n)$, but we attempt to find the function with the smallest order. For example, the growth function may be

$$f(n) = 3n^3 + 4n - 5.$$

Certainly, a function of $O(n^4)$ satisfies $g(n)$. However, a function of $O(n^3)$ also does, so we choose the smaller order and say that $f(n)$ is $O(n^3)$.

Other complexity classes may have a time complexity that is logarithmic or exponential. There is an order to the complexity classes. Table 10.2 summarizes the most common complexity classes and arranges them in decreasing order of complexity.

TABLE 10.2. Common Complexity Classes.

Name	Order
Exponential	$O(c^n)$
Polynomial	$O(n^c)$
Logarithmic	$O(log\ n)$
Linear	$O(n)$
Constant	$O(1)$

To find the complexity of a growth function, follow these steps:

1. Ignore the constant terms.
2. If nonconstant terms are summed, choose the term with the highest complexity and ignore the others.
3. If nonconstant terms are multiplied, the order is the product of each term's order.

PRACTICE 10.4!

Determine the time complexity of an algorithm with the growth function

$$f(n) = \log(n/2)n^3 - 10 \log(n) + 4n^2 - 5n + 10$$

Effect of Growth Rate

The effect of a rapid growth rate on the time it takes to complete an algorithm can be catastrophic in real-world applications. Consider an algorithm that classifies chemical compounds according to some characteristic (e.g., two-dimensional structure). The algorithm may be algorithmically correct and may be tested on a small set of compounds. As the number of compounds increases, the time that it takes to complete the classification also increases. Assume that three programmers write three different versions of code to perform the classification. The first programmer's solution has a growth rate of $O(n^2)$, the second programmer's solution is $O(n\ log\ n)$, and the third is linear, or $O(n)$.

Given that each of the three algorithms can classify 100 compounds per second, Table 10.3 summarizes the amount of time that it would take to classify larger sets of compounds. When a 5,000-compound set is input, the $O(n)$ algorithm takes a little over eight minutes. The $O(n^2)$ algorithm takes over an hour to compute. Sets of 10,000

TABLE 10.3. Computation time of three algorithms of varying complexity.

Number of Compounds	$n/10$ sec	$(n\ log\ n)/23$ sec	$n^2/100$ sec
10	1	1	1
100	10	20	100
1,000	100	300	10,000
2,000	200	661	40,000
3,000	300	1,044	90,000
4,000	400	1,442	160,000
5,000	500	1,851	250,000
10,000	17 min	1 hr	11 days

compounds are not unreasonable for this application. An algorithm of $O(n^2)$ becomes infeasible for an input set of that size. By contrast, $O(n\ log\ n)$ or $O(n)$ algorithm scales well enough to be feasible.

If an algorithm is going to be used only for small input sets, the complexity of the solution is not that important. However, if larger data sets are to be used, the complexity of the algorithm is very important.

Finding Growth Rates of Algorithms

Thus far, we have exemplified algorithms in just a few code segments. Several types of algorithms in real applications suffer from rapid growth rates and deserve special consideration. Among these are search algorithms and sort algorithms. Searching and sorting are performed in many real-world applications, especially those using large databases. In this section, we will describe two sorting algorithms and then determine the growth rate of each.

The first sorting algorithm is called the *selection sort*. The general idea of the algorithm is to walk through each item in the list. Each item is then swapped with the smallest remaining item in the list. Figure 10.13 shows a pseudocode description of the selection sort algorithm.

In Figure 10.14, we present a function definition for selection sort. For purposes of illustration, we have not used MATLAB's built-in functions as shortcuts. We could have used the MATLAB built-in *min* function. However, we want to perform timing tests on our algorithm. Since MATLAB's built-in functions are compiled and highly optimized, mixing built-in functions with external ones would be like comparing apples and oranges.

```
for each item
    find smallest of the remaining items
    swap current item with the smallest (from previous step)
loop
```

Figure 10.13. A pseudocode description of selection sort.

Figure 10.15 shows the definition of the helper function *swap*. Since *swap* is used by other functions, it is not defined as a subfunction of *selectionSort*.

The growth rate of *selectionSort* can be determined by noticing that the algorithm is fundamentally a nested loop, nested to a depth of two. The outer loop, which begins at line 8, executes n times. The inner loop, which begins at line 11, executes $n - 1 + n - 2 + n - 3 + \ldots + 2 + 1$ times. This sum equals $n(n - 1)/2$, which is $O(n^2)$. The *swap* function is called in the outer loop and is thus called a maximum of n times. The n^2 term dominates, so we can say that the *selectionSort* algorithm is $O(n^2)$.

The *quick sort* is a more efficient sorting algorithm, with a methodology that partitions the vector that is to be sorted into two parts. The first part contains values less than or equal to a value called the *pivot value*. The second part contains values greater than the pivot value. The algorithm is repeated recursively for each partition. Figure 10.16 shows a pseudocode description of the quick sort algorithm, taken from [1].

```
1    function Out = selectionSort(A)
2    % selectionSort(A)
3    %      Implements the selection sort algorithm. Select
4    %      the minimum of the remaining items and swap it
5    %      with the current item.
6    Len = length(A);
7    % loop through all but last item
8    for Index1 = 1 : Len - 1
9      % find minimum of remaining items
10     lowIndex = Index1;
11     for Index2 = Index1 + 1 : Len
12       if A(Index2) < A(LowIndex)
13         LowIndex = Index2;
14       end
15     end
16     % if minimum item is smaller, swap
17     if A(Index1 > A(LowIndex)
18       A = swap(A, Index1, LowIndex);
19     end
20   end
21   Out = A;
```

Figure 10.14. Definition of the *selectionSort* function.

```
1 function Out = swap(A, N, M)
2 % swap(A, N, M)
3 %    Swaps elements N and M in vector A.
4 Temp = A(N);
5 A(N) = A(M);
6 A(M) = Temp;
7 Out = A;
```

Figure 10.15. Definition of the *swap* helper function.

The method for finding a pivot point does not have to be very sophisticated. The median of the vector is the best pivot value. However, the median can be costly to compute. A simple method is to start with the first element of the vector and find the first two unequal values. The second of these is then taken as the pivot point. Figure 10.17 shows the function definition for this simple method.

```
Find a pivot value
Split the vector into two parts around the pivot value
Repeat the algorithm on the left part
Repeat the algorithm on the right part
```

Figure 10.16. A pseudocode description of the quick sort algorithm.

```
 1 function PivotValue = findPivot(A, Len)
 2 % pivotValue = findPivot(A, Len)
 3 %     Returns element closest to median of
 4 %     vector A with length Len.
 5 pivotValue = 0;
 6 for Index = 2 : Len
 7   if A(Index) < A(Index - 1)
 8     PivotValue = A(Index-1);
 9     break
10   elseif A(Index) > A(Index - 1)
11     PivotValue = A(Index);
12     break
13   end
14 end
```

Figure 10.17. Function for finding a pivot point.

The next section of the quick sort algorithm splits the vector along the pivot point. The goal is to efficiently move all of the elements less than or equal to the pivot value to the left side of the vector and move all of the elements greater than the pivot value to the right side.

Figure 10.18 shows a solution to the splitting problem. The gist of the algorithm is to keep two pointers, called left and right. The left element is swapped with the right element. Then the left pointer is incremented and the right pointer is decremented. Both then "walk toward each other" until they meet.

Figure 10.19 defines the main *quickSort* function. The algorithm calls *findPivot* and *split*, as well as the *swap* function. You can define each of these functions as either subfunctions or private functions to *quickSort*. You should be able to follow the pseudocode algorithm as you walk through the main function.

A base case has been added (Pivot==0) to stop the recursion. In addition, a small optimization handles the case of vector size two. This optimization has been coded without using recursion, in order to save stack space and avoid exceeding the recursion limit.

In the next section, we will evaluate and compare the computational speed of the quick sort and selection sort algorithms.

```
 1 function [A, Right] = split(A, Pivot, Len)
 2 % [A, Rght] = split(A, Pivot, Len)
 3 %    Splits vector A so that elements < Pivot are
 4 %    on the left and elements >= Pivot are on the
 5 %    right. Returns split vector A and right = index
 6 %    of the first element >= pivot.
 7 Left = 1;
 8 Right = Len;
 9 while Left <= Right
10    % swap left and right elements
11    A = swap(A, Left, Right);
12    % increment left marker
13    while A(Left) < Pivot
14       Left = Left + 1;
15    end
16    % decrement right marker
17    while A(Right) >= Pivot
18       Right = Right - 1;
19    end
20 end
```

Figure 10.18.   Function for splitting a vector around a pivot point.

10.3.2 Array Optimization Techniques

As you know by now, MATLAB is designed for array computation. The basic data type is an array, and the MATLAB function library contains many functions that are highly optimized for array computation.

You should become acquainted with the efficiency gains that can be made by using array computation effectively. The first part of learning to do so is to master subscripting. The MATLAB colon operator provides a powerful means for accessing and manipulating arrays. You can use the logical indexing feature for filtering arrays. Another way to use arrays effectively is to learn vectoring operations. Frequently, you can avoid program loops by selecting vector operations.

Subscripting

The colon operator is a powerful method for accessing and manipulating an array. The *end* keyword has a second meaning when used with subscripting: In a subscript, *end* refers to the last element of the array. For example, the following command returns the fifth through the last elements of a vector:

```
> A = [1 3 5 7 9 11 13 15];
>> A(5:end)
```

```
 1 function Out = quickSort(A)
 2 % Out = quickSort(A)
 3 %     Implements a quick sort algorithm. Recursively
 4 %     partitions subsets of A.
 5 Len = length(A);
 6 % find a pivot point
 7 Pivot = findPivot(A, Len);
 8 % base case
 9 if Pivot == 0
10    Out = A;
11 elseif Len == 2
12    % avoid recursion if Len = 2
13    if A(1) > A(2)
14      Out = [A(2), A(1)];
15    else
16      Out = [A(1), A(2)];
17    end
18 else
19    % split the array along the pivot point and
20    % call each partition recursively
21    [A K] = split(A, Pivot, Len);
22    out = [feval(@quickSort, A(1:K)) ...
23            feval(@quickSort, A(K+1:Len))];
24 end
```

Figure 10.19.   The main *quickSort* function.

```
ans =
      9    11    13    15
```

The next example returns the last half of an array, including the middle element if the size of the array is odd:

```
>> A = [1 3 5 7 9];
>> A(floor(end/2)+1 : end)
ans =
      5    7    9
>> B = [2 4 6 8];
>> B(floor(end/2)+1 : end)
ans =
      6    8
```

You can use the colon operator to return a modified array. For example, the following command returns a vector in reverse order:

```
A = [ 1 3 5 7 9];
>> A(end:-1:1)
ans =
     9     7     5     3     1
```

Multidimensional Subscripting

Recall that you can access a multidimensional array by using subscripts in each dimension or by using a single subscript. Consider the following two-dimensional array A:

```
>> A = [1   14   21;   43   2   8;   12   3   91]
A =
      1     14     21
     43      2      8
     12      3     91
```

The use of subscripts in two dimensions provides an index into a row and then a column, as in the following example:

```
>> A(2,1)
ans =
     43
```

A single subscript is an index into a single column formed by concatenating column one, column two, column three, etc.:

```
>> A(6)
ans =
     3
```

Logical Indexing

A powerful method for selecting elements from an array is logical indexing. A relational operator or a function that returns True (1) or False (0) may be applied to an array. For example, the expression $A > 10$ returns an array of the same order as A. Each element i in the array contains a one if $A(i) > 10$ is true and a zero otherwise:

```
>> A>10
ans =
     0     1     1
     1     0     0
     1     0     1
```

A logical expression may also be used as a subscript of an array. In this case, the elements that satisfy the expression are returned. For example, applying the expression $A > 10$ as a subscript of A returns the elements that are greater than 10 in column order:

```
>> A(A>10)
ans =
     43
     12
     14
     21
     91
```

It may be helpful to read the statement $A(A > 10)$ as "return A such that $A > 10$".

The MATLAB *find* function returns the subscripts, rather than the elements, of a logical expression. Note the difference between the following use of the *find* function and the previous example:

```
>> find(A>10)
ans =
       2
       3
       4
       7
       9
```

In this case, the *find* function returns the indices of the five elements of *A* that are greater than 10. The indices are returned in column order, using one-dimensional subscripts.

You can use the results of the *find* function to replace the found elements. This trick makes use of the fact that an assignment of a scalar to a subarray replaces each element of the subarray with the scalar. In the following example, we assign to *B* the indices of the elements of *A* that are greater than 10, and then we assign 1,000 to each of those elements in *A*:

```
>> B = find(A>10);
>> A(B) = 1000
A =
              1        1000        1000
           1000           2           8
           1000           3        1000
```

Vectorization of Algorithms

The vectorization of an algorithm refers to the replacement of loops with array functions. The following *for* loop computes the sum of the square root of the numbers from 1 to 300:

```
Y = 0;
for Index = 1:300
   Y = Y + sqrt(Index);
end
```

The following array operation produces the same results:

```
>> sum(sqrt(1:300))
ans =
   3.4726e+003
```

The MATLAB built-in array operators are generally much faster than loops.

Now let us try a slightly more complicated problem. In this example, we want to sort the odd-numbered columns of a matrix, but leave the even-numbered columns alone. The MATLAB sort function will perform the sort, but the following code segment will also do the job with the use of a loop:

```
for Index = 1:size(A,2)
   if rem(Index,2)  ~= 0
      A(:,Index)  = sort(A(:,Index));
   end
```

```
    end
    disp(A)
```

To test the code, we generate a 4×4 matrix of pseudorandom numbers:

```
>> A = rand(4)
A =
    0.7036    0.3654    0.6739    0.3603
    0.4850    0.1400    0.9994    0.5485
    0.1146    0.5668    0.9616    0.2618
    0.6649    0.8230    0.0589    0.5973
```

The execution of the aforementioned code will result in the following matrix:

```
    0.1146    0.3654    0.0589    0.3603
    0.4850    0.1400    0.6739    0.5485
    0.6649    0.5668    0.9616    0.2618
    0.7036    0.8230    0.9994    0.5973
```

Note that columns one (1) and three (3) are sorted, but columns two (2) and four (4) are not.

We can obtain the same results with the following single line of code:

```
>> A(:,1:2:end) = sort(A(:,1:2:end))
```

If you are interested in array manipulation and vectorization, use the Help feature to look up the following built-in MATLAB functions: *rot90, repmat, fliplr, flipud, flipdim, permute, ipermute, triu, tril,* and *filter.* You can use these functions in conjunction with the colon operator, the *find* function, and logical subscripting to vectorize many algorithms.

10.3.3 Profiling Code

Measuring Elapsed Time

The reason that you should vectorize your program code is not to make the code more concise. In fact, the vectorized versions are usually *less* readable than the versions with loops. The reason to vectorize code is to take advantage of MATLAB's built-in array optimizations. In most cases, the vectorized versions will execute much faster than the versions with loops. In this section, we will show you how to time a segment of code. In addition, we will show you how to create reports that detail the timing results of a function.

One way to measure elapsed time is to use the functions *tic* and *toc*. The *tic* function starts a timer, and the *toc* function stops the timer and returns the elapsed time. As an example, you can use the *tic* and *toc* functions to measure the elapsed time taken to execute a loop that computes the sum-of-square roots. In order to accentuate the differences in elapsed times, we are going to increase the loop count to 300,000. If you copy the following commands into a script file and run it, the program should output the elapsed time:

```
tic
Y = 0;
for Index = 1:300000
    Y = Y + sqrt(Index);
end
```

```
toc
elapsed_time =
    4.0560
```

If you now run the vectorized version of the solution, you should get a shorter elapsed time:

```
tic;
sum(sqrt(1:300000));
toc;
elapsed_time =
    0.3810
```

The exact elapsed times will be different on your computer. In fact, you run the scripts more than once, you will probably get slightly different elapsed times on each run. However, the differences in elapsed time should be similar in magnitude. The vectorized version is an order of magnitude faster.

The Profiler

The MATLAB profiler is a tool that provides a detailed report of the execution characteristics of a segment of code. The profiler shows how much time is spent executing each function and each line of code within each function. The report that is generated can help you quickly determine which parts of an algorithm are consuming the most time. Then you can focus your efforts on the offending segments of code.

The two basic commands that are used for profiling are *profile* and *profreport*. The *profile* command is used to

- turn profiling on or off
- control the level of detail in the report
- produce reports

The *profreport* command generates a report of all code executed during the profiling. The report generator creates a report in HTML format and invokes the default web browser to view the results.

You can turn profiling on with the following command:

```
profile on
```

In this mode, the profiler collects statistics on any subsequently executed code. The use of the *history* flag will cause the profiler to keep a history of all function calls, in addition to collecting statistics on those calls:

```
profile on -history
```

The number of calls in the history is limited to 10,000.

The following arguments of *profile* suspend the profile, resume profiling, and clear all profiling data, respectively:

```
profile off
profile resume
profile clear
```

You can obtain the profiler status at any time by using the *status* flag.

```
>> profile status
ans =
```

```
        ProfilerStatus: 'off'
          DetailLevel: 'mmex'
      HistoryTracking: 'off'
```

You can optionally use the functional form of *profile* to store the status results within a program:

```
>>my_status = profile('status');
```

To generate a report or plot, use the *report* or *plot* flags of the *profile* function. The results are automatically displayed in your default web browser. If a *pathname* parameter is given, the results are saved in the designated location. A number of HTML files are generated. The primary HTML file is given the *basename* with an *html* extension. The relevant commands are as follows:

```
profile report
profile report <pathname>
profile plot
```

The easiest way to see how these commands work together is through an example. Usually, you will be using the profiler to locate the places in your code that are consuming the most time. In this example, however, we will use the profiler in a slightly different manner: to compare the efficiency of two different sorting algorithms.

The *testSort* function in Figure 10.20 sorts a vector twice, once using the *selectionSort* function and once using the *quickSort* function. The *testSort* function then compares the outputs to verify that they produce the same results.

```
function [Out1, Out2] = test_sort(A)
% test_sort(A)
%    This function sorts vector A using two different
%    sorting algorithms.
%    selectionSort - O(n^2)
%    quickSort - O(n log n)
out1 = selectionSort(A);
out2 = quickSort(A);
if isequal(Out1, Out2)
  disp('Both functions returned the same output.')
end
```

Figure 10.20. Sort a vector using two sorting algorithms.

You can use the commands that follow to generate a profile of the *testSort* function. Then you can use the results to compare the execution time of the two sorting algorithms. The second line generates a 1×500 array of pseudorandom numbers:

```
>> profile on
>> A = rand(1,500);
>> testSort(A);
Both functions returned the same output.
```

```
>> profile report 'C:\temp\sort_results'
>> profile clear
```

The first page in the report that is generated shows the information displayed in Figure 10.21. The total time taken for this exercise will vary, depending on your computer's speed. The relative times should be similar to the results shown in the figure.

The function list displays each function that was called during the program's execution. The *testSort* function calls all of the other functions except *profile*. The *time* column lists the time taken for each function (including all functions that are called by the designated function.) Thus, *testSort* consumes 100% of the time, since it calls all the other functions. The *profile* command's time is inconsequential.

MATLAB Profile Report: Summary

Report generated 17-Nov-2001 10:04:26

Total recorded time:	3.20 s
Number of M-functions:	5
Number of M-subfunctions:	2
Clock precision:	0.010 s

Function List

NAME	TIME		CALLS	TIME/CALL	SELF-TIME	
testsort	3.20	100.0%	1	3.204000	0.02	0.6%
selectionsort	2.44	76.2%	1	2.443000	2.35	73.4%
quicksort	0.74	23.1%	653	0.001135	0.29	9.1%
quicksort/ split	0.39	12.2%	326	0.001199	0.26	8.1%
swap	0.22	6.9%	1740	0.000127	0.22	6.9%
quicksort/ findPivot	0.06	1.9%	653	0.000092	0.06	1.9%
profile	0.00	0.0%	1	0.000000	0.00	0.0%

Figure 10.21. A Sample Profile Report.

The column titled *self-time* displays the time taken by each function alone (i.e., ignoring any functions that it calls). Thus, *testSort* consumes 100% of the total time if its calls are included. However, *testSort* consumes only 0.6% of the total time if its calls are not included. This makes sense, because *testSort* does not do much except call other functions.

The comparison that is of interest is the ratio of the total amount of time taken by *selectionSort* and all of its calls to *quickSort* and all of its calls. For n = 500, *quickSort* appears to be about three times faster than *selectionSort* (0.74 second vs. 2.44 seconds).

The Profile Report also presents a detailed analysis of each function called. In Figure 10.22, each line of code for *selectionSort* is shown, along with the amount and percentage of time it takes the line to complete execution. Line 12 appears to consume the most time.

```
100% of the total time in this function was spent on the
following lines:


            5:  %    with the current item.
 0.01   0%  6:  Len = length(A);
            7:  % loop through all but last item
           10:  LowIndex = Index1;
 0.02   1% 11:  for Index2 = Index2 + 1 : Len
 1.55  64% 12:     if A(Index2) < A(LowIndex)
 0.02   1% 13:        LowIndex = Index2;
 0.01   0% 14:     end
 0.71  29% 15:  end
           16:  % if minimum item is smaller, swap
 0.01   0% 17:  if A(Index1) > A(LowIndex)
 0.11   5% 18:     A = swap(A, Index1, LowIndex);
           19:  end
```

Figure 10.22. Detailed profile of the *selectionSort* function.

On the basis of its indices, Line 12 enters the array *A* twice and makes a comparison of the two values found. Line 12 is also executed many (Len − 1) times. Why do you think that the *end* statement in line 15 consumes 29% of the total time? It is because the computation of the criteria for exiting (or remaining in) the *for* loop is performed at the end of each loop. When line 15 is reached, the counter *Index2* is incremented and is then compared with *Len*.

10.4   INTERFACING WITH OTHER LANGUAGES

MATLAB provides a mechanism for interfacing with modules written in other programming languages, such as C, FORTRAN, and Java. The connection works in both directions. That is, a MATLAB program may call a FORTRAN routine, or a FORTRAN program may call MATLAB functions.

This interface is a very useful feature. Someone may have spent a great deal of time writing an efficient solution to a problem that you need to solve. If the solution was written in a language different from that in which your application was written, then you might be faced with the task of translating the code. Translating code from one language or operating system to another is called *porting*. For example, you might have to port from C to MATLAB or from MATLAB to Java. The MATLAB interface to other programming languages allows you to take advantage of code written in FORTRAN, C, or Java without having to *port* the code to MATLAB.

Likewise, you may be writing a program in another language and wish to use a MATLAB function. You can call the MATLAB engine from within C, FORTRAN, or Java code. In the next section, we show one of the ways to interface with other languages: how to create a C extension module and call it from MATLAB.

10.4.1 Calling Extension Modules

A module that is external to MATLAB is called a MATLAB extension module, or *MEX file*. The MEX file is created by compiling and linking the source code from the native language (e.g., the C language).

One disadvantage of using MEX files is that they are platform specific. That is, you create MATLAB source code on a Microsoft Windows machine and then load it into the MATLAB interpreter on a UNIX machine, the code will usually run. By contrast, a MEX file that is compiled and linked on one particular platform (e.g., Microsoft) will definitely not run on another (e.g., Linux).

The first step in creating a MEX file is to configure your system so that it can identify the location of the external language's compiler. MATLAB interfaces with a variety of compilers on the MS Windows and UNIX platforms.

In what follows, we present an example of compiling a C program on the MS Windows platform.

MEX Configuration

To configure your system with a compiler, type the following at the MATLAB prompt:

```
>> mex -setup
Please choose your compiler for building external
interface (MEX) files:

Would you like mex to locate installed compilers [y]/n?
```

Choose **Y** (yes). The names of the compilers that are available on your system will appear. MATLAB includes its own C compiler called *Lcc*.

```
Select a compiler:
[1] Lcc C version 2.4 in C:\MATLABR12\sys\lcc

[0] None

Compiler:
```

Choose a compiler. In this example, the only available compiler is the MATLAB C compiler, *Lcc*. Choose item **[1]** and confirm the choice:

```
Please verify your choices:

Compiler: Lcc C 2.4
Location: C:\MATLABR12\sys\lcc

Are these correct?([y]/n): y

The default options file:
"C:\WINNT\Profiles\kuncicky
\ApplicationData\MathWorks\MATLAB\R12\mexopts.bat"
is being updated from
C:\MATLABR12\BIN\WIN32\mexopts\lccopts.bat...
```

Creating a C source file

There are several different C files that are appropriate for building a MEX file in the MATLAB distribution. These files are in the MATLAB root in the following directory:

```
<MATLAB ROOT>\extern\examples\mex
```

The components of a MEX file may include one or more computational functions that perform the desired work. Every MEX file must have one function that is used as a connector or gateway between MATLAB and C. The connector function is named *mexFunction* and is defined as follows:

```
void mexFunction(int nlhs,mxArray *plhs[],int nrhs,
                 const mxArray *prhs[])
{
}
```

The parameters of *mexFunction* are as follows:

- *nlhs* - an integer containing the number of output arguments
- *plhs* - a pointer to an array of mxArrays
- *nrhs* - an integer containing the number of input arguments
- *prhs* - a pointer to an array of input arguments

You are not expected to know the C programming language to understand the material presented in this section. As an example, we will use the most basic C program, named *hello*, because all it does is print the string "Hello, world." We will not use any of the aforementioned arguments in this example. Figure 10.23 shows the C code for the *hello* program. Type the code into the MATLAB editor and save it as *test1.c*.

```
/* A simple example MEX source file */
#include <mex.h>
void mexFunction(int nlhs,mxArray *plhs[],int nrhs,const
mxArray *prhs[])
{
  mexPrintf("Hello, world! \n");
}
```

Figure 10.23.   The MEX version of the *hello* program.

Compiling and Executing a MEX Program

To compile the MEX *hello* file, first change the directory to the file's location and invoke the MEX compiler:

```
>> cd (['c:\Dave\Examples'])
>> mex test1.c
>>
```

If everything works correctly, the compiler will perform its work silently and then return to the MATLAB prompt. The C source file has been compiled into a dynamic-link library (*DLL*) and can be called from the MATLAB prompt as follows:

```
>> test1
Hello, world!
```

Disadvantages of MEX Files

The first limitation of MEX files, mentioned earlier, is that they are operating-system dependent. The DLL just created will not execute on the Solaris or Linux operating system. If the program had been written as an M-file, it would run on any platform on which MATLAB runs.

The second limitation is that data structure conversions from MATLAB to C require an understanding of the MATLAB data storage methods. Recall that all data structures in MATLAB are built on the basic array type. Scalars, cell arrays, strings, etc., are special cases of the MATLAB array type. The C data structure that is used to hold MATLAB data structures is called an *mxArray*.

10.4.2 Source-Code Control

Programs of the size that are used in this text are not representative of real-world software applications, which may require tens or hundreds of thousands of lines of source code. The code may be written by a team of programmers, and the programmers who maintain the code may not be the same ones who originally wrote it. The software application may have many different versions, and the code for each version must be catalogued in some way so that it may be retrieved.

You can see that the task of organizing and keeping all of these versions among a number of programmers is a formidable one. This task is called *source-code control*. Fortunately, specialized applications called source-control systems, or SCS's, exist just for maintaining source code. An example of an SCS is the Revision Control System, or RCS, a GNU-licensed public-domain tool. Another example is ClearCase, a proprietary product developed by the Rational Software Corporation.

An SCS helps you manage multiple revisions of files by keeping a complete history of the changes that were made to the files. The history allows you to see how and when a file was changed or to quickly return to a previous version of a file. This kind of management is important for files that are edited frequently or that are being edited by multiple users.

Most source code control systems work by retaining a repository of the source code. Before modifying the source code, the programmer checks it out of the repository. After modifying the code, the programmer checks it back into the repository.

There are two methods of maintaining consistency among versions of code. Source code control systems use one of these two methods. The first method uses locking. Before a programmer can check code out of the repository, the system tests to see if someone else has the code checked out. If so, the second programmer is denied access. The *locking method* maintains consistency by ensuring that only one person at a time is working on the code. This is a strong advantage. The disadvantage of the locking method is that a module may be large enough that two programmers need to work simultaneously on different sections of the same module.

The second method of maintaining consistency among versions is called the *merge method*. In this method, more than one programmer may check out the code simultaneously. However, when the code is checked back in, the system notices whether others have made changes while someone has been working on the code. If so, the system attempts to merge the changes. If the system cannot automatically merge them, then it asks the user to merge the two versions of the code before allowing the check-in to be completed. The advantage of the merge method is that several programmers may work on the same module simultaneously. The disadvantage is that some merges may be difficult to make. In either type of system, it is important for programmers to communicate well and to divide tasks.

The MATLAB editor provides a mechanism for checking code into and out of a source control system (SCS). Each SCS works differently, and it is not within the scope of this text to describe the setup for each, so we will not do so here. If you are using a UNIX system, you may already have RCS installed. Connecting to RCS from the PC requires a PC version of RCS and mounting the UNIX file systems on your PC. Check with your system administrator for help in setting up a repository or finding existing repository locations.

KEY TERMS

algorithm error	interactive response time	run-time errors
asymptotic complexity	locking method	selection sort
big-*O* notation	merge method	source-code control
breakpoint	MEX file	space complexity
bug	NaN	space efficient
debugging	order of complexity	space-time trade-off
DLL (dynamic-link library)	porting	time complexity
error handling	quality assurance	time efficient
exception handling	quick sort	trap
exceptions	regression test	

NEW MATLAB FUNCTIONS, COMMANDS, AND RESERVED WORDS

dbclear—clears a breakpoint
dbcont—continues execution (during debugging)
dbquit—quits the debug mode
dbstack—displays current function-call stack
dbstatus—shows all breakpoints
dbstep—steps forward one or more lines of code (during debugging)
dbstop—sets breakpoints
dbtype—adds line numbers to M-file and displays the source code
echo—turns echoing of script files on or off
end—(second meaning) indicates the last index of an index expression
error—causes a function to be terminated after displaying a message
find—returns nonzero elements of an array
inf—positive infinity, usually returned upon a division by zero or an overflow
keyboard—stops the program and passes control to the keyboard
lasterr—returns the last error made
Lcc—MATLAB's built-in C compiler
NaN—not a number, returned upon certain error conditions, such as 0/0
pause—pauses execution for a given number of seconds
profile—turns the profiler on or off
profreport—creates a report of profiled code
round—rounds to the nearest integer
tic—turns on the timer
toc—turns off the timer
try ... catch—tries to execute code and catch errors

SOLUTIONS TO PRACTICE PROBLEMS

10.1.   line 1–the formal parameter is defined to be 'Character', but 'C' is used in the code (syntax error)
line 4–the logical *and* operator is "&", not "and" (syntax error)

line 4–"C < 57" should read "C<=57", so the digit 9 will be classified incorrectly (algorithmic error)

line 6–"elseif" should be "else" (syntax error)

10.2. Change lines 5 and 6 to read as follows:

```
5  if length(N) ~= 1 | round(N) ~= N | N <= 0
6      error('Input must be a non-negative scalar
          integer.')
```

10.3. A correct solution is

```
function Out = sort_cols(A)
% sort_cols - sorts columns of matrix A in
%                    ascending order.
for i = 1:size(A,2)
  if rem(i,2) ~= 0
    A(:,i) = sort(A(:,i));
  end
end
Out = A;
```

10.4. The constant 10 is ignored. Of the other summed terms, the term $\log(n/2)n^3$ dominates. The division by the constant 2 can be ignored. Thus, $f(n)$ is $O(n^3 \log(n))$.

Problems

Section 10.2

1. Find four errors in the following function, and identify each as a syntax error or an algorithmic error:

```
1 function fib(N)
2 % fib(N) - Returns the Nth Fibonacci number.
3 switch N
4    case {1}
5       out = 1
6    else
7       out  = feval(@fib, N-1) + feval(@fib, N-2);
8 end
```

2. Correct the errors in the code in Problem 1. Then add code to check for valid inputs. Do not accept character arrays, nonintegers, zero, nonscalars, or negative numbers. Sample output is as follows:

```
>> fib(1.1)
??? Error using ==> fib
Argument should be a natural number.
```

3. Write a function called *my_power* that computes the exponentiation of a matrix. Use a *try* ... *catch* statement to test whether the matrix is square. If the matrix is not square, truncate one dimension until it is square. Then perform

the exponentiation. Return the result together with a message indicating that the matrix was truncated. Sample output is

```
>> A = [3 2; 4 5; 6 7];
>> A^2
??? Error using ==> ^
Matrix must be square.

>> my_power(A,2)
Matrix has been truncated to make square.
ans =
      17      16
      32      33
```

4. The command `errordlg('error string')` displays a graphical error dialog box. Modify the *my_factorial* program in Figure 10.8 to produce separate error dialog boxes for each of the following errors:

- Input is not a scalar
- Input is not an integer
- Input is less than or equal to zero

Section 10.3

5. What is the order of complexity of an algorithm with the growth function $f(n) = n^5 - \log(n^2) - 4n$.

6. Make a convincing argument that the growth function $f(n) = 3n^3 + 4n - 5$ is $O(n^3)$. (*Hint*: Show that $f(n) \le c \cdot g(n)$ for all $n \ge n_0$, $c = 12$ and $n_0 = 1$).

7. Write a script that compares the sorting times for a randomly generated 500-element vector obtained with the use of (a) *selectionSort*, (b) *quickSort*, and (c) MATLAB's built-in *sort* function.

8. Write a single MATLAB command that creates a $1,000 \times 1,000$ matrix with each cell containing the number five.

9. Create the following matrix:

```
A =[ 1   3   5 4;
     2  -2   6 2;
     3   2   0 0;
     6   0  -2 1 ]
```

Write a single MATLAB command that returns the sum of the negative elements of *A*.

10. Write a script that profiles the *my_factorial2* function in Figure 10.8. To get better results, create a loop that calls *my_factorial2*(15) 500 times. What line of code uses the most time?

REFERENCE

[1] Aho, A., Hopcroft, J., and Ullman, J. [1983]. *Data Structures and Algorithms*. Reading, MA: Addison-Wesley.

Appendix A
The ASCII Character Set

Table A.1 shows the ASCII character set. You read the table by appending the column number to the row number of a character. For instance, the ASCII code for 'K' is row 7 and column 5, or 75.

There are a number of special characters, such as *nul* and *soh*. These nonprintable characters have special meaning for a monitor or printer. For example, the *cr* or carriage return character (ASCII 13) indicates that the monitor or printer should move the cursor or print head all the way to the left. The *bs* or backspace character (ASCII 8) indicates that the cursor is to be moved one space to the left.

MATLAB stores characters in 2 bytes (or 16 bits) in a superset of the ASCII character set called Unicode. To see the decimal representation of a character in MATLAB, convert the character to an unsigned 16-bit representation by using the *uint16* function:

```
>> uint16('A')
ans =
    65
```

To convert an integer to its ASCII character representation, use the *char* function:

```
>> char(65)
ans =
A
```

TABLE A.1. The ASCII character set.

	0	1	2	3	4	5	6	7	8	9
0	nul	soh	stx	etx	eot	enq	ack	bel	bs	ht
1	nl	vt	ff	cr	so	si	dle	dc1	dc2	dc3
2	dc4	nak	syn	etb	can	em	sub	esc	fs	gs
3	rs	us	sp	!	"	#	$	%	&	'
4	(	)	*	+	,	−	.	/	0	1
5	2	3	4	5	6	7	8	9	:	;
6	<	=	>	?	@	A	B	C	D	E
7	F	G	H	I	J	K	L	M	N	O
8	P	Q	R	S	T	U	V	W	X	Y
9	Z	[	\	]	^	_	`	a	b	c
10	d	e	f	g	h	i	j	k	l	m
11	n	o	p	q	r	s	t	u	v	w
12	x	y	z	{	|	}	~	del		

Appendix B

Compilers and Interpreters

One of the differences between MATLAB and many other programming languages such as FORTRAN and C++ is that MATLAB is an interpreted language, rather than compiled language. It is worth discussing the difference between an *interpreter* and a *compiler*.

Programming languages are implemented by converting or translating the programming code, called *source code*, into machine instructions, which are then executed by the CPU Programming source code is written in a textual language such as MATLAB. Figure B.1 contains an example of MATLAB source code.

The source code is translated by the MATLAB engine into a series of instructions that are specific to a particular CPU. The group of binary instructions or *machine code* particular to a CPU type is called the processor's *instruction set*. Examples of a CPU are the Intel Pentium or Sun's SPARC processor.

The reason that high-level source code exists is that machine code is barely intelligible (except to the computer). Machine code is a *binary code* and is not easy to read. A binary code is a series of zeros and ones, for example 01110011101110. Virtually no one can write more than the simplest program when using binary code.

Moreover, each processor type has a symbolic representation of its machine code, which is called *assembly language*. Assembly language is not much more readable than binary code. Figure B.2 shows a section of assembly code. Can you describe what the assembly code in Figure B.2 does? Figure B.3 shows the same action written by using the MATLAB language. Although you may not have written a computer program, can you guess what the code in Figure B.3 does?

The advantage of writing code in an assembly language is that the idiosyncrasies of the particular processor may be used to write very efficient code. This is important in writing code that is frequently used (e.g., code that operates a network router or switch).

Both compilers and interpreters take source code and eventually produce machine code. The main difference between a compiler and an interpreter is the time when the translation occurs. An interpreter analyzes each line of source code and translates the code into machine language as the code is executed. A compiler translates the source

```
A = 0;
Index = 1;
while A <= 100
    A = A + Index^2;
    Index = Index + 1;
end
```

Figure B.1. Example of a MATLAB program's source code.

```
            mov     cx, stop
            sub     cx, start
            jl      Continue
            inc     cx
Body:       stmt
            loop    Body
Continue:
```

Figure B.2. Example of assembly code.

```
for Index = start:stop
  stmt;
end
```

Figure B.3. MATLAB code equivalent to assembler in Figure B.2.

code and converts it into *object code*. The object code may be linked with other object code and an executable file is produced. There are several important differences between an executable file and an interpreted program:

1. The executable file can now be run without the help of an interpreter or compiler. It is a stand-alone program. This is different from the use of an interpreter, in which case the source code is reinterpreted each time it is executed.
2. The executable file can only be run on the processor for which it was compiled. If it was compiled for a Sun SPARC processor, it will not run on an Intel Pentium.
3. The executable file usually executes faster than an interpreted program. This is because the executable has already been translated into the processor's native machine language. The interpreter must perform the translation anew each time.

This being said, many modern languages have an intermediate solution: the translation of source code into *byte code*. Byte code is binary code that is not restricted to use on a single type of processor. Byte code can be thought of as being partially compiled. Thus, it generally executes faster than interpreted source code. However, unlike completely compiled code, byte code is portable.

There is a catch here: The byte code can only execute on a machine that has a byte-code interpreter installed. Java is an example of a language that can be compiled to byte code. The byte code can be executed on any machine that has a Java byte code interpreter, which is called a Java *virtual machine*.

Appendix C

MATLAB's Data Structures

C.1   INTRODUCTION

The data structures for a programming language consist of the mechanisms that the language provides for organizing data. A language typically provides primitive built-in data structures such as integers and characters. The *primitive data structures* are the basic elements from which more complex data structures are built. In addition, a language typically provides means for constructing more complex data structures. Languages vary considerably in the choice of primitive data structures. For example, the programming languages Lisp and Python support lists as primitive data structures, while C and MATLAB do not.

MATLAB was originally written in the programming language FORTRAN. The FORTRAN language was designed for use by scientists and engineers. FORTRAN's primitive data structures at that time consisted of scalars such as integers and floating point numbers.

A data *constructor* is a more complex data structure, which is built from primitive data structures. The original FORTRAN data constructor was the array. Certain control structures, such as loops, were optimized to perform array computations efficiently.

The *primitive* data structure in MATLAB is the array. All other primitive and constructed data types are derived from an ARRAY object. The designers of MATLAB have highly optimized the computations on arrays, thereby simplifying the programmer's optimization task.

For instance, when programming in FORTRAN, a programmer could optimize certain computations by being aware of whether a matrix was stored in *row-major* order or *column-major* order. This is not necessary for the MATLAB programmer, since array computations are internally optimized for the built-in MATLAB functions.

The data types that MATLAB supports are all built on the ARRAY object. The primitive data types consist of characters and nine different numeric types. The data constructors include numeric arrays, strings, cell arrays, sparse matrices, objects, logical arrays, empty arrays, structures, the java class type, and function handles. These will each be discussed next.

C.2   CHARACTERS AND STRINGS

Characters are stored as 16 bit unsigned integers. The integers represent 16-bit ASCII Unicode. Characters are entered by using single quotes; for example

```
>> C = 'W'
C =
W
```

If the single quotes were not used, then MATLAB would try to assign a variable named W to C. Because the quotes are used, MATLAB assigns the character W to C.

Strings are groups of characters and are entered by using single quotes as delimiters. A string is stored as an array of characters, starting with the index one (1). Characters within strings can be accessed by using the array name, followed by the index in parentheses. The second character in the string C = 'New Orleans' can be accessed by using the notation C(2).

To verify this to yourself, type the following in the Command window:

```
>> A = 'America'
A =
America
>> A(6)
ans =
c
```

The string *America* is stored as a 1×7 array of characters and may be accessed by using array subscripts. Look in the Workspace window to verify the size and type of *A*.

To verify that a name is associated with type *char*, use the *ischar* function:

```
>> ischar(A)
ans =
     1
```

The *ischar* function returns true (1) if the name is of type char, otherwise it returns zero (0).

C.3   NUMERIC TYPES

MATLAB's numeric data types include integers and floating-point numbers. To use the various numeric data types effectively requires an understanding of the underlying storage mechanism for numbers.

C.3.1   Integers

There are six different integer types. These include 8-bit, 16-bit, and 32-bit signed and unsigned integers, named, respectively, int8, int16, int32, uint8, uint16, and uint32.

In this section, we will discuss how integers are stored internally. It is important to have a general understanding of how numbers are stored internally.

All data on a digital computer are stored in binary representation. A single, binary storage unit is called a *bit* and, typically, an 8-bit unit is called a *byte*. Each bit can exist in one of two states: on or off. Here's an example of a byte containing 8 binary bits:

```
10111001B
```

To avoid confusion, binary numbers are sometimes written in text with a B trailing the number. A decimal number is sometimes written with a D trailing the number, and a hexadecimal number is written with a trailing H. The trailing letters are not stored internally in the computer.

An 8-bit byte can store 2^8 different numbers and, more generally, an n-bit unit can store 2^n different numbers. A 16-bit integer (signed or unsigned) is stored by using 16 bits or 2 bytes. Numbers are stored in multiples of 8 bits, since computer registers and computer memory word sizes are usually multiples of 8 bits.

The unsigned integer storage mechanism is straightforward. Each integer is stored in its binary representation. The 8-bit unsigned integers are represented as follows:

```
  0D = 00000000B
  1D = 00000001B
  2D = 00000010B
  3D = 00000011B
  . . . .
  . . . .
254D = 11111110B
255D = 11111111B
```

The 16-bit unsigned integer format can be used to represent integers from zero to $2^{16}-1$, or 65,535. The 32-bit unsigned integer format can be used to represent integers from zero to $2^{32}-1$, which is more than 4 billion.

Signed integers are usually represented by using *twos-complement notation*. The twos-complement of a binary number is the complement of the number plus one.

The complement of a binary number is computed by simply replacing each one with a zero and each zero with a one. For example, the complement of the 3-bit binary number 011 is 100. The twos-complement of 011 is 100 + 1 = 101.

The positive integers up to $2^{(n-1)}-1$ are represented by using unsigned binary notation, where n is the number of bits. The negative integers down to $-2^{(n-1)}$ are represented in twos-complement notation.

PRACTICE C.1!

The representation of signed integers can be confusing. Let us assume a 3-bit representation, so that we can check our answers with this table:

```
 0D = 000B
 1D = 001B
 2D = 010B
 3D = 011B
-4D = 100B
-3D = 103B
-2D = 110B
-1D = 111B
```

Here, 3-bit integers from −4 to +3 are represented in signed integer notation. The same method is used on a computer to store 8-bit, 16-bit, and 32-bit signed integers, though some processors may swap bytes internally.

Because $2^{(3-1)}-1=3$, we can represent the positive integers from 1 to 3 with 3 bits. Since $-2^{(3-1)}=-4$, we can represent the negative integers down to −4.

Find the signed binary representation of −3 as follows:

1. The unsigned binary representation of 3D = 011B.
2. The complement of 011B = 100B.
3. Adding one, we get 101B.

Find the decimal equivalent of signed 111B as follows:

1. Since the leftmost bit is a one, the number must be negative.
2. Subtracting one, we get 110B.
3. The complement is 001B.
4. The decimal number is −1.

An integer can be created in code by using the integer type as a function name. For example, to create an unsigned 8-bit integer named *A* with the value 3, type the following:

```
>> A = uint8(3)
A =
        3
```

Use the *whos* command or look in the Workspace window to verify that *A* is stored in a single byte, as shown here:

```
>> whos A
   Name        Size         Bytes  Class
   A           1x1              1  uint8 array
```

The same integer functions that are used to define integers are also used to convert a number into an integer type. For example, to convert the number −5.623 into a 16-bit signed integer, type

```
>> A = int16(-5.623)
A =
       -5
```

When converting to an integer from a floating-point number, the fractional digits are truncated. If a number is assigned to an integer representation that is too small to hold the number, it is truncated to the largest available number. Recall that the largest number that can be stored in an 8-bit unsigned integer is 11111111B or 255D. Thus, as shown here, the integer 257 is truncated to 255 when converting to an 8-bit unsigned integer type:

```
>> B = uint8(257)
B =
      255
```

PRACTICE C.2!

Test your understanding of integer representation.

1. What is the unsigned 8-bit binary representation of the decimal integer 6?
2. What is the signed 8-bit binary representation of the decimal integer −5?
3. What is the decimal equivalent of the signed 8-bit number 11111111B?
4. What is the decimal equivalent of the unsigned 8-bit number 01111111B?

C.3.2   Floating-Point Numbers

The floating-point types are *single precision* and *double precision*.

There are three components in a floating-point number: a sign, a mantissa, a base, and an exponent. Floating-point number is denoted in decimal notation as follows:

$$-5.23 \times 10^{\wedge}3.$$

Here, the sign is negative, the mantissa is 5.23, the base is 10, and the exponent is 3.

One **IEEE** floating-point standard defines the storage of single precision numbers to be 1 sign bit, 8 bits of exponent, and 23 bits of mantissa, with the base assumed to be 2. The total single precision number is stored in 4 bytes (32 bits).

A double precision number is stored using 1 sign bit, 11 bits of exponent, and 52 bits of mantissa. The total double precision number is stored using 8 bytes (64 bits).

Arrays of numbers may be stored as integers or single precision numbers. Though all data types support basic array operations, such as subscripting and reshaping, **MATLAB** computations are always performed using double-precision arithmetic. The reason you would define an array as integer or single precision is to use memory more efficiently. When actually performing computations, you should first convert the array to double precision.

The conversion to double precision is done by using the *double* function. The *double* function takes a numeric array as an argument. In the next example, we convert the 8-bit unsigned integer A to a double precision floating-point number by using the *double* function. The result is assigned to B and the *whos* function is used to verify that the unsigned integer representation of 3 requires 1 byte, and the double representation requires 8 bytes. Your workspace should look like this:

```
>>A = uint8(3);
>> whos A
  Name        Size            Bytes  Class
  A           1x1                 1   uint8 array
>>B = double(A);
>> whos B
  Name        Size            Bytes  Class
  B           1x1                 8   double array
```

If the double function is passed a double precision argument, the result is the same as the input: Nothing is changed.

MATLAB's default data type is an array of double. Type the following at the Command window prompt:

```
>> A = 5
A =
     5
```

Note that although we have entered an integer, MATLAB converts the number 5 to a 1×1 array, containing a double floating-point value. Use the *whos* command to verify this. Your workspace should look like this:

```
>> whos A
  Name        Size            Bytes  Class

  A           1x1                 8   double array
Grand total is 1 elements using 8 bytes
```

PRACTICE C.3!

Create the 5-element array [3, 4, 5, 6, 7] as three different numeric types: uint8, int16, and double. How much storage is needed for the array in each case?

C.4 CELL ARRAY TYPE

Note that until now, each member of an array is of the same type. You cannot define a standard numeric array that contains some integers and some floating-point numbers. You cannot convert a single entry in an array from integer to double or vice versa. However, you can convert the type of an entire array at once.

A *cell array* is an array type for which each entry may be of a different type. Some cells may hold integers, and others may hold double numbers. A cell may even hold strings or other arrays, including other cell arrays.

To avoid confusion with the accessing methods of regular arrays, the delimiter for cell arrays is a set of curly braces, {}. To assign elements to a cell array, enclose the elements in curly braces. For example, to create the cell array *A*, which contains the string 'foo', the number 3.4, and the array [3, 5, 7], type the following:

```
>> A = { 'foo', 3.4, [3, 5, 7]}
A =
    'foo'    [3.4000]    [1x3 double]
```

Note that MATLAB doesn't display the contents of nonscalar elements when a whole cell array is printed. In order to save space, only the size and type of nonscalar numeric arrays are shown.

The contents of a cell array element are accessed by using subscripts enclosed by curly braces. To copy the contents of the third element of *A* into *B*, type the following:

```
>> B = A{3}
B =
    3    5    7
```

To make a copy of a cell, use subscripts enclosed by parentheses. For example, to copy the third cell of *A* into *B*, type

```
>> B = A(3)
B =
    [1x3 double]
```

What is the difference? In the first example, a 3-element array was copied into *B*. In the second example, a cell containing a 3-element array was copied into *B*.

C.5 STRUCTURE ARRAY TYPE

At times, it is convenient to access the elements of a data structure by using named labels instead of subscripts. For example, you can create a cell array to hold the name, social security number (SSN), grades, and grade-point average (GPA) of a student by typing

```
>> Student = {'Mick Savage',
              '267-34-3123',
              [48, 90, 95, 73, 100],
              81.2}
Student =
    'Mick Savage'
    '267-34-3123'
    [1x5 double]
    [    81.2000]
```

To access the GPA of the student, type

```
>> Student{4}
ans =
    81.2000
```

If there were a large number of attributes for each student, it would become very tedious to remember what subscript to use to access the student's GPA instead of the student's post office box, for example. If there were a large number of attributes, you would have to create some sort of lookup table to decode them. It would be more convenient to access the GPA with the use of a label. This can be accomplished by using a *structure array*.

A structure array can consist of dissimilar elements. Attributes are accessed with labels, instead of subscripts. The label for a single attribute is called a *field*. A field is designated by using dot notation. For example, to create a structure array containing the same student information used in the previous cell array, type

```
>> Student.name = 'Mick Savage';
>> Student.SSN = '267-34-3123';
>> Student.grades = [48, 90, 95, 73, 100];
>> Student.GPA = 81.2
Student =
       name: 'Mick Savage'
        SSN: '267-34-3123'
     grades: [48 90 95 73 100]
        GPA: 81.2000
```

To access the student's GPA, type

```
>> Student.GPA
ans =
    81.2000
```

Isn't this more intuitive than using subscripts to access the student's GPA? Imagine a real-world student record that might have 50 or 60 fields. You would need to refer to a decoding table to know what each field meant.

A structure array can be expanded into a two-dimensional array by using subscripts. For example, to add a second student's name, type the following

```
>> Student(2).name = 'Susan Bassett'
>> Student(2)
ans =
       name: 'Susan Bassett'
        SSN: []
     grades: []
        GPA: []
```

Note that the fields for SSN, grades, and GPA have been created for the second student, although nothing has been assigned to them. The collection of fields for a single entry is called a *record*. Every record in a structure array contains the same fields, even if some of the fields are empty.

A new field can be added to an existing structure array, but the field will be added to all records in the array. For example, we can add a library card number field to the student array by typing

```
>> Student(1).LibNum = '13266'
```

Every student now has a field named LibNum. A field can be removed from every record by using the *rmfield* function. The syntax of the *rmfield* function is

```
s = rmfield(Structure_Array,'fieldname')
s = rmfield(Structure_Array,FIELDNAMES)
```

The *Structure_Array* parameter is the name of a structure array. The *fieldname* parameter is the name of a single field. The alternate *FIELDNAMES* parameter is a variable that can contain a character array of field names or cell array of strings.

For instance, to remove the SSN field from the student structure array and assign the results to a structure array of the same name, type

```
>> Student = rmfield(Student,'SSN')
Student =
1x2 struct array with fields:
    name
    grades
    GPA
    LibNum
```

The field names of a structure array can be viewed by using the *fieldnames( )* function:

```
>> fieldnames(Student)
ans =
    'name'
    'grades'
    'GPA'
    'LibNum'
```

C.6   TYPE ASSIGNMENT AND CHECKING

In MATLAB, types are assigned to names at run-time. This is different from *statically typed languages* such as C++, Ada, FORTRAN, or Pascal. In a statically typed language, the name of a variable or parameter is associated with a particular type in the declaration section of the program code. The type association is known at compile time. Within the scope of the definition, the type association does not change until the code is modified and recompiled. In Pascal, a variable is defined and associated with a particular type in the *var* section of the program code. The following Pascal code segment states that the variable *x* is to be associated with the *integer* type:

```
var
   x: integer;
begin
  x := 5.45;
end;
```

Type checking is performed when the Pascal code is compiled. The compiler will notice that the number 5.45 cannot be assigned to an integer, and the compilation will fail.

In contrast, MATLAB associates names with types as the code is executed. This is called *dynamic typing*. The type of a variable is not known until the program is executed.

There are several ways to determine the type of an object. One method is to use the *who* and *whos* commands. Type the following session in the Command window:

```
>> A = [3, 5, 7]
A =
      3     5      7
>> who A
Your variables are
A
>> whos A
   Name        Size             Bytes  Class
   A           1x3                 24  double array
   Grand total is 3 elements using 24 bytes
```

The *who* command displays the names of the variables in the current workspace. The *whos* command displays the variable names along with the size, structure, and type (or class) of the variables.

Another way to view the types of objects in the workspace is in the Workspace window. While typing commands in the Command window, view the names, sizes, and types of the objects in the Workspace window. For example, type the following in the Command window:

```
>> A = 5
A =
      5
```

In the Workspace window, note that the name *A* is associated with the type *double array*. This confirms what was mentioned previously, that scalars are stored as 1×1 arrays. In addition, the default numerical type is the *double type*. You can also see that a 1×1 double array requires eight bytes of memory storage.

Now type the following in the Command window:

```
>> B = 'r'
B =
r
```

The resulting type for *B* is a 1×1 array of type *char*, requiring two bytes of storage. Type the following command, which assigns *B* to *A*:

```
>> A = B
A =
r
```

In a statically typed language that performs strong type checking, the previous command would result in a compile time error. Note what happens in MATLAB. The variable *A* is not only assigned the value 'r', but the type has now changed. The name *A* has been reassociated with a different object and all of the new object's characteristics.

The concept of stringent or strict type checking is sometimes confused with the concept of early or late binding. Some statically typed languages, such as C, are weakly typed. This means that a programmer can easily confuse types, for example, mixing pointers and integers. Other statically typed languages, such as Pascal and Ada, are strongly typed. Some dynamically typed languages, such as Python, are strongly typed. The type checking just occurs later than in a statically typed language.

Is MATLAB a strongly or weakly typed language? In most cases, MATLAB performs strong type checking. MATLAB does not allow mathematical operations on integer types. For example, if you try to perform multiplication on an integer, an error will result:

```
>> A = uint8(5)
A =
     5
>> B = 2.5 * A
??? Error using ==> *
Function '*' not defined for variables of class
   'uint8'.
```

One weakness in the MATLAB typing system is the representation of characters. Most languages store characters internally as an integer, according to some code, such as the ASCII code. In some cases, it may be helpful to be able to subtract or add the integer representations of two characters—for example,

```
>> 'c' - 'a'
ans =
     2
```

This tells us that the character 'c' follows the letter 'a' by two positions if we were to enumerate the alphabet. However, in most languages, a character cannot be added to a real-valued number, as shown here:

```
>> A = 'c'
A =
c
>> B = 3.4 + A
B =
   102.4000
```

To allow the addition of a real-valued number and a character makes no sense. This is an example of weak typing.

C.7   REVIEW OF DATA TYPES

The major MATLAB data types are summarized in Table C.1. All types are built on the array type. Scalars are considered 1×1 arrays. The default type is an array of double precision numbers.

TABLE C.1.   Summary of MATLAB Data Types.

Category	Types	Access Method
Characters, strings	char	subscripts ( )
Integer	uint8, uint16, uint32, int8, int16, int32	subscripts ( )
Floating Point	single, double	subscripts ( )
Cell Array	cell array	subscripts {}
Structure Array	struct array	subscripts ( ) and field names

The character, integer, and floating point types require that each element of the array be of the same type. For example, one element cannot be an integer if other elements of the same array are floating point numbers.

Cell arrays and structure arrays may contain elements of mixed type. The difference between a cell array and a structure array is the access method. Elements in a cell array are accessed with the use of subscripts. Elements in a structure array are first accessed by subscript, but within each element (called a record) the fields are accessed by field name.

Several data types have not been covered. We have not mentioned the way MATLAB handles imaginary numbers. In addition, user-defined types, java classes and function handles have not been covered.

SOLUTIONS TO PRACTICE PROBLEMS

C.2. 1. 0000 0110
2. 1111 1011
3. -1
4. 127

C.3. 1. 5 bytes
2. 10 bytes
3. 40 bytes

Problems

1. Execute the following MATLAB commands:

- `A = uint16([3 4 5]);`
- `B = 1:50;`
- `C = {'foo', [3, 4, 5]};`

What are the sizes and types of the variables A, B, and C?

TABLE C.2. 8-bit binary–decimal conversions.

Signed Binary	Unsigned Binary	Decimal
00001010		
	NA	-100
	00000000	
		64

2. Fill in the blank 8-bit binary-decimal conversions in Table C.2.
3. Create a cell array that contains these 4 elements:

- the character string 'Olympics',
- a double array of the sequence 1 to 10,
- an unsigned 16-bit integer array of the sequence from 1 to 10, and
- a signed 32-bit integer array of the sequence from 1 to 10.

Use the colon operator to create the sequences. What is the total size of the cell array?

4. Create a structure array where each record is called *Bridge*. Create a record by using the following named fields and values:

- *LoadLimit* – 4020.4
- *Lanes* – 4
- *Name* – 'Red River Bridge'
- *Length* – 0.8

Appendix D

The MATLAB Notebook

D.1   INTRODUCTION

The MATLAB Notebook is a feature that supports the creation of MATLAB macros inside of a Microsoft Word document. The macros may be evaluated by the MATLAB engine. The Notebook is useful for embedding MATLAB code into reports and technical papers.

A Word document that contains embedded MATLAB commands is called an *M-book*. Commands are embedded in *cells*. There are three kinds of Notebook cells:

- input cells
- output cells
- autoinit cells

An *input cell* consists of MATLAB commands. *Output cells* consist of the results of commands. *Autoinit* cells consist of commands that are automatically executed when an M-file is opened.

Cells may be grouped in various ways. A *cell group* consists of multiple contiguous commands without any other text. A *calc zone* consists of a group of commands that may be mixed with other text. These groupings allow you to perform operations on a group of commands with a single action.

The operations for an M-file consist of various ways of evaluating the cells:

- evaluate a single cell
- evaluate a cell group
- evaluate a calc zone
- evaluate an entire M-file
- repeatedly perform an evaluation (loop)

In the next sections, we will demonstrate how to configure your system to use MATLAB notebooks. Then, we will demonstrate the creation and use of an M-book.

D.2   CONFIGURING THE NOTEBOOK

Release 12 of MATLAB Notebook supports the following versions of Microsoft Word:

- Microsoft Word for Windows 95
- Microsoft Word 97
- Microsoft Word 2000

(*Note*: The MATLAB notebook feature will not work unless you have a supported version of Microsoft Word on your computer.)

Before the notebook feature can be used, it must be configured for your system. A MATLAB script will guide you through the setup process. At the MATLAB prompt, type

```
>> notebook -setup
```

Follow the instructions on the screen. When you are prompted for the location of the Word executable and template files, you may have to search a little to find them on your system. A common location for them is

```
C:\Program Files\Microsoft Office\Office\Winword.exe
```

and

```
C:\Program Files\Microsoft Office\Templates\Normal.dot
```

If you do not find the files in these locations, try using the Microsoft Search feature to locate them. From the Start menu on your desktop, choose **Find → Files or Folders**. If you are working in a computer lab, the files may be located on network drives, and they may be difficult to locate. Talk with the lab assistant or system administrator for help in locating Winword.exe and Normal.dot.

D.3   CREATING AN M-BOOK

A MATLAB notebook is also called an M-book, so the terms MATLAB notebook and M-book are used synonymously in this text. To create a new M-book, type the following command at the MATLAB prompt:

```
>> notebook
```

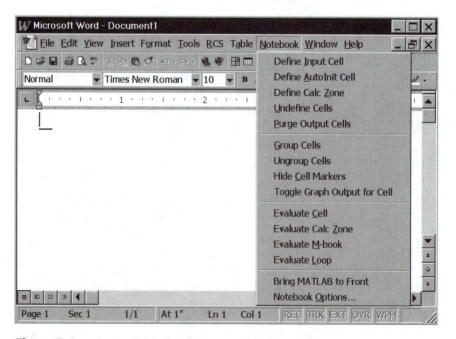

Figure D.1. The Notebook drop-down menu in Microsoft Word.

The *notebook* command invokes Microsoft Word with an additional item on the Menu bar titled "Notebook." Choose **Notebook** from the Menu bar. You should see the drop-down menu in Figure D.1.

D.4 USING AN M-BOOK

To learn about the items in the Notebook menu, let's walk through an example. First, create a notebook and then type the text shown in Figure D.2 into the new Word document. It is not important that you understand the MATLAB code in Figure D.2 at this time. However, it is important that you precisely type the MATLAB commands shown in Figure D.2.

D.4.1 Defining Cells

To create an executable cell from text in a notebook, first select the line

```
[x,y] = meshgrid([-4 : 0.1 : 4]);
```

by clicking the left mouse button and dragging it across the selection until it is highlighted. Then, choose **Notebook → Define Input Cell** from the Menu bar. The selection should become bold, the font should change to Courier, and the color of the text should change to green. Large, bold square brackets should enclose the new cell. This is depicted here in black and white:

```
[[x,y] = meshgrid([-4 : 0.1 : 4]);]
```

Perform the same action for the other two MATLAB commands in the notebook. When finished, you should have three separate input cells as depicted in Figure D.3, except your cells will be colored green.

First, generate a grid of *x,y* coordinates:

```
[x,y] = meshgrid([-4 : 0.1 : 4]);
```

Next, create 3D points based on *x* and *y*:

```
z = x.^2 + y.^2;
```

Finally, plot the results:

```
plot3(x,y,z)
```

Figure D.2. Initial typed text of a notebook.

First, generate a grid of *x,y* coordinates:

```
[[x,y] = meshgrid([-4 : 0.1 : 4]);]
```

Next, create 3D points based on *x* and *y*:

```
[z = x.^2 + y.^2;]
```

Finally, plot the results:

```
[plot3(x,y,z)]
```

Figure D.3. Notebook with three input cells defined.

D.4.2   Evaluating Cells

You can evaluate each cell individually by selecting a cell and then choosing **Notebook → Evaluate Cell** from the Menu bar. If you sequentially evaluate the three cells, an output cell should appear in the notebook as shown in Figure D.4. The output cell will contain a three-dimensional plot. If the output cell does not appear, check your input cells for typing mistakes.

By default, the output cell will be placed in the Word document immediately below the last evaluated input cell. The output cell can be cleared by selecting it with the mouse and then choosing **Notebook → Purge Output Cell** from the Menu bar.

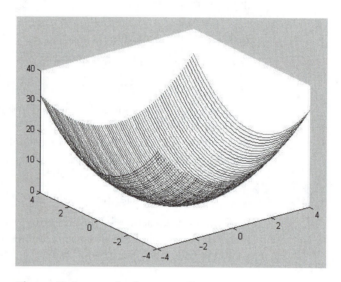

Figure D.4.   Notebook output cell.

D.4.3   Combining Cells

Cells can be combined into *cell groups*. However, cell groups can only contain MATLAB commands. Other text cannot be embedded in a cell group. If text exists in the selection, it will be moved outside the new cell group.

Cells and text can be combined into a *calc zone*. The advantage of combining cells into cell groups or calc zones is that the cells can then be evaluated in a single command.

Try this by creating a calc zone for your entire document:

1.   Make sure that you have purged the output cell.
2.   Select all of the text in your document with the mouse.
3.   Choose **Notebook → Define Calc Zone** from the Menu bar.

The entire calc zone should now be enclosed in another set of large, bold, square brackets.

Now the three cells can be evaluated at once by choosing **Notebook → Evaluate Calc Zone** from the Menu bar. The three-dimensional graph should reappear in the output cell. Before moving on to the next example, purge the output cell and delete the outer square brackets that define the calc zone.

D.4.4   Automatic Cell Evaluation

An *autoinit* cell is a cell that is automatically evaluated when the notebook is opened. An explicit evaluation command is not necessary. Test this by selecting the

The power of compound interest is magic! The best investment strategy is time. That means we should start investing while we are young. A friend of mine is a risky investor and has placed $1,000 into an investment that is expected to return 10% annually. I have taken a more conservative strategy and placed $1,000 into an investment that is expected to return 6% annually. Ignoring the risk factor, let us write a MATLAB program that graphs the hypothetical returns of our investments for the next 20 years.

Although you have learned very few MATLAB commands, this example should be easy for you to follow: Copy the first part of this program into the MATLAB editor (down to the first plot command) then save and run it! Continue to type in code a line at a time, then press the F5 key to save and run the modified program. Watch the effect on the plot as you add new commands.

Figure 2.26 shows the results of executing the complete program. You can see from the graph that my friend will triple his money in just over 11 years, while it will take 19 years for me to triple mine!

```
% compound_interest.m
% This program computes and plots the principal + interest (P+I)
% for a $1,000 investment over a 20 year period.
% Two interest rates are used: 6% and 10%, compounded annually.

% Create a 1x20 array named 'Years' containing the numbers
% 1, 2, . . ., 20.
Years = [1:20];
% Create a 1x20 array named 'Safe' containing P+I at 6%.
Safe = 1000* (1 + 0.06).^Years;
% Create a 1x20 array named 'Risky' containing P+I at 10%.
Risky = 1000* (1 + 0.10).^Years;

% Plot the Safe array.
plot (Safe);
% Tell MATLAB to hold that plot, because we're going to plot
% a second array.
hold on;
% Plot the Risky array.
plot (Risky);

% The next 6 commands place the labels and title on the graph.
% Create the title. The \bf notation indicates bold font.
title ('\bf Rates of Return on $1000 Investment');
% Label the X-axis.
xlabel ('\bf Years');
% Label the Y-axis.
ylabel ('\bf Dollars')
% Create the graph labels and place a grid on the graph.
text (Years (15), Safe (15), '\bf 6%', 'Vertical Alignment', 'top');
text (Years (16), Risky (16), '\bf 10%', 'Vertical Alignment,' 'top');
grid on;
```

Figure D.5. Program dealing with compound interest.

first input cell:

```
[[x,y] = meshgrid([-4 : 0.1 : 4]);]
```

Then, choose **Notebook → Define AutoInit Cell** from the Menu bar. The bold, green text should change to bold, blue text. Perform the same action with the second and third cells in the example. To test the automated evaluation, save the Word document and then reopen it. The three cells will be automatically evaluated when the file is opened and the three-dimensional graph will be generated in the output cell.

The ability to combine MATLAB commands and documentation in the same report is a very useful feature. Some instructors require that homework and projects be turned in as a MATLAB notebook.

D.5   SAVING A MATLAB NOTEBOOK

A MATLAB notebook is stored as a Word file with a DOC extension. Save the notebook by choosing **File → Save** from the Word Menu bar. Although you initially created the notebook by using MATLAB, it should now be opened by using Word.

Problems

1. Create a notebook and copy the program about compound interest in Figure D.5 into the notebook. If you create an M-file, you can simply cut and paste the program into the notebook. Convert the commands into input cells.

2. Modify the notebook that you created in Problem 1. Change the interest rates to 8% and 11%, respectively. Execute the modified cells. How long will it take to triple the $1,000 investment at 11% annual interest?

Appendix E
Importing External Data

E.1   INTRODUCTION

MATLAB provides several ways to import and export data from other applications. Computer applications tend to store data in two general formats: text and binary. A *text-formatted file* uses a standard character representation, such as the ASCII standard. Any text editor or application that understands ASCII text will be able to read the file.

ASCII stands for The American Standard Code for Information Interchange and it is pronounced *ask-ee*. The ASCII code is a standard seven-bit code that was developed in the 1960s and maps characters to the decimal numbers 0–127. For example, the character 'a' is represented internally in many computers by the number 97.

A *binary-formatted file* contains data in application-specific or proprietary formats. For example, a Microsoft Word document is stored in a proprietary format. An MP3 audio file is stored in a format that only an audio software can understand.

You can import both text data and binary data into MATLAB. In interactive sessions, the easiest way to import data is by using the Import Wizard. We will show by example how to import a text file and a binary image file into your workspace.

E.2   IMPORTING TEXT DATA

Before we describe importing text data, create a sample text file. You can do this by using any ASCII text editor (e.g., Microsoft Notepad or the MATLAB editor). To use the MATLAB editor, choose **File → New → M-file** from the Menu bar. Type the following into the editor:

```
1  3  5  7  9  11
0  2  4  6  8  10
-1  1  3  5  7  9
```

Now save the file with the name "text_data.txt." By default, MATLAB will save the file in a folder named "Work."

To launch the Import Wizard, choose **File → Import Data** from the Menu bar. The Import dialog box should appear as depicted in Figure E.1. Click on the arrow to the right of the box labeled "Files of type" and then observe the types of files that MATLAB can import. Scroll down and select **Text** from the menu. If you are not in the

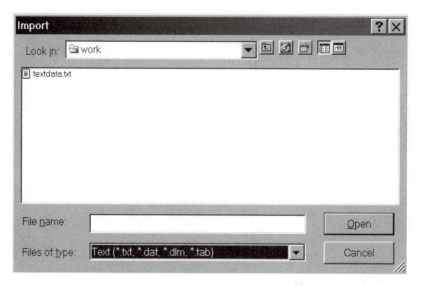

Figure E.1. The Import dialog box.

Work folder, click on the arrow to the right of the box labeled "Look in," and locate the folder named "Work." Select your newly created file **text_data.txt** and click the *Open* button.

The Import Wizard window should appear as depicted in Figure E.2. Note that all or part of the file to import is shown in the Preview pane. MATLAB tries to guess the *delimiter* for your file. A delimiter is a character that is used to separate columns of data. A file in which the separator is a comma is called a *comma-delimited* file. You can select the delimiter if MATLAB did not guess correctly.

You can also type another delimiter in the box titled "Other." For example, on UNIX systems, many of the administrative files use a colon as a delimiter.

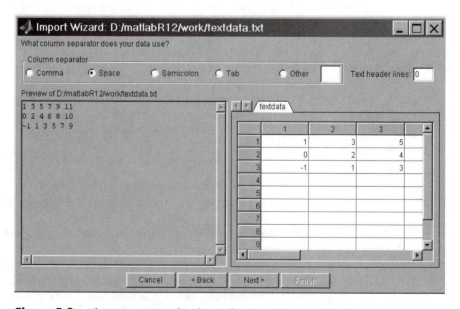

Figure E.2. The Import Wizard with text data.

If your file has one or more header lines that do not include data, specify the number of header lines in the box titled "Text header lines." The grid on the right side of the wizard screen shows the data as MATLAB will arrange it. If the grid correctly depicts the file's data, then click on the **Next** button. If the preview is correct, choose **Finish**.

Alternatively, you can import text data at the MATLAB command line.

The *importdata* function loads data from a filename into your workspace. The *importdata* function takes two arguments. The first argument is the filename and the second optional argument is a delimiter. For example, the following command loads a tab-delimited file named *foo.txt* into the variable A:

```
>>A = importdata('foo.txt', '\t')
```

E.3   IMPORTING BINARY DATA

A number of binary formats are recognized by MATLAB, including image formats (such as GIF and JPEG), audio formats (such as AU and WAV), video formats (such as AVI), and MATLAB's binary data format MAT.

As an example, let's import an image file in JPEG format:

1. Choose **File → Import Data** from the Menu bar. The Import dialog box should appear as depicted in Figure E.2.
2. In the window labeled *Files of type*, choose **JPEG compliant**.
3. In the file locator box labeled "Look in," locate and click on the folder named **demos**. Choose the file named "banner.jpg." The Import Wizard should appear as depicted in Figure E.4.
4. The Preview pane in Figure E.3 describes the file *a 24 bit truecolor JPG image*. The other pane contains two tabs. One tab is titled with the variable name of the imported data. In this example, the name is "banner." Click on the **banner** tab to see a truncated view of the stored data, in this case a 10 × 10 × 1 view.

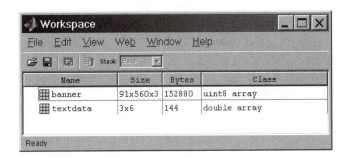

Figure E.3.   Storage formats of imported data.

5. Click on the **Image Preview** tab and then click on the **Show Image** button to preview the image.
6. To complete the importing process, choose **Finish**. The Import Wizard will now create an array to hold the image file.
7. Open the Workspace window and note that the example file *banner.jpg* has been saved as a three-dimensional array of type *uint8*. (See Figure E.4.) The type *uint8* is an unsigned integer representation in which each digit occupies one byte (or 8 bits) of memory.

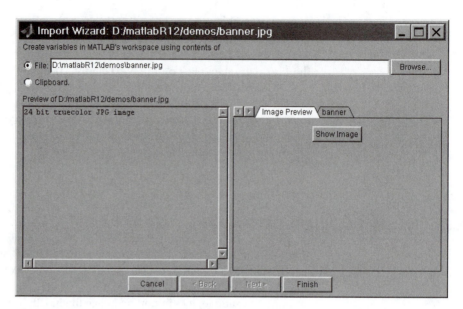

Figure E.4. The Import Wizard with binary image file.

The text data from the previous example (*importing text data*) has been stored as a 3 × 6 array of double floating-point numbers. Note the size of the array is 144 bytes, implying that each of the 18 numbers in the array takes 8 bytes of storage.

Alternatively, the *importdata* function may be used to import binary data from the command line. MATLAB uses the file extension of the data file to attempt to determine the binary file format. You do not use the delimiter argument when importing binary data.

Index